NICK HOLDSTOCK is an award-winning writer of fiction and journalism whose work appears in *The Guardian*, *The Times Literary Supplement*, the *London Review of Books*, and *Financial Times*. He is the author of three non-fiction books about China, *The Tree That Bleeds* (Luath, 2011), *China's Forgotten People* (IB Tauris, 2015) and *Chasing the Chinese Dream* (IB Tauris, 2017). He is also the author of a novel, *The Casualties* (St Martins, 2015) and the forthcoming short story collection, *The False River*. He is a frequent commentator on China for a variety of international media outlets.

CHINA'S FORGOTTEN PEOPLE

XINJIANG, TERROR AND THE CHINESE STATE

NICK HOLDSTOCK

I.B. TAURIS

LONDON • NEW YORK • OXFORD • NEW DELHI • SYDNEY

I.B. TAURIS
Bloomsbury Publishing Plc
50 Bedford Square, London, WC1B 3DP, UK
1385 Broadway, New York, NY 10018, USA

BLOOMSBURY, I.B. TAURIS and the Diana logo are
trademarks of Bloomsbury Publishing Plc

First published in Great Britain 2015
This edition published 2019

Cover design: Namkwan Cho
Cover image © Mark Ralston/AFP/Getty Images

A catalogue record for this book is available from the British Library.

A catalog record for this book is available from the Library of Congress.

ISBN: 9781788319799
ePDF: 9781788319829
eBook: 9781788319812

Typeset by Newgen KnowledgeWorks Pvt. Ltd., Chennai, India
Printed and bound in Great Britain

To find out more about our authors and books visit
www.bloomsbury.com and sign up for our newsletters.

CONTENTS

*'Even in the best circumstances the
position of a minority is uneasy.'*

ALBERT HOURANI
A History of the Arab Peoples

Map1: Provinces and Regions in the People's Republic of China

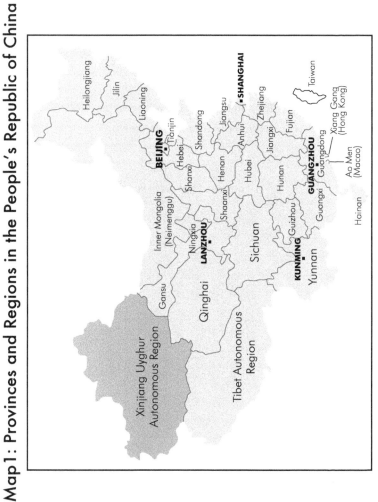

Map 2: The Xinjiang Uyghur Autonomous Region

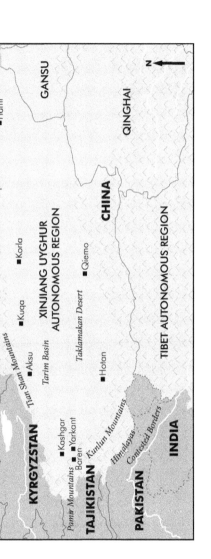

A NOTE ON PLACE NAMES

This book is about a contested region; choosing what to call it is thus a political issue. For some, the use of 'Xinjiang' endorses China's claims to the territory, just as the use of 'East Turkestan' is often taken to support the idea that the region should be independent. Perhaps the most neutral choice is to refer to the region by its current legal name: the Xinjiang Uyghur Autonomous Region (XUAR). However, to avoid littering the text with acronyms, or having to repeat these four words many times a page, I have opted to abbreviate this to 'Xinjiang'. My choice of other place names reflects what I take to be the convention in scholarly and media discourse, and should not be taken to indicate any particular political stance on which is the 'correct' name. Hence in some cases I use the Chinese name for a place (such as 'Yining', rather than 'Ghulja', its Uyghur equivalent), whereas in others I opt for its Uyghur name (such as 'Kashgar' rather than 'Kashi').

PREFACE

They come for you in the middle of the night. Although you have been expecting them – they have taken friends, relatives, people you went to school with – when the fists bang on your door it is still a shock.

When you ask the three policemen what you have done, all they say is 'Don't talk'. But once you are in a room without windows this is all they want you to do. They ask simple questions that are not simple. They say, 'Do you smoke?' 'Do you drink?' They read out texts from your phone. They ask about conversations you had yesterday, last month, last year. They say, 'Why did you go to that foreign country?' 'Who do you know in that country?' If you look at the policeman, he'll ask why you're looking at him. If you look down at the floor, he'll ask why you're not looking at him.

They hit you. They hit you again. They do not let you sleep. This goes on for two days. Eventually you sign something just so they will stop even though you know they won't. But you are not a criminal. You have been charged with nothing. You have made mistakes, you are suspicious, but now you will be helped.

And so even though you are handcuffed and shackled, the place they take you to next is not a prison. If there is no bag over your head, you will see a long building with high walls and bars on the windows that is surrounded by barbed wire and armed guards. Inside, they take your clothes and make you change into a blue tracksuit and then shave your head. The lights are too bright. You are taken to a cell in which are crowded people of all ages, even the elderly, people who look like farmers, people who look like professors. Then a voice speaks from the wall and everyone moves out of the cell, down the corridor, shuffling as if chained. There are cameras everywhere.

In the dining hall no one tries to sit. They know, as you will soon know, that before they can eat they must stand and loudly thank the country, the President, the Party.

Lunch is stale buns and vegetable soup with no vegetables. Afterwards you are allowed to rest in your cell, but you can only sit on your bed: lying down is forbidden.

In the afternoon you perch on a hard stool in a classroom and learn to sing the national anthem, then other political songs. Videos explain the correct way to think, to speak, to dress. After three hours you are cold and uncomfortable and want to move. The instructors keep giving you rules to remember, slogans to chant. They say, 'Admit your mistakes.'

Dinner is the same as lunch. At 8 pm you are allowed to sleep, but the light is never turned off.

Next morning you stand outside at 6.30 am to watch the flag being raised. After breakfast there are more songs to sing, more rules to learn, and every word in them counts. Someone is always listening, always watching, even if you can't see them.

Next day is the same.

Inevitably, people break. An old man shouts that he will not criticise his religion and is then placed in handcuffs for twelve hours. A young man who keeps interrupting the lessons is strapped into a metal chair for three days until his legs and buttocks are swollen.

At the end of your first week you are tested. There are written exams about the rules and laws; you must write your responses to the videos. You must say how grateful you are to the Party, you must praise it, praise the President, convince them you are loyal. You must stand up and criticise your previous wrong actions, your previous wrong thoughts.

Two weeks pass. Three, four. You do not know when you will be able to leave.

*

This glimpse of a totalitarian scenario might seem like a Stalinist bad dream, an Orwellian nightmare. But some version of this is now the experience of an estimated one million people in Xinjiang, a vast region in western China that's so far from Beijing it's in another time zone. The questions asked by the police will have differed; there will have been more or less violence; the pretext for the detention will have varied. Having a full beard; abstaining from alcohol; speaking their native language in school; having WhatsApp on their phone; owning extra food, a tent, a compass, too many knives; travelling abroad; speaking with someone who has travelled abroad; praying; fasting; not allowing officials to sleep and eat in their house; being related to someone who has done any of the above – any of these 'mistakes' can result in being taken to an internment camp.

What all the detained have in common is that in the eyes of the Chinese state they are suspicious because of their ethnicity. Roughly 60 per cent of Xinjiang's approximately 24 million people are from ethnic groups who aren't Han Chinese (the ethnic majority in China). By far the largest group are the Uyghurs, who, like the Kazakhs, Hui, Kirghiz and many of the other peoples in Xinjiang, are predominantly Muslim. Though the constitution of the People's Republic of China explicitly guarantees freedom of religious belief for state-approved religions, the government has long regarded the non-Han peoples in Xinjiang as a population it needs to tightly control. Since the 11 September 2001 attacks, China has claimed to be the target of Islamist terrorists with links to the Taliban and al-Qaeda (claims that this book examines in more depth).

The first reports of the camps appeared in late 2017, but the Chinese government denied their existence for a year, despite the persuasive evidence of satellite imagery, official documents and the testimonies of some of the very few people who have been released (the opening section of this book draws heavily on their brave accounts). International concern built to the point that in August 2018 a United Nations human rights panel stated that Muslim minorities in Xinjiang were 'being treated as enemies of the state based on nothing more than their ethno-religious identity'. At a time when ethnic minorities are subject to increasing repression – in Myanmar, Ethiopia, Turkey, Iraq and many other places – the mass detention in Xinjiang is a worrying example of an authoritarian regime committing human rights violations on a vast scale.

When the Chinese authorities finally admitted the camps' existence in October 2018, they initially described them as centres that offered 'transformation through education' or 'counter-extremism education', before switching to the more innocuous-sounding 'vocational training centres'. According to Shohrat Zakir, the Xinjiang governor, the camps aimed to 'get rid of the environment and soil that breeds terrorism and religious extremism'. He claimed that the centres offer training in various skills and Mandarin-language instruction (most of the non-Han Chinese people in Xinjiang have their own languages). In addition to providing a corrective to 'extremist' thoughts, he said they thus also sought to reduce poverty (some of the causes of which, as this book argues, stem from government policies).

Zakir was so determined to emphasise the benign nature of the camps that he made them sound like holiday camps, claiming that 'the dormitories are fully equipped with radio, TV, air conditioning, bathroom and shower. Indoor and outdoor sports venues for basketball, volleyball and table tennis have been built, along with reading rooms, computer labs, film screening rooms, as well as performance venues such as small auditoriums and open-air stages.' He went on to comment, in the very particular way that Chinese Communist Party

(CCP) officials often combine the absurd and the terrible, that many of the people in the camps 'had never participated in such kinds of art and sports activities, and now they have realized that life can be so colourful'. State-run TV subsequently showed upbeat footage of shiny classrooms, people playing sports and suitably grateful inmates.

The Chinese government's sudden transparency did not extend to specifying the numbers of people in the camps, or their locations. At the time of writing there are thought to be around 180 facilities throughout Xinjiang (and there are most likely many more). There are camps in villages, towns and cities, some in repurposed schools and factories, but many others in newly built facilities.

Constructing a large-scale network of detention so fast – three years ago few of these facilities existed – has required immense bureaucratic effort and massive financial investment, which naturally begs the question of why. Even before the camps were conceived, Xinjiang was probably the most heavily securitised part of China, with armed police, soldiers and paramilitary organisations spread all over the region, particularly since the riots in Urumqi, the provincial capital, in 2009. There have been many waves of mass arrests and compulsory political study sessions in Xinjiang, but these were short-term campaigns whose aim was to root out a few 'bad apples' (even if this involved arresting tens of thousands of people to do so). Both the physical presence of the camps and the official rhetoric surrounding them signal a shift towards a more enduring strategy for Xinjiang. As Zakir put it, 'We have laid a good foundation for completely solving the deeply-rooted problems that affect the region's long-term stability.'

Though he was referring to 'religious extremism' (and perhaps poverty), it's arguable that for the CCP the 'deeply rooted problems' stem from the complex history of Xinjiang and its peoples. These have produced cultures, traditions and identities that implicitly challenge the secular, nationalistic (and mostly mono-ethnic) identity the CCP wishes to promote. The camps can't be properly understood without a greater appreciation of the way that throughout the 1990s, 2000s and the present decade, the lives and concerns of Uyghurs, Kazakhs and other Muslim people in Xinjiang have been marginalised by the Chinese state (events this book explores in more detail).

And yet – why now? What made the authorities embark on a campaign of political indoctrination reminiscent of the ideological excesses of the Cultural Revolution? The CCP is such an opaque institution that it's hard to explain (let alone predict) the direction of policy, but it seems likely the coincidence of three factors was crucial in the formation of the camps. The first was the ascension to power of Xi Jinping in late 2012, which, while some observers felt might be the start of a more liberal, more open China, has been completely the opposite: China is a much less freer place than it was five years ago.

The second, related development was the launching of Xi's ambitious Belt and Road Initiative in late 2013, a program of infrastructure development and investment in Europe, Asia and Africa, what some have called a New Silk Road. Xinjiang is 'a core region' of this plan, partly due to its massive energy reserves of gas, coal and oil, but mainly because it accounts for a lot of China's western border (on its own, Xinjiang borders eight nations). This alone would probably have led to tighter restrictions on daily life in Xinjiang, though perhaps not on the scale of the camps.

But the third factor that has produced the current system of apartheid in Xinjiang was two events that didn't take place in the region, one in Beijing in October 2013, the other in Kunming in March 2014. These decisively altered how many, both inside China and outside, viewed Xinjiang and its peoples.

INTRODUCTION

It was a cool, dry Saturday night in the city of eternal spring. Kunming, the capital of China's south-western Yunnan province, has a pleasant climate and is popular with both Chinese and foreign tourists for its scenery and local culture. On 1 March 2014 its main railway station was bustling with thousands of people: some of them visitors to the city, others students and migrant workers returning to their jobs in distant cities after Chinese New Year. Given the large volumes of human traffic that China's stations have to deal with, it's unsurprising that most offer little in the way of welcome or comfort. The ticket halls, waiting rooms and entrance halls are vast stone-floored spaces whose ceilings can seem as distant as those of cathedrals. There's little natural light; train information is written in red neon. Bells ring; gates are opened; tunnels and overpasses fill with a sudden crush. To gain access to the platforms one needs to pass through a ticket check and a security inspection, but the station forecourt and ticket hall are open to anyone. The entry and exit of so many people, at all times of day and night, mean that there's a constant minor chaos.

Kunming's main railway station is no different. With so many people coming and going, it's unsurprising no one paid much attention to the eight mask-wearing figures in black clothes who appeared outside shortly after 9 p.m. Even if someone had taken notice, it's unlikely they would have thought them cause for concern: though protests and riots in China are far from rare, there is relatively little violent crime.

So when the masked figures produced long knives from their dark clothing and started attacking people outside the station, it must have

1

been hard to believe. A man working in a nearby shop recalled: 'Two women said to me, "There's fighting outside, they're killing people." I said, "Don't talk nonsense, it's very safe here." But people really were being killed.'

Once people realised what was happening they tried to escape. Over 100 people sought refuge in the Chongqing Restaurant; some had to stand on the tables: 'They were terrified and crying. Some couldn't even speak,' said the owner later.

Others attempted to find safety in the station. A student in the ticket hall recalled: 'There were still many people lined up to buy tickets, and the people came pouring in shouting "Murder!"'

Wang Ji and an old school friend of hers, Mr Cao, were also in the ticket hall. They had just collected their tickets when the attackers entered. The first thing Mr Cao saw was a man in a mask holding a long knife: 'He came in and immediately hacked a man in the neck [...] As soon as that person collapsed, he moved on and stabbed someone else.'

Cao and Wang fled, but there was only one exit; the man slashed Wang's head as she ran. They went to the closest hospital, but by the time they got there it was already full of the wounded.

Not everyone managed to escape. One man from the distant north-eastern city of Harbin described how his mother was caught: 'She tripped over a chair. I failed to pull her up. One attacker thrust a knife into my mother's throat. Instead of pulling it out, he drew another knife he had with him and continued to chop her.'

Another victim was 59-year-old Xiong Wenguang. He and his wife Chen Guizhen were migrant workers from the Yunnan countryside who had come home for the New Year holidays. Their train to Zhejiang province in the east wasn't due to leave until next morning, but because they couldn't afford a hotel they thought it best to wait in the station. When Xiong saw a man with a long knife coming towards them, he pushed Chen out of the way, saving her at the cost of his own life.

The attackers moved through the station, from victim to victim, killing indiscriminately. Liu Guilin, who runs a cramped, windowless shop whose metal shelves are packed with instant noodles and snacks, afterwards described the chaos: 'Two men were killed right in front of me, one had his throat cut, the other [was stabbed] in the chest. There was blood everywhere.'

Liu was one of a small group of men who managed to defend themselves with metal parasols, steel rods and fire extinguishers. Another man, nicknamed 'Big Buffalo' for his height, also fought off the attackers successfully.

It took the armed police almost 20 minutes to arrive. By then 29 people were dead, and over 140 were wounded. When the police did enter the station, they shot and killed four of the attackers, but the other four escaped. The wounded were taken to hospital. The authorities quickly sealed off the station. Photos posted online of the scene showed scattered luggage, pools of blood, the grieving and the dead.

The following day hundreds gathered to light candles outside the station, next to which they placed white chrysanthemums, a traditional flower of mourning in China. By then speculation was rife about who was responsible. Many already blamed the Uyghurs, a predominantly Muslim ethnic group concentrated in the Xinjiang Uyghur Autonomous Region, a vast yet sparsely populated area in the far west of the country: 'Xinjiang people are not human beings,' wrote one user on Weibo, China's version of Twitter. Another wrote: 'So it was indeed the Uyghurs who did this! I am baffled. Under the good circumstances and favourable developmental environment of our country at present, why are you people still making trouble? […] Are you just inherently wretched?'

While these remarks weren't necessarily representative of public opinion – many netizens urged caution and restraint – they were drawing on a narrative of Uyghur violence that was well established. Five months previously, in October 2013, a car crashed into a wall and exploded on the edge of Tiananmen Square in Beijing. Five people were killed, including the three passengers, and more than 40 were injured. The Beijing police described it as 'an act of terrorism by suspects from

Xinjiang', and though they did not specify the ethnicity of the perpetrators, the implication was that they were Uyghur.

The Chinese government blames both the attack in Kunming and the Tiananmen explosion on radical Islamist organisations that aim to promote what it calls the 'three evils' of 'terrorism, separatism and religious extremism'. It claims these terrorists are directed by hostile foreign forces aligned with al-Qaeda and the Taliban, and that their aim is to separate Xinjiang from China in order for it to become an independent Islamic state. The government's common response to any suggestion that Xinjiang, an autonomous region, might secede is to argue that the region has been an integral part of China since ancient times, and that people in Xinjiang have no reason to be dissatisfied. Publicly, the authorities take pains to stress that there's no ethnic conflict: in March 2014 Nuer Bekri, the top official in Xinjiang, claimed that the 'terrorist activities don't represent any particular ethnicity'.

Despite Bekri's claims, the association in many people's minds (both within and outside China) between Uyghurs and violence has never been stronger. Yet this is a comparatively recent perception, one that has been shaped as much by media coverage and the opinions of self-designated security experts as by the facts, as known, about actual events in Xinjiang. When I first went to live in the region in autumn 2001, few people outside China had heard of Xinjiang or Uyghurs. The region was an obscure, somewhat exotic part of China, mainly known to Central Asian scholars and tourists on Silk Road package tours. When I told people I was going to a part of China where the majority of people were Muslim, they usually looked at me in disbelief (this still happens). Back then, when major events occurred in Xinjiang, such as the brutal suppression of a protest in 1997 in Yining, a small city on the Kazakh border, they barely registered internationally, except within the reports of organisations like Human Rights Watch or Amnesty International.

Even within China, Xinjiang was a place that most Chinese citizens knew little about, and had usually never been to. The region is so far from Beijing that it's in a different time zone; it used to take three days to get to Xinjiang by train. This didn't stop people from having stereotypes. In the late 1990s most of the opinions I heard were positive, if somewhat patronising. My colleagues and students at the college in Hunan province where I taught were convinced not only of the beauty of girls in Xinjiang, but also that life there was colourful and, most of all, that Uyghurs were very good at singing and dancing.

This book explores the way in which the public image of Uyghurs in China and abroad has shifted over the last two decades from that of benevolent minstrels (or an oppressed minority) to that of Islamist terrorists intent on separating the region from China. It is a story of how the Chinese government altered its portrayal of dissent in the region in accordance with changes in the geopolitical context, in particular with regard to US foreign policy, and the impact this has had on the lives of Uyghurs living in the region. Rather than making the region safer, the arrests, executions and heightened surveillance of Uyghurs in Xinjiang have only fostered resentment.

In parallel, there have also been changes in how events in Xinjiang, and by extension, Uyghurs, are portrayed in much of the Western media. Though motivated by different considerations (that is, newsworthiness rather than political convenience), there has been a gradual convergence of the official Chinese account and that of many Western news outlets. The nadir of this tendency occurred in March 2014, when Fox News, *The Times* and the *Daily Mirror* (a British tabloid newspaper) speculated that Uyghurs might be responsible for the disappearance of Malaysia Airlines flight MH370. The *Daily Mirror* article described Uyghurs as 'Islamic militants in China' and talked about their 'known terrorist links'. Fox News repeated the accusation and described Xinjiang as a 'radical Islamist enclave'.

It's easy to dismiss both the Fox report and the *Daily Mirror* article as lazy journalism (there wasn't any evidence for a link between Xinjiang, Uyghurs and the fate of the plane), but they were indicative of the general tenor of coverage of the region. While there are journalists who provide balanced, careful accounts of what happens in Xinjiang, the dominant trend is now to present the region and its people through a lens that emphasises sensationalised ethnic conflict to the exclusion of almost everything else. To this end, many news outlets describe Xinjiang as a 'volatile' or 'restive' region, and write about the region almost exclusively in terms of violence.

Of course, sensationalist reporting is not confined to China: it's more or less endemic to foreign coverage, whether it be of the Middle East, the Balkans or Africa. In Xinjiang, and elsewhere, this kind of coverage has the pernicious effect of presenting places and peoples in a very restricted manner, and of obscuring the complexity of what's actually happening, including the real (and usually diverse) causes of the conflict.

In the case of Xinjiang, the growing focus on violence and 'terrorism' has obscured discussion of the worsening conditions for Uyghurs in the region. Though many news reports refer to the economic and social disadvantages that Uyghurs face (few are employed in Xinjiang's main industries, most of which are state-owned), as well as the numerous religious restrictions imposed on them, these and other human-rights concerns have arguably become a secondary component of Western media coverage.

One of the main aims of this book is to provide a corrective to those accounts. After outlining the social and cultural factors that make the region unique, I explore the historical and political forces that have shaped both 'Xinjiang' and the modern Uyghur ethnic identity. The chapters then focus on the major incidents, both peaceful and violent, that have taken place in Xinjiang or been linked to it over the last 25 years: in Baren in 1990, in Yining in 1997, in Urumqi in 2009, and then in Beijing, Kunming and Urumqi in 2013 and 2014. Only by separating fact from conjecture, exaggeration and, in some cases, pure invention, can there be any chance of understanding these events and their causes, even if it means admitting that there are incidents in Xinjiang where we simply can't establish what happened, and why, with any degree of certainty.

I also argue for the importance of placing events in Xinjiang within a wider Chinese context, so as to understand the degree to which the inequalities there are specific to the region (and by implication, to Uyghurs). The fact that Uyghurs and Han farmers in central China might be the victims of the same policy doesn't lessen the injustice experienced by either; but it should make us hesitate before attributing every problem in Xinjiang to ethnic discrimination.

On a broader level, this book asks questions about the ways we talk and think about rights, protests and ethnicity in China. I propose that there is an equal, perhaps more subtle danger in thinking about Uyghurs in Xinjiang as an ethnic minority oppressed by an authoritarian (and ethnic-majority) state. This narrative runs the risk of blinding us to the ways in which ordinary people adapt (and, in doing so, resist) the constraints placed on them by authority. It's also my contention that not enough attention has been paid to Uyghur popular culture, which is perhaps a better indicator of what many Uyghurs think than the actions of a group of people who attack a crowd with knives. This book's examination of some aspects of contemporary Uyghur culture also aims to serve as a reminder that Uyghurs are not, as is commonly implied, an ethnic minority whose *raison d'être* is resenting the Chinese government.

I also present the contrasting stories of two Uyghurs who challenged Chinese government policy in the region, and paid a heavy price: Enver Tohti, who helped expose the cancer epidemic caused by China's nuclear-testing programme in Xinjiang, and Rebiya Kadeer, who heads the World Uyghur Congress (WUC), the main organisation that campaigns for Uyghur rights. It argues that 'the Chinese communist reign [...] can be considered the darkest chapters [*sic*] in the history of Uyghurs. Under the current conditions, the very existence of [the] Uyghur nation is under threat.'

The story of how the problems in Xinjiang came to be seen as a narrative of Islamist terrorism is for the most part bleak. Over the 15 years I have been following events in the region, from 2001 – when I spent a year living in Yining – up to my most recent visit, in autumn

2013, there has been little good news. At best, there have been periods when no incidents were reported, and it was possible to think, perhaps naively, that the situation was improving in a gradual, undramatic way, one that would, by its very nature, slip beneath the radar of the media. But then there would be a report of a knife attack, or shooting, or – depending on whom you believed – a peaceful protest on which the police opened fire. In the following weeks there would be claims and counter-claims about what had happened, and what it meant; the only certainty was that the situation of Uyghurs in the region had got worse.

So when, as is customary, I end the book by offering predictions about the future for Uyghurs in Xinjiang, they are far from optimistic. Most, if not all, of the forces that make life difficult, and sometimes dangerous, for Uyghurs living in Xinjiang are unlikely to lessen greatly in the near future. But I also think (or perhaps hope) that when we clear away some of the haze of misrepresentation that arises from much of what is said and written about Xinjiang, and about what 'the Uyghurs' apparently want and believe, it may be possible to identify ways in which some Uyghurs in Xinjiang, especially the younger generation, are adapting to the pressures and constraints of their society, and in doing so, creating possibilities (and perhaps identities) that will allow them to endure.

1

DRAWING BOUNDARIES

It was noon and the market was packed. The stalls were selling tights, packs of henna, crystal sugar, dried grapes, rubber-bunged medicine bottles of what appeared to be blood. Then I saw the husks, their niches, and thought *pomegranates*. The women's heads were covered by brightly coloured scarves, the men's by many kinds of hat: homburgs, trilbies, pork pies, stiffened skullcaps. The faces looked Turkish, Russian, Iranian, but they were definitely not Chinese. The same was true of the words they were saying: they could have been any of those languages, but they were not Mandarin. At the end of the stalls a man with a cloudy eye was selling books written in Arabic.

There was then a space full of chairs and tables where parts of sheep were being consumed. A boy was fanning kebabs with cardboard, making the coals glow. There was smoke and yelling, a pile of rams' heads; chunks of yellow lung were being dropped in bowls.

Further on I saw men trickling into a mosque. Its gate was decorated with green and orange tiles; next to it an old woman knelt on the ground, her head covered, one bony hand outstretched. After that there were no more stalls, just low houses with cyan walls, turquoise doors and decorated shutters. Clay ovens were baking bread; old men slammed chess pieces down; a flock of sheep flowed through. It could have been a neighbourhood in many places: Uzbekistan, Kyrgyzstan or even Turkey. But it would be untrue to say I was confused about where I was. I never forgot I was in Kashgar, in south-west Xinjiang, and, above all, in China. I knew this, and yet – it didn't quite make sense.

'XINJIANG' OR 'EAST TURKESTAN'?

When I first visited Xinjiang in 2000 I was living in a small town in Hunan province, and the two couldn't have been more different. The countryside around Shaoyang was a patchwork of rice fields that went vivid green in spring. South Xinjiang, where Kashgar is located, was a vast expanse of pale desert abruptly broken by oasis towns. In Hunan the people were almost exclusively Han (the ethnic majority that makes up 92 per cent of China's population) and the only language I heard and saw was Chinese. But in Kashgar there was much greater ethnic diversity. Apart from Uyghurs – the largest ethnic group in Xinjiang, who account for 44 per cent of its population, according to the 2010 census – there were also Uzbeks, Kyrgyz, Tajiks, Kazakhs and Hui. The Uyghur language was totally different from Chinese, which is unsurprising, given it's from a different group of languages: Uyghur is part of the Turkic family, which also includes Kazakh, Uzbek and Kyrgyz.

Uyghur food was nothing like the boiled rice and wok-fried dishes I ate in south China. Instead there were thick soups, chunks of mutton with rice and carrots, long wheat noodles, savoury pasties and, best of all, circles of freshly baked nan bread.

When people invited me into their small courtyard homes built of brick and adobe, the customs of hospitality were also different from those of the Chinese people I knew. Instead of perching on hard chairs and drinking green tea, I reclined on floor cushions and drank black tea while eating dried fruit and nuts from a low table. The fashions of my hosts were also different. Many of the women wore loose, brightly coloured dresses and covered their hair with scarves. Some of the men wore a stiffened hat with intricately patterned embroidery (known as a *doppa* in Uyghur).

The trip was a bewildering experience that challenged many of my ideas about life in China. Most surprising was the obvious centrality of Islam to Uyghur communities – most people don't expect religion to be prominent in communist societies, given the history of Marxist

opposition to it. The most quotidian signs of piety are mosques, ceme-
teries and stalls selling religious publications in markets. The first of
these range in size from small prayer rooms that can accommodate 50
people to those that can hold several thousand, with the largest being
the Id Kah mosque in Kashgar.

A less conspicuous expression of faith is the shrines (in Uyghur,
mazar) based around the tombs of local saints. These are found throughout Xinjiang, though mostly in the south. People make pilgrimages to
mazar throughout the year, both at religious festivals and when they
want to ask for the saint's intercession with a personal problem (a spiritual, physical or mental ailment) or one that affects their community,
such as a drought. *Mazar* take a variety of forms. The simplest are
branches planted in the ground with strips of cloth threaded in between;
the most elaborate involve an actual tomb around which hundreds of
poles with coloured flags sprout from the desert (the flags derive from
Buddhist customs). There are also *mazar* based around a natural feature,
often a tree. In Yining there used to be a tree in the centre of a main
road whose branches were covered with small red strips of cloth that
had been tied by women hoping to conceive.

Such shrines have been associated more with Shi'a than Sunni
Islam, especially with Sufi practices. *Mazar* also show the influence of
shamanism: shrines are often surrounded by ritual offerings that range
from goat horns and horses' tails to metal crescents and bricks. There
are also small handmade dolls made from cloth, or miniature cribs, left
by women to petition the saint to help them conceive. The influence of
these other belief systems is opposed by some Muslims, who argue that
they encourage the worship of beings other than Allah.

In press reports and articles that feature Uyghurs the main fact sup-
plied about them is that they are Sunni Muslims. Though accurate, this
statement needs to be qualified. Both the degree of religious belief and
participation vary greatly among Uyghurs, to the point that for some
Uyghurs the notion of being 'Muslim' is more a cultural marker than
a description of faith. This is not to downplay the importance of Islam

to many Uyghurs' sense of identity, but just to acknowledge the diverse ways in which this is expressed. Some Uyghurs' religious observance is limited to eating only halal food, while others go to Friday prayers and fast during Ramadan. Some attend prayers at the mosque five times a day, never smoke or drink, go on the hadj and donate money to Islamic charities. All of them would consider themselves Muslims (if not necessarily approve of each other).

One might even argue that to say that Uyghurs are 'Muslim' isn't to say much. It certainly isn't very revealing about their actual religious beliefs and practices. Most Uyghurs follow the Hanafi school of Islamic jurisprudence (which permits prayer in a non-Arabic language), but the complex interplay of spiritual influences that have passed through Xinjiang during its history means that many Uyghur beliefs and customs (such as *mazar*) are leavened with influences from Sufism, Zoroastrianism, Buddhism and shamanism. The relative importance of these for different Uyghur communities tends to vary between regions – in the west of Xinjiang, shamanic influences from Central Asia have been stronger, while in the south Buddhist practices from India have had more of an influence. Though the pre-Islamic influences came first, actual spiritual practice for many Uyghurs, especially in the countryside, is a hybrid of orthodox Islamic customs and these older traditions.

Considering the widespread adherence to Islam among Uyghurs in Xinjiang, the linguistic similarity of Uyghur to many Central Asian tongues and the considerable overlap in diet, social customs and culture between the region and the neighbouring post-Soviet republics, the question many visitors end up asking (as did I) was how a place with such different traditions came to be part of the People's Republic of China.

The cultural distinctiveness of Xinjiang is also reinforced by its physical location. The region is so far to the west that it's in a different time zone from the rest of the country. 'Xinjiang time' is two hours behind the time used elsewhere in China (known as 'Beijing time'). In Xinjiang the latter is displayed in most public places, and is used for train times, for flight departures and in all schools, hospitals and government offices. Most Uyghurs follow Xinjiang time, while most Han follow Beijing time. There is, however, some allowance made for the time difference. Elsewhere in China, lessons in colleges and schools usually begin at 8 a.m., but in Xinjiang they usually don't start until 10 a.m. (8 a.m. Xinjiang time).

The huge size of Xinjiang alone can make it seem like a separate region stuck onto the rest of China. It's about the size of Western Europe, and China's largest administrative region by a considerable margin. Mountains define most of Xinjiang's boundaries. To the north-east, the Altai Mountains separate it from Russia and Mongolia, while in the north-west the Tian Shan ('Heavenly Mountains') mark the boundary with Kazakhstan and Kyrgyzstan. The Tian Shan also bisect the region horizontally, dividing it into north and south.

The result of this natural boundary is that the region has been treated as at least two separate parts, both historically and in modern times. The northern part, the Zhungar Basin, is steppe and semi-desert, and in the past was used mostly as pastureland and for growing cereal crops. At present it's where most of Xinjiang's manufacturing is located, as well as the capital, Urumqi. In the north of Xinjiang the Han Chinese form a clear majority, though only due to massive migration from inner China since 1949.

The region south of the Tian Shan, the Tarim Basin, is dominated by the Taklamakan Desert. This vast area is the result of the 'rain shadow' cast by the Himalayas and Pamirs, which form the southern extent of Xinjiang and steal the moisture out of the tropical air from the Indian Ocean. Only a series of scattered oases, fed by snowmelt from the mountains, makes agriculture (and settlement) possible in the region. This is where at least 80 per cent of the Uyghur population live.

Two smaller areas are also significant, both partitioned by mountains from the rest of Xinjiang. In the east, the Turpan Depression is one of the hottest, driest places in China. Its few oases specialise in high-quality, intensely sweet fruit, especially melons and grapes. On the far western side of Xinjiang, the Ili valley is separated from the Zhungar

Basin by the Borohoro Mountains, and from the Tarim Basin by the main range of the Tian Shan. The largest city in the region is Yining (known in Uyghur as Ghulja).

Xinjiang's geography has thus divided it into four separate areas, while also presenting a major natural barrier between the region (or rather, regions) and other Turkic peoples to the west. However, these physical barriers are not impermeable. Goods, ideas and peoples have been crossing these mountains for thousands of years, sometimes in large migrations: in the 1920s and 1930s many entered the region to escape Soviet collectivisation; in 1962, 60,000 fled from the Ili region to escape famine. As a result there's a sizeable Uyghur diaspora throughout Central Asia, primarily in Kazakhstan (220,000), Uzbekistan (55,000) and Kyrgyzstan (49,000).

The question of how Uyghurs came to be part of China isn't just an academic matter, but one that's crucial to understanding some of the explanations for why those masked figures killed 29 people in Kunming, or why three Uyghurs blew up their vehicle in Tiananmen Square in 2013. Ultimately, it's an issue of legitimacy. This book will go on to chronicle the many shifts in Chinese government policy and their effects on the people of Xinjiang, but the issue of whether Uyghurs *should* be part of China, instead of having their own country (or at least a greater say in their own affairs) is at the heart of the conflict. There are numerous present-day causes of Uyghur resentment of the Chinese state – religious and cultural repression, economic discrimination, the imposition of family-planning regulations – but behind all of them is a question that everyone should ask of their government: by what right does it claim to represent them? Even authoritarian, non-elected regimes like the Chinese Communist Party need to justify their use of power. The Chinese government's general strategy is to appeal to a sense of nationalism and common 'Chinese' culture and history stretching back thousands of years (in Chinese, *Zhonghua minzu*). In other words, China tells the same kind of story to its citizens as most other nations do.

This kind of unifying nationalism is especially important in states that have a high degree of ethnic diversity, like the United States and China (which has 55 other ethnic groups besides the Han). Coupled with this is a promise that the state is concerned with ensuring the common welfare of *all* its citizens, whatever their ethnicity. For the Chinese government, the reason why Xinjiang and, by extension, the Uyghurs are part of China is that this has *always* been the case. According to this narrative, the Communist Party is just the latest Chinese regime to exercise its rightful authority over the territory, the goal of which is the betterment of the lives of all the peoples of Xinjiang.

But many Uyghurs today have a very different sense of who they are, and where they came from. They don't feel 'Chinese'. This means that any unpopular decision by the Chinese state or its representatives has the potential to be seen as the oppressive act of an alien, occupying power. It's impossible to understand why some Uyghurs feel this way without knowing something of the historical forces that have shaped both the boundaries of present-day Xinjiang and the Uyghur identity. The opposing stories told about the history of Xinjiang and the Uyghurs are crucial to the ongoing struggle to define not only the status of Xinjiang, but also the position of Uyghurs in China.

It's also important to realise that the current borders of the region, as well as the idea of its being a single entity, are both recent developments. 'Xinjiang', which means 'new territory' in Chinese, is a name that only dates back to 1884. It wasn't until the mid-eighteenth century, during the rule of the Qing dynasty, that the region became one administrative unit. Before then the distribution of peoples and powers in the region was heavily influenced by the north–south divide created by the Tian Shan mountains, and within these regions there were also often multiple sources of authority.

The result of all these different kingdoms and empires has been a profusion of names for its parts, most of which reflect a particular political stance. Within China, the region was known as the 'Western regions' until the Qing renamed it. There wasn't an equivalent word for the whole territory among the different peoples of the region – the north–south division was the main distinction. From the seventeenth century, the northern part was known as Zhungaria, a reference to the Zhungar Mongols who controlled the area during that period. The southern part was usually referred to as Altishahr, a Uyghur word meaning 'Six Cities', which may not have been meant in a literal sense – there is no consensus about which were the six cities. What seems more likely is that the word indicated a general sense of similarity among many of the peoples living in the Tarim Basin. However, the fact that other names were used by its peoples for parts of Altishahr – the area around Kashgar, a south-western oasis town, was often called Kashgaria – also suggests that perceived differences between the peoples there (by city or religion) were often just as important.

Among foreigners, Altishahr was known as 'East Turkestan', a term coined by nineteenth-century Turkologists, who argued for an even wider affinity, this time between the peoples of the Tarim Basin and those of 'West Turkestan' – the area in Central Asia that roughly corresponds to the post-Soviet states of Uzbekistan, Kazakhstan, Tajikistan, Kyrgyzstan and Turkmenistan. 'East Turkestan' is now generally used by those who believe that 'Xinjiang', or at least the region south of the Tian Shan, should not be considered part of China.

The story of how present-day 'Xinjiang' arose is inseparable from the story of how the modern Uyghur identity came about. 'Uyghurs' aren't a group of people whose fortunes and movements can be tracked through time: to think so is to confuse race and ethnicity. What defines Uyghurs (and any other ethnic group) is a sense of communal identity based around religious beliefs, social traditions, a shared language and culture, and some degree of physical resemblance. The term 'Uyghur' does have a long history, which has allowed some Uyghur scholars to argue that Uyghurs have been in the region for more than a thousand years. However, not only do the peoples the term originally referred to have little or nothing in common with Uyghurs in the modern era, there were also centuries when no such identity existed. To relate the history of the 'Uyghurs' is thus not to tell the story of one group of people – rather, it is to tell the story of how the different elements of modern Uyghur identities came together into their present form, and thus also to tell a larger story of the rise and fall of kingdoms and empires, and the conflict of faiths.

HOW THE WEST WAS 'WON'

Before the early twentieth century, 'Uyghur' was generally used to refer to a confederation of Turkic peoples who ruled territory from the mid-eighth to the ninth century that roughly corresponds to what is now Mongolia. The kingdom's official religion was Manichaeism, the core tenet of which was the idea of a conflict between a good, spiritual world of light and a dark, material world of evil. At its height, the kingdom extended west to the Caspian Sea and to the Pacific in the east. But after a famine and civil war, it succumbed to an invasion by another alliance of tribes, the Yenisei Kyrgyz, in AD 840.

Those who fled south established two separate kingdoms in what is now Gansu province in China (where it lasted three centuries before being absorbed into another kingdom), and in the Turpan region in present-day eastern Xinjiang. In the latter there were already Indo-European people, whose traditions influenced the Uyghurs. Over time many converted to Buddhism, and they gave up their alphabet in favour of the Sogdian alphabet (at the time Sogdian was the lingua franca of the Silk Routes). At the beginning of the thirteenth century the Uyghurs of Turpan willingly became subjects of Genghis Khan's Mongol Empire, but the regime ended when it was overcome by the independent armies of Chaghatai Khan, Genghis Khan's second son. In the mid-fourteenth century these peoples fragmented into a number of separate kingdoms.

After so many linguistic, religious and cultural shifts, it's arguable that by the beginning of the fifteenth century there was no Uyghur identity per se – there was nothing for it to signify. At most, a case can be made that during the reign of the Turpan kingdom some of the elements – Islam and Turkic-ness – which would come to define *modern* Uyghur identities became established in the region. The south-west area, around present-day Kashgar, was conquered by the Karakhanids, an alliance of Muslim Turkic tribes, in the tenth century. Their territory extended into present-day Afghanistan and western Kyrgyzstan; by the start of the eleventh century Islam had spread east to the Buddhist kingdom of Hotan. Its progress was halted by the waves of Mongol invaders in the twelfth and thirteenth centuries, though by the middle of the fourteenth century many of these Mongols had also been converted.

The spread of Islam in the Tarim Basin was also encouraged by the missionary activities of Sufi mystics, who converted through demonstrations of healing, or by showing themselves to be unharmed by trials of fire, a method of persuasion that owed much to the shamanic practices already present in the region. Just as Christianity in Europe during the early centuries of the Church often relied on finding similarities with existing pagan beliefs – to which the new faith became an additional layer of doctrine, often without displacing the older practices – so Islam built on existing systems of faith.

But though Islam was prevalent in the Tarim Basin in the fifteenth and sixteenth centuries, the next main power in the region, the Zhungar Mongols, had different spiritual traditions. They were an alliance of nomadic tribes from western Mongolia who mostly believed in a sky god and other shamanic spirits, though there were also some Tibetan Buddhists and Nestorian Christians.

The Zhungars began the process of integrating the different parts of the region into what would eventually be 'Xinjiang'. At the beginning of the seventeenth century their state controlled the area to the north of the Tian Shan, but over the course of the century, and especially after a meeting of various tribes and lamas in 1640, Tibetan Buddhism became the designated Mongol religion. This became a unifying factor, and, through an alliance with the Tibetans, both strengthened and legitimated the Zhungar state, enough to allow it to seize the Tarim Basin and Turpan region in 1678–80. But the Zhungars didn't try to govern the southern region (unlike their successors the Qing, and after that the Republican forces, then the Communists). Instead they were content to extract tribute in various forms, ranging from cash to gunpowder and minerals (such as silver from Kashgar), and also labour power.

One of the most significant aspects of the last of these was their transferral of small numbers of people from the western Tarim regions to the Ili valley to work on agricultural projects. These people would come to be known as 'Taranchi', which in Chaghatai (a now-extinct Turkic language) means 'farmers'. Though it would be anachronistic to say that these people were Uyghurs – there was still no such identity – some of their descendants would claim this identity several centuries later.

The Zhungars' attempt to expand their state eastwards brought them into conflict with the Khalkas, another Mongol people, who were close allies of the Qing (their soldiers had been part of the force that seized Beijing). The Qing and the Zhungars fought intermittently until the mid-eighteenth century, when the Qianlong emperor sent a huge army to eradicate not only the Zhungar state, but most of its population as well. The emperor was determined to prevent any future threat from the Zhungars, and explicitly told his generals to starve the civilian population. It's estimated that around a million Zhungars died as a result.

The genocide also offered the Qing the opportunity to address its empire's overpopulation through resettlement and developing the region's agriculture. However, despite its imperial agenda, there is no evidence that the Qing intended to expand any further, into the region south of the Tian Shan: it had been difficult enough to gain support for the high cost of its Zhungar invasion. The cost of controlling the region since then has remained high for all regimes – even now the Chinese government has to subsidise the region massively, despite its relatively high GDP.

Betrayal, and a consequent wish for revenge, was what pushed the Qing into invading the Tarim Basin. When some of its allies in the region slaughtered the garrison in Yining then fled south, Qing forces pursued and conquered the oases. The Qianlong emperor faced opposition, but argued that it promoted stability, as holding the entire region meant it could act as a buffer zone against future invasions (an argument that would subsequently be often invoked).

The ideological legacy of this is still present in the Chinese government's rhetoric about Xinjiang's being an integral part of China. According to James Millward, a professor of history at Georgetown University, the idea that Xinjiang was an essential part of China was 'something no Chinese would have argued before the nineteenth century'. Even in the Republican period of the early twentieth century, a number of Chinese historians questioned the idea that peripheral regions conquered by non-Han dynasties could legitimately be claimed by the Chinese nation. It wasn't until 1959, ten years after the founding of the People's Republic of China, that the official view of Xinjiang's history, oft-repeated since, was crystallised in the formulation: 'Xinjiang has since ancient times been an inseparable part of the motherland.'

Only a very selective historical view allows the present Chinese government to claim that the region has *always* been a part of China, one which requires glossing over the eight centuries when the area wasn't part of any regime based in that territory, either in part or as a whole. To make such a claim requires projecting Xinjiang's Qing-era borders back into the past, so that its history is best understood as a steady march towards an inevitable present. According to this interpretation, if the dynasty ruling in China had diplomatic relations, trade relations or a military pact with the states in the region, that should be seen as equivalent to its being under Chinese rule. And since Xinjiang has *always* been part of China, then it logically follows that no 'Chinese' regime can be said to have annexed or conquered it. According to the Chinese government, the gradual incorporation of the territory should instead be thought of as a process of 'unification'.

This kind of logic produces absurd claims like the Ministry of Information's statement that everyone who has *ever* lived in Xinjiang has been a Chinese citizen: 'From ancient times until today, many ethnic groups have lived on the territory of Xinjiang. Every ethnic group who has ever laboured, existed, and multiplied in Xinjiang has been a member of the Chinese nation.' This is wrong, firstly because the Chinese nation is a modern creation, and secondly because so few of the dynasties that have ruled China (as we define it now) have exercised any control over the region. As for recent attempts by some Chinese scholars to recruit *mythical* figures like Xiwangmu, 'the Queen of the West', into this fabrication of history, they smack of desperation.

My aim here is not to dispute China's claim to the territory; it is merely to highlight the way in which the history of the region is routinely distorted to meet political ends. An unfortunate consequence of this distortion is that it has engendered similar claims among many Uyghur historians and activists, who regularly promote a version of history that stresses the continuity of Uyghurs in the region. For example, on the website of the World Uyghur Congress (WUC), the 'Brief History of East Turkestan' section claims that 'the Uyghurs have a history of more than 4,000 years in East Turkestan. Throughout the history [*sic*], independent states established by the ancestors of Uyghurs and other indigenous people thrived and prospered in the lands of East Turkestan.'

In a similar vein, the section presents a string of disparate episodes of unrest against the Qing as a cohesive campaign, arguing that the people of the region 'revolted 42 times against Manchu rule with the purpose of regaining their independence'. This continuity is even stretched into the present, as the dramatic proclamation ending the section shows:

> Despite all the brutal and destructive campaigns by the Chinese gov-
> ernment against the[ir] identity and existence, the Uyghurs and other
> indigenous people of East Turkestan refuse to be subjugated by China
> and are carrying on resistance torch [*sic*], handed down to them by
> their ancestors, against Chinese occupation.

This kind of statement is the product of the rhetorical arms race that has been going on between the Chinese government and groups like the

WUC for the last several decades, in which one grand claim to exclusive ownership of the territory is met by another. On an ideological level, each side is trying to do the same thing: build an idea of 'the nation'. It's understandable that activist groups like the WUC need a simple, easily communicated message, and want to stress Uyghurs' rights to be awarded greater autonomy as indigenous people. But the result is that they are perpetuating the same kind of misrepresentation as the government they oppose.

THE QING EXPANSION

The Qing hadn't intended to occupy the entire region, but it quickly adapted. During the early phase of its rule it brought in reforms that transformed the demographics and economy of the area (many of which would later be emulated by the Communists). Like the Zhungars, the Qing ruled mainly from the north, with military and civilian authority concentrated in Huiyuan, a new town built in the Ili valley in the north-west. It also continued the Zhungars' agricultural reforms by moving more farmers from the south to join the Taranchi, and established a network of state farms known as *tuntian*, whereby soldiers worked fields that were adjacent to their garrisons. This was a practical necessity for provisioning the army, given the distance of the region from the imperial centre. By 1800 there were 34,000 Taranchi in the Ili region, which in addition to increasing cotton and food production also encouraged cultural convergence between the Turkic-speaking peoples in the north and south.

Convicts and exiled dissidents provided labour for irrigation and mining projects, with the most severe offenders being sent furthest into Xinjiang – the murderers generally went to Yining in the far north-west. The view of Xinjiang as essentially a penal colony persisted into the early 1980s. The novelist Ma Jian described the west as 'a place of banishment, populated by political prisoners, descendants of Turkic migrants, and the ghosts of buried cities'.

However, the Qing did not rely solely on coercion – merchants and other civilians from inner China were offered tax incentives to resettle in the region, and in some cases the cost of relocation was covered as well. The main trading centre was established in the north-east of what had been Zhungaria. The Qianlong emperor named the new town 'Dihua', which means 'to enlighten'. By 1762, more than 500 shops had been opened there, and its population was a mixture of Han Chinese, Manchus and Hui (Chinese-speaking Muslims, originally from Persia and Central Asia, who are still China's largest Muslim ethnic group), with very few people from the Tarim Basin. In the twentieth century, this settlement would become the capital of the region, and be renamed Urumqi (which means 'beautiful pastureland' in Mongolian).

While the initial phase of Qing colonisation was undoubtedly ambitious in some respects, it was cautious in others. In keeping with its original aims, the majority of projects were in the north of Xinjiang. Before 1830 there was very little resettlement of civilians from inner China in the Tarim Basin, most likely for fear of provoking local resentment. On an administrative level, the Qing also had the good sense to recruit local elites into its system of governance, who thus had less incentive to undermine Qing rule. Many of these seem to have been unpopular, either on the basis of their collaboration or because they ruled corruptly. Some were known as 'dogs with human faces'.

The first century of Qing rule brought much-needed stability to the region. The agricultural programmes increased harvests to the point that grain was sometimes cheaper than in inner China, though the cost of the occupation was still heavily subsidised by Beijing. The progress in agriculture also led to an increase in handicrafts, in particular leather goods, carpet-weaving and jade-carving (which are all still major industries in the region, as five minutes in any souvenir shop in Xinjiang will tell you).

In the 1830s the Qing's idea of its mission in the region changed. Incursions into south Xinjiang by the forces of the neighbouring Khoqand kingdom (centred around the Fergana valley in present-day

Uzbekistan) demanded a reassessment of how they governed that area. The result was permission for Han civilians to migrate to the Tarim Basin, where they set up colonies that had both an agricultural and a military purpose.

When resistance to Qing rule began in the 1860s, the causes stemmed from both inside and outside the region. The Qing dynasty had been economically and militarily weakened by fighting the Opium Wars against foreign powers in the east. There was thus less funding for the Xinjiang authorities, who responded by raising taxes and auctioning official positions. The resulting misrule and financial hardship created resentment against the Qing. The fact that the use of the term 'Altishahr' seems to date from this period suggests that having a common enemy helped bind the indigenous population together, fostering awareness of what they had in common (such as being Turkic or Muslim).

However, this couldn't have occurred without some pre-existing regional identity. In his recent book *The Sacred Routes of Uyghur History*, Rian Thum proposes that one of the means by which this was fostered was the network of pilgrimage routes between *mazar* in southern Xinjiang. Each major shrine had a story about a local saint who was buried there, and most of these stories were recorded on manuscripts that were shared and amended by a community of readers and listeners (the latter especially, given the strong tradition of oral recitation in Islam). The transmission of these spiritual histories within and between the oases encouraged a shared sense of the past that was rooted in an attachment to particular places. While the label 'Uyghur' wouldn't be reintroduced until the early twentieth century, it would not have been meaningful without the existence of this deep cultural and linguistic affinity among the peoples of southern Xinjiang.

REBELLION

Some Uyghur nationalists present the uprisings in 1864 as a struggle for independence, but there's little evidence that this was their aim, at least initially. They began after a rumour spread that the governor was planning to have all the Hui in Xinjiang killed to prevent them rebelling (something that, given the genocide against the Zhungars, was not unfeasible). The uprising started in Kuqa, then spread to other cities in north and south Xinjiang. While in most places unrest began with the Hui, the other Turkic peoples usually joined forces with them.

One way to interpret this is that the Turkic peoples were supporting their fellow Muslims, and this was probably true to some degree. But there had been attacks against the Qing by other Muslim forces during the previous two decades, none of which were well supported by the Turkic peoples. The reason they supported the Hui was not that they had faith in common, but that they shared the same grievances.

The uprisings removed the administrative unity that the Qing had brought to the region; in its place there was once again a series of disconnected cities ruled by local Turkic elites. In 1865 Kyrgyz forces took advantage of this relative power vacuum by invading from the west, and quickly took Kashgar. Their triumph was short-lived, as one of their commanders, Ya'qub Beg, who led a force of Andijanis (from a region in present-day Uzbekistan), took control of the city. After this he conquered the rest of the region, with the exception of the Ili valley, which was under Russian control. His rule was unpopular, as he taxed his subjects heavily and imposed a much stricter form of Islam than had generally been observed in the Tarim Basin.

Given the major investment the Qing had made in the region, one might expect the decision to reconquer to have been uncontested. But some thought it wasn't worth the expense. Li Hongzhang, an elder statesman of the Qing court, argued that Xinjiang was 'useless' as it had so few resources, and that the empire's limited finances were better spent on naval defence. He was opposed by General Zuo Zongtang, who argued that Russia couldn't be allowed to gain control of Xinjiang, which was thus worth preserving as a buffer zone.

Even if Li's arguments had prevailed, it wouldn't have saved the Qing, which was already too weak. But if the region had been left in the hands of Ya'qub Beg and his successors, it seems at least possible that it wouldn't be part of the People's Republic of China today. One possible future is that it might have become first a Soviet republic, then a Turkic state.

Zuo Zongtang's plans were approved, despite their tremendous cost – a sixth of the annual budget for the country. The planning of the expedition took longer than the fighting. Zuo spent three years organising the campaign, but only needed three months to retake the north of Xinjiang in 1878. Though the Qing hadn't always been popular among the different peoples of the region, there were certainly some who preferred its rule to Ya'qub Beg's regime, judging by this popular song:

> From Peking the Chinese came, like stars in the heaven
> The Andijanis rose and fled, like the pigs in the forest.
> They came in vain and left in vain, the Andijanis!
> They went away scared and languidly, the Andijanis!
> Every day, they took a virgin, and
> They went hunting for beauties.
> They played with dancing boys.

But although the Qing faced little opposition, rebuilding its former regime wasn't possible. 'Since the chaos, the old system has been entirely swept away,' commented one general. The former capital in Huiyuan, in the Ili region, had been damaged so badly by Ya'qub Beg's forces that Urumqi had to become the new centre. Another change was that the new administration was staffed with Han Chinese rather than Manchus or local Turkic elites – 55 per cent were from Hunan, Zuo's home province.

There was also an attempt to move beyond purely military forms of control, principally through changing the education system. Zuo argued that 'if we wish to change their peculiar customs and assimilate them to our Chinese ways, we must found free schools and make the Muslim children read [Chinese] books'. Students were also given Chinese names, and in 1908 Chinese became the main language of instruction.

The overall aim of both the increased role for Han Chinese and the new cultural policies was to promote the integration of Xinjiang into China proper. Though the Qing Empire didn't last much longer – in 1911 it was overthrown and a republic established – many of these basic goals and methods would be continued by the Communists after 1949.

INDEPENDENCE?

The demise of the Qing didn't make much immediate difference to the peoples of the region. Though there were political assassinations and skirmishes between remnants of the Qing regime and the new authorities, there were no uprisings or calls for a new nation (as there were in Tibet and Mongolia). One explanation is that there wasn't yet a sufficient sense of similarity among the Turkic peoples in Xinjiang, coupled with the fact that there wasn't sufficient resentment of either the Qing or its replacements. When people in the south of Xinjiang described which group they belonged to, most said *Musulman* ('Muslim'), *Turki* or the name of the place where they lived. While 'Muslim' qualified as a larger, regional identity, it wasn't the same as an ethnic identity, or, perhaps, a nationalistic attachment to place. But as Rian Thum cogently argues, this lack of a consistent label for the people of Altishahr is only problematic from a contemporary perspective:

> The modern fixation on stable ethnonyms is itself a product of nationalist thought. We should not be surprised to find a non-modern, non-nationalist system of identity using a less rigid vocabulary.

Perhaps the biggest impact of the Qing's demise was the loss of a subsidy from a central authority, which meant that Xinjiang had to become financially self-sufficient. To achieve this, the new Republican governor, Yang Zenxin, developed the region's agriculture and transportation, but more importantly encouraged trade with Russia. By the end of the 1920s Xinjiang was doing ten times more trade with the Soviet Union than with the rest of China. Though it would be an exaggeration to say that Xinjiang was a de facto independent state at this point, it could be argued that it was the most autonomous it had been since its borders were fixed by the Qing (and more than it would be after the Communists took over, despite being dubbed an 'autonomous region' in 1955). Lest this sound like some principled exercise in self-determination, it should be stressed that Yang was more a warlord than a governor – he usually had his political opponents killed, sometimes at a banquet he'd invited them to. He would certainly not have wanted to encourage the growth of any kind of ethno-nationalist sentiment that might challenge his authority.

It wasn't only goods that passed between Xinjiang and the Russian lands to the west. David Brophy, a professor at Sydney University, argues that the intellectual debates that took place in the Altishahr diaspora in Tashkent played an important role in the growth of modern Uyghur identity. After reading the work of European historians about the ancient Uyghurs from Mongolia who settled in Turpan, some Taranchi and Kashgari intellectuals adopted the name to describe themselves. As early as 1910, one poet was using the pen name 'Child of the Uyghur'. While these intellectuals may have been only a small, elite group, the fact that by 1913 over 50,000 seasonal labourers were travelling from south Xinjiang to the region every year showed that there was clearly potential for these ideas to be spread.

However, in the early 1920s there was still no consensus (let alone acceptance) of what constituted being 'Uyghur'. Though some historians have argued that the term 'Uyghur' was first revived at a workers' meeting in Tashkent in 1921, Brophy argues that it was used to indicate not just Turkic people or Muslims, but everyone from Xinjiang, including Han Chinese. The debate about the name's applicability continued during the decade, with some opposing the concept entirely on the grounds that 'Taranchis' and 'Kashgaris' were linguistically separate and thus two completely different ethnic groups.

Many factors are involved in the development of a shared identity, but a sense of opposition – a 'them' against which an 'us' can be formed – is often the strongest (as the Chinese government has discovered to its cost in both Xinjiang and Tibet). After Yang Zenxin was killed in 1928, his successor, Jin Shuren, introduced a series of punitive taxes that led to widespread discontent, culminating in a rebellion in Hami in 1931. There were also local causes: land was being confiscated from farmers and given to Han settlers from other parts of China (a complaint that would recur during the Communist era). For the next two years Xinjiang was in chaos, with Republican troops, local forces and the armies of Ma Zhongying, a Hui warlord from Gansu province, all competing for control of the region. Though Hui and Uyghur troops often fought alongside one another, this wasn't always the case, something that should caution against the idea that religious differences, rather than a general sense of injustice, were the main forces driving the conflict.

Jin's rule didn't last long – in April 1933 he was ousted in a coup and replaced by Sheng Shicai, who was heavily supported by the Soviet Union (in return for mineral and oil resources). In January 1934 they sent troops and planes to Urumqi, where Sheng was under siege from the army of Ma Zhongying. The planes dropped chemical weapons on Ma's army, which retreated to south-west Xinjiang and took control of Kashgar. In some respects, this was just another occupation of a city that had been conquered and lost many times in the preceding centuries. But from the perspective of many Uyghur nationalists today, it cut short the first real expression of modern Uyghur identity.

The Turkic Islamic Republic of East Turkestan (ETR) had only just been established in the Kashgar and Hotan region in November 1933. More than 20,000 attended its inauguration, at which students sang: 'Our flag is a blue flag, our horde is a golden horde, Turkestan is the homeland of our Turk people, it has become ours.' The fact that the ETR's first coins were minted as being from the 'Republic of Uyghuristan' indicates the growing currency of the 'Uyghur' ethnonym, though the fact that its leaders were also Kyrgyz and from other Turkic peoples suggests that the term was still not being used in the narrower sense in which it is used today. The establishment of the ETR undoubtedly helped towards this, as well as creating an iconography – the flag of a white crescent and star upon a turquoise background – that many Uyghur nationalists still use.

Though it may seem like remarkably bad luck that the ETR ended so swiftly – and at the hands of an army that was only there as a result of a forced retreat – it's unlikely that it would have survived much longer, given it had few resources and no foreign backers. If Ma's armies hadn't ended it, Sheng's forces surely would have.

Sheng didn't only rely on the Soviets for military and economic assistance. In the mid-1930s he also imported their approach to classifying people: 'Uyghur' thus became the official name for the Muslim Turkic people of south Xinjiang (though the name 'Taranchi' was retained). Like many other imperial powers before them (and since), the Soviets wanted a simple way to understand the peoples in the territory they acquired. Though this sometimes involved an attempt to study their culture and language, it often resulted in ethnic labels that failed to reflect how people saw themselves and others. One purpose of this was to divide the population enough to prevent them uniting against a common foe, and in the short term this was often achieved. But ultimately these labels often ended up creating a shared identity among people who hadn't thought of themselves as having a history and culture in common, with the result that they began to aspire to self-governance, which was arguably one cause of the eventual break-up of the Soviet Union.

While the official recognition of 'Uyghur' ethnicity cannot be credited with introducing the term, it did promote its acceptance. Of equal importance in doing so was the network of Cultural Promotion Societies (CPS) that existed throughout Xinjiang. The Soviets encouraged the creation of such societies for each of the recognised ethnic groups in Xinjiang, and they were primarily responsible for organising education in these communities. The first CPS had been created during the ETR, and both it and the later Soviet-backed CPS groups helped foster a sense of ethnic identity by stressing the linguistic similarities of those involved. By the beginning of the 1940s the term 'Uyghur' was being used throughout the region, though it probably took several more decades before it was entirely accepted.

Although the term didn't technically include the Taranchis of the Ili region, the links between the Turkic peoples of south and north Xinjiang were stronger than they had been in the 1920s. One indication of this was provided by an uprising that began in the Ili region in 1944. Sheng's popularity had plummeted since 1937, when he launched a series of purges that detained thousands of people, especially intellectuals and nationalists. The cause of the Ili uprising was his attempt to requisition 10,000 horses for military use. Those who couldn't supply horses had to pay a fine. This hit the nomadic herders in the region hardest, who started a guerrilla insurgency. They managed to overwhelm the north-west part of the region (though not Urumqi), and declared the founding of the second East Turkestan Republic. The kinship between the second ETR and the first was made even more explicit by their use of the same flag. Uyghur activists still use this flag in demonstrations and on their websites, and claim both republics as evidence of Uyghur self-rule before the founding of the People's Republic of China. Though there's an element of truth to this, the facts of the second ETR, like the first, don't entirely fit the narrative. Though Uyghurs were heavily represented in its leadership, the second ETR aimed to represent a much broader set of interests than just Uyghur nationalism. It was both secular and Islamic, and aimed to represent all the non-Han peoples of the region.

Another reason it's hard to see the second ETR as a fully fledged independence movement is that it was heavily indebted to the Soviet Union for most of its troops and equipment. In 1942 Sheng had switched his allegiance from the Soviets to the Guomindang forces (the ruling party of the Chinese Republic after 1928), and had the former's forces and advisers expelled from the region. By supporting the Ili rebellion the Soviets were able to re-establish their influence in Xinjiang.

Having a powerful backer was not the only respect in which the second ETR was more fortunate than the first. The Guomindang were

31

too busy fighting the Japanese (and, to a lesser extent, the Communists) to start another military campaign. As a result the ETR was allowed to develop, and Soviet influence in the region grew, to the point that a consulate was opened in Yining. Even today, the building still stands (though it is now a restaurant), along with several others from that era, such as a long two-storey building with wooden floors that serves as the administrative offices of a teachers' college (where I taught in 2001).

Unsurprisingly, the Guomindang didn't trust Sheng (especially after he tried switching back to the Soviets). They sent in their own troops to undermine him; in August 1944 he agreed to a transfer. His replacement, Zhang Zhizhong, was probably the most accommodating Chinese official the region has ever had. Under his leadership, the Guomindang formed a coalition with the ETR in 1946. He consulted with prominent Uyghur intellectuals who favoured autonomy within China, and made Uyghur and Kazakh official languages of Xinjiang, including in education. He also wanted non-Han Chinese people to occupy 70 per cent of official positions, and introduced elections for county assemblies. Zhang even went so far as to suggest a radical level of autonomy for the region, arguing: 'We Chinese comprise only 5% of the population of Sinkiang [Xinjiang]. Why have we not turned over political powers to the Uigurs and other racial groups?'

The coalition was widely praised in the media. One newspaper went so far as to say that it meant Xinjiang 'was more advanced than China proper' and 'a model for other provinces', a claim not repeated since, or likely to be. Though many others in the Guomindang were less enthused by Zhang's progressive views, the measures were implemented nonetheless. In many cases, the results were less than inspiring, especially in the elections. In southern Xinjiang there was so much intimidation and so many electoral irregularities in the Guomindang-run districts that not even one Turkic candidate was elected. As for the changes in the bureaucracy, although some Han officials were replaced, the number fell short of the promised percentage. The changes made both Chinese officials and many non-Han peoples dissatisfied: the officials resented being displaced, while the non-Han peoples were unhappy that the pledge had only been partially fulfilled. The failure of this well-meaning attempt at positive discrimination to please anyone would be repeated during the Communist era, when preferential policies in family planning (and, to a lesser extent, education) were equally unpopular.

The other well-meaning – though equally ill-fated – initiative that Zhang introduced was the sending of non-Han song-and-dance performers from Xinjiang to inner China, so as to increase appreciation for the musical culture of the region. While this initiative should, in itself, be lauded, in hindsight it's hard not to see this as the (at least partial) originator of the stereotype in mainstream Chinese culture of members of ethnic minorities as colourful performers.

The coalition between the ETR and the Guomindang was never likely to last – their interests were too different. The treaty fell apart, and Zhang was replaced. By summer 1949 the People's Liberation Army (PLA) was in neighbouring Gansu and Qinghai provinces. There's an unconfirmed story that Stalin told the Guomindang commander in Urumqi that if he declared independence for the region he would offer military assistance. Whatever the truth of this, the Guomindang commander chose to have his 80,000 troops surrender. And so, in October 1949, the Communists took control of Xinjiang.

2

'LIBERATION': THE COMMUNIST ERA BEGINS

Xinjiang has frequently been characterised by the Chinese government as a 'backward' region in need of (socialist) modernisation, often with the implicit suggestion that the culture of its people is equally retrograde, especially compared to that of the Han. As recently as 2009 the Ministry of Information wrote that the 'Han are superior in the areas of their economic cultural level, science and technology, and their labour resources'. But in 1949 the region was clearly one of the poorest in the new People's Republic. Much farmland was fallow, livestock was decimated and the irrigation systems established by previous rulers were in disrepair. There were few hospitals (especially outside cities), no railways and almost no significant industry. The scarcity of land fit for cultivation, coupled with high mortality rates, meant that Xinjiang had one of the lowest population densities in China, despite accounting for one-sixth of its total area. Of its roughly 4.3 million people, 70 per cent lived in the south, which was the economic centre.

The official version of the incorporation of Xinjiang into the People's Republic of China is that it was a 'peaceful liberation' welcomed by all the peoples of the region, who became 'masters of the state'. But the conduct of the new authorities suggests that the situation was more volatile. After all, this was a region where there had been scattered uprisings and violence against predominantly Han Chinese authorities for a long period. While there wasn't a mass uprising against the change in regime, the 'liberation' wasn't unopposed. For the next few years there were conflicts between former Guomindang troops and bandits, and in 1954 a brief uprising took place in Hotan.

The main potential source of organised resistance, the ETR, had already been dissolved. After 'liberation' most of its leaders flew to Beijing to negotiate with Mao, but the plane crashed on the way. Exactly what caused the crash is unknown, with the result that there has been speculation ever since over whether Mao (or Stalin) had them killed. Some of the ETR's surviving leaders, such as Mehmet Emin Bugra and Isa Yusef Alptekin, escaped to Turkey in the early 1950s. In March 1952 Turkey offered asylum to 2,000 Uyghurs who had fled into India and Pakistan, and to another 900 the following year. Turkey was a stable base from which Alptekin and Bugra conducted low-level political activism, publishing journals and newspapers and attending conferences.

As for the legacy of the ETR, the Communist Party presents its achievements very differently to Uyghur nationalists, who view it as a proto-independent Uyghur state. Though between 1951 and 1952 there were purges of Turkic leaders with links to the ETR, from the safe distance of decades later the ETR is now praised by the Communist Party for its contribution to the struggle against the Guomindang. In Yining there is a street named after Ahmetjan Kasimi, one of the ETR leaders who perished in the crash. In a nearby park there is a monument to him and the other leaders, bearing a quote from Mao: 'May their spirit live forever!' it proclaims.

Despite the lack of major opposition, the Communists were cautious. Their main objective during the first decade was to develop the region's economy. In this respect (and in many others), their strategy echoed the Qing's. Between 1952 and 1954 they began forming a network of state-managed farms, factories and mines whose aims were to develop agriculture and industry, in particular land-reclamation and mining. The manpower for these projects came from around 100,000 demobilised PLA troops, to which were later added convicts, demobilised Guomindang soldiers and roughly 100,000 settlers from inner China (especially from Shanghai) who were lured with slogans like: 'Put your weapons aside and pick up the tools of construction.' There was also a very questionable initiative involving 40,000 female 'volunteers', mainly from Hunan and Shandong provinces, who were sent to Xinjiang to try to redress the greater proportion of Han males in the region. Many of these women were virtually forced into marriage to soldier farmers. Instead of being given military status, these women were relegated to 'housewife' status, which lacked the same salary and pension as their male counterparts. By also blocking their means to return to their hometowns, this policy made their situation so precarious that marriage was the only secure option.

For them, as for many others, there was a huge gap between actual conditions in Xinjiang and what they had been promised. Instead of factory jobs and hot baths there was mostly hardship: 'We lived in holes in the ground, and all we did night and day was hard labour,' recalled Han Zuxue in 2009, who was a teenager when he left his home in far-off Henan province. 'At first we cried every day but over time we forgot our sadness.'

The migration and resettlement of this huge labour force was overseen by the Xinjiang Production and Construction Corps (XPCC), also known as the *bingtuan*, an organisation with a dual role. Though its major function was ostensibly to coordinate agricultural development, it was also there to keep order, hence its slogan: 'On one shoulder a rifle, on the other a hoe.' The XPCC put the migrants and former soldiers to work clearing land, building dams and digging canals. In just over a decade it tripled the amount of land being cultivated in Xinjiang and began to shift the economic focus of the province to northern cities like Urumqi, Karamay, Kuytun and Shihezi, which became centres of commerce, industry and transportation.

This great effort to develop Xinjiang was part of the overall strategy of national reconstruction following several decades of war. It was the first time the region was subject to policies that hadn't been specifically created for its particular social and economic conditions. One example was the Xinjiang government's decision in 1954 to apply the same restrictions on people's movements as in the rest of China. In 1950 the national government had brought in laws to prevent urban migration to ensure that there were enough people working the land. People had to stay where their *hukou* (a household registration document) placed them, which for most Uyghurs meant remaining in the countryside. Over the next few decades, as the state encouraged progressively more Han Chinese from other parts of China to migrate to Xinjiang, the population grew steeply. Around 400,000 joined the *bingtuan* between 1954 and 1966, as well as a further 2 million refugees during the famine of the Great Leap Forward of 1959–61. Though not all of them stayed in Xinjiang, those that did were able to settle in towns and cities (either because they already had an urban *hukou* or were granted one).

In some cases this transformed small towns with a Uyghur majority into cities where they were in the minority. The population of Korla, a county town of fewer than 30,000 people on the northern edge of the Tarim Basin, where in 1949 Han people represented less than 2 per cent of the population, tripled after 1955. By 1965 Han people were more than half the population. Yet in other places, where non-Han were still the majority, many of these settlers did make an effort to learn the local language and become part of the community.

The eventual outcome of this in-migration was that by the 1980s the rural–urban divide also had an ethnic dimension, which would lead to profound economic disadvantages for Uyghurs, as we shall see in Chapter 3. But this wasn't an intended consequence of the policy, just an unfortunate by-product of its being applied in the same way as in the rest of the country. The more general point this suggests is that we should hesitate before assuming that *every* instance of inequality suffered by non-Han peoples in Xinjiang is the result of ethnic discrimination.

Collectivisation was another national policy that profoundly altered Xinjiang society. The Communists regarded private landownership as a feudal, unjust practice: such land had to be confiscated and returned to the people. Though there were many such confiscations in Xinjiang – land was mostly taken from religious organisations and the rich – that it did so more slowly, especially in areas with many nomadic people (like the Ili region) suggests that many officials in Xinjiang were being cautious, and with good reason. Most couldn't communicate directly with the local people, whose customs they were wholly unfamiliar with. This was also something officials had been warned about: an article in the *Xinjiang People's Daily* newspaper in 1950 by Wang Zhen, the leader of the PLA in the region, spoke out against 'Great Hanism' – the rigid application of policies developed for other parts of China, with little consideration of local conditions, or consultation with minority officials. At the beginning of Communist rule such sentiments were not just rhetoric. *Bingtuan* were initially established only in north Xinjiang, in predominantly Han areas, and Islamic education in madrasas was allowed until the mid-1950s.

A concerted effort was also made to recruit non-Han people to join the new administration, with some success. Uyghurs, Kazakhs and other minorities became well represented at lower levels of government, though their holding of higher positions was invariably nominal, with a Han deputy usually possessing the real authority (an arrangement that continues today). The chairman of the region, Saifudin Aziz, who was one of the few surviving ETR leaders (he had taken the train to Beijing), had little real influence in the region, which until 1967 was actually governed by Wang Enmao and his supporters. Wang was the first governor of the region, despite being only 36 and without any administrative experience or much education. But his revolution-ary credentials were excellent: he was a veteran of the Long March (the Red Army's prolonged retreat from the Guomindang between October 1934 and October 1935) and the political commissar of the PLA's First Field Army. He drew heavily on the army when picking his staff – during his governorship around 40 per cent of top officials had an army background.

In addition to transforming the land, the Communists also changed the administrative boundaries of Xinjiang. Despite proposals that the region be declared a socialist republic, as the Soviets had done with their territories in Central Asia, it was instead designated an 'autonomous region': that is, it would have more influence on policy than a province but still be ruled by the central government. (Autonomous regions were also created in Tibet, Guangxi, Ningxia and Inner Mongolia.) While Saifudin would toe the party line for the rest of his long political career – he would consistently be one of the strictest opponents of separatism and Soviet influence – his one major contribution was to urge that the region's name reflect its ethnic composition. In the early 1940s Xinjiang's population was just under 4 million, roughly 75 per cent of whom were Uyghur. At that point, Han Chinese weren't even the second largest ethnic group in Xinjiang: there were 326,000 Kazakhs, 187,000 Han, 92,000 Hui and 65,000 Kyrgyz. Saifudin told Mao that 'autonomy is not given to mountains and rivers. It is given to particular nationalities.' (By 'nationalities' he meant ethnic groups.)

As a result, the Xinjiang *Uyghur* Autonomous Region came into being in 1955. The adoption of this name may have further boosted the sense among some Uyghurs that they had a claim to all of Xinjiang, not just the south, where they were concentrated. The associated rhetoric of minorities being 'masters in their own house' would also have raised many Uyghurs' expectations that they might have some input into decisions that affected them. However, one crucial difference between the autonomous regions the Communists created and the Soviet republics they were modelled on was that the latter had the right to secede, something that was expressly forbidden in the new Chinese constitution.

The logic of 'recognising ethnicity' was also applied to internal governance. Areas with high concentrations of a particular ethnic group were labelled 'autonomous prefectures' (after 'province', 'prefecture' is the second-largest administrative level in China, and often just refers to a city). These were established all over China; in Xinjiang five were created: one for Hui (in Changji), two for Mongols (in Bayinguoleng and Bortala), one for Kazakhs (in Ili) and one for Kyrgyz (in Kizilsu). The stated intention was to ensure these peoples' rights by making them *dang jia zuo zhu* ('masters of their own house'), but several features of the policy call this into question. One was that the titular ethnic group often wasn't the largest group in the area; another was that the amount of land each minority was awarded was often more than its share of the population (for instance, in Bayinguoleng, which accounts for a third of Xinjiang's total area, Mongols were only 35 per cent of the population). Gardner Bovingdon, a professor of Central Eurasian studies at Indiana University, proposes that the Communists may have hoped to promote territorial disputes among the non-Han peoples, with the aim of preventing solidarity among them while also attempting to undermine the demographic superiority of Uyghurs.

Wang's efforts to govern Xinjiang differently were thwarted by the nation's changing political climate. When Mao initiated the Hundred Flowers campaign in 1956 to encourage criticism of party rule (or, as he put it, 'to coax the snakes from their holes'), the grievances aired in Xinjiang were far stronger than the 'gentle breeze and mild rain' that had been requested. Non-Han peoples complained that in spite of Xinjiang's 'autonomous' status they had no control over policy, and denounced the XPCC as 'Han colonists'. They also castigated local officials for only using Chinese, and complained that whenever they voiced criticisms of the party they were labelled 'separatists' (complaints still heard today). The party responded in exactly the manner it had earlier criticised: in 1958 more than 1,500 people were branded 'local nationalists', many of whom were jailed. The same year, Saifudin gave a lamentable speech that refuted the accusations of Great Hanism, and justified the preponderance of Han officials in top positions by saying it was due to their advanced revolutionary experience.

Wang Enmao went further in 1960 when he spoke of his belief that 'the complete blending of all the nationalities' was necessary for the continuing development of Xinjiang. The assumption behind this was that if the minorities were sufficiently assimilated then their ethnic identity would fade away until there was only (Han) Chinese culture left. Chinese history is full of references to 'barbarians' and their inferior culture – before 1949, part of the Chinese characters used for non-Han peoples implied that they were animal-like (which perhaps finds an echo in the common stereotype among Han Chinese that Uyghurs are 'wild' or 'untamed'). In recent years a version of this idea has been expressed by references in official discourse to the low 'quality' (in Chinese, *suzhi*) of people in minority areas.

The modern notion of Han racial and cultural superiority has its roots in the ideas of Sun Yat-sen, the Republican president. Sun argued that the true Chinese nation was composed of five races – Han, Hui, Manchus, Mongols and Tibetans – with the result that 'All under heaven is shared by everyone'. Some scholars argue that Sun's racial theories played a major role in creating the idea of a 'Han Chinese' identity, and to some degree, the idea of 'China' as a nation. Sun saw this as necessary to unite the population against the Qing; before this, regional differences in language and culture were probably as significant in determining identity as perceived similarities (not unlike the Turkic peoples of Xinjiang). But Sun didn't see the 'Republic of Five Races' as an alliance of equals. In 1924 he described the Han as the 'single, pure race' of the Chinese nation, and took a strong line on the need for assimilation, arguing that 'the dying out of all names of individual people inhabiting China, such as Manchus, Tibetans, etc.' was a necessary step to have a unified nation (summed up by the Chinese phrase *minzu tuanjie*).

While it would be simplistic to argue that this belief has been the sole aim of all Chinese government policy in Xinjiang, some version of this argument has been frequently articulated by Chinese officials and intellectuals during the Communist era. In 1957 Premier Zhou Enlai described assimilation as 'a progressive act if it means the natural merger of nations [i.e. ethnic groups] advancing towards prosperity. Assimilation as such has the significance of promoting progress.'

Though the motivations behind many party decisions are often obscure, when it comes to a number of policy areas, especially education and religion (which I will discuss later), it's hard to avoid drawing the conclusion that some 'blending' of the Uyghurs is one of the intended outcomes. There's certainly not much ambiguity in this statement from the Ethnic Unity Education Board: 'The fading away of ethnicity is an inevitable result of ethnic self-development and self-improvement. It is a global process realised across the world. It is the final result of ethnic development at its highest stage.'

THE CHAOS OF THE CULTURAL REVOLUTION

The deterioration of Sino-Soviet relations had major ramifications in Xinjiang. Some of this was due to tensions originating in the long Soviet involvement in the region – they had been awarded preferential access to its oil and metals for 30 years – but the abrogation of these treaties in the late 1950s failed to prevent the rift from widening. The real problem was the ideological differences between Mao and Khrushchev after the latter criticised Stalin's policies – and therefore, by extension, Mao's, which had often followed those of his Soviet counterpart.

The lowest point of Sino-Soviet relations occurred in 1962, when famine caused by the disastrous agricultural policies of Mao's Great Leap Forward forced 50,000 people to flee from the Ili region into Kazakhstan. The border was closed, and the PLA and the forces of the XPCC occupied the area. This was met by a protest of tens of thousands (mostly Uyghurs and Kazakhs) in the main square, which soon degenerated into a riot. Government buildings were attacked and officials (both Han and minority) were taken prisoner and beaten. The crowds had to be dispersed by gunfire.

This incident accelerated the exodus of Russians from the region. In 1949 there had been 20,000 Russians in Xinjiang; by the 1970s there were around 500. There were also purges and arrests in Xinjiang in the early 1960s of those deemed to have pro-Soviet viewpoints. The Chinese Communists were so worried about possible alliances between Uyghurs and peoples living in Soviet territory that they changed the written form of Uyghur (which at the time used a Cyrillic alphabet) to a Latin script. Any communication with relatives in the Soviet Union was viewed with great suspicion. If a person received a letter, the police might take him or her in for questioning.

There were also continuing efforts to boost patriotism among non-Han peoples, such as the song 'Ode to the Motherland', which was introduced into Uyghur schools in 1962 and remained part of the curriculum until the end of the 1980s:

> China is my dear mother, the place of my birth, I am her son
> To her I am bound with my body and all my love.
>
> My focal point is my party, it is my companion, my leader
> Each fight it throws me into is a pleasure for me.
>
> This red epoch of mine is my pride, my glory
> I am proud of being a singer and constructor of this time.

Though the Sino-Soviet split had major consequences for Chinese society, a far greater turbulence soon engulfed the country. In May 1966, Mao launched his Great Proletarian Cultural Revolution, whose stated intent was to eradicate all traditional, capitalistic and non-revolutionary elements from society, especially intellectuals. The general tenor of this campaign can be seen from the announcement in the *Xinjiang People's Daily* in June 1966 that the Cultural Revolution was 'unfolding in the region like a tempestuous storm, exposing the representatives of the bourgeoisie who had wormed their way into the party, wiping out all monsters and freaks'. The vulnerability of Xinjiang to yet another mass campaign originating in Beijing was further proof the region wasn't autonomous in any meaningful sense.

But while the political rhetoric in Xinjiang was of the same tenor as that in the rest of the country, Wang Enmao initially managed to keep the disorder within limits, with the result that the top officials were not subjected to intense criticism and retained their posts. This was anathema to the cohort of Red Guards – the revolutionary Maoist youth – who arrived from Beijing in August 1966. They wouldn't have seen the irony of their claims that Wang was a de facto separatist, and that Xinjiang was being run as an 'independent kingdom'.

For the next three years there were clashes between the Red Guards from outside the province and those loyal to Wang Enmao. The most dramatic sign that things were slipping from Wang's control was the clashes in January 1967 in Shihezi, a new town that was the headquarters of the main *bingtuan* division near Urumqi (and whose population was, and is, almost entirely Han). A radical faction attempted to seize control of a textile factory, and detained several veteran XPCC officers. The following day ten trucks of soldiers turned up, and in the ensuing fighting dozens were killed.

Factional fighting continued in Xinjiang until the end of the 1960s, usually without significant involvement of non-Han peoples. The closest thing to their mass participation was a plan for a rally against Wang's 'Great Hanism', with tens of thousands projected to attend, but this was prevented by intervention from the PLA and the *bingtuan* on the orders of Zhou Enlai, the Chinese premier, who feared that the rally might foster unity among the Turkic peoples.

The non-Han peoples' lack of involvement in the conflicts between the different Red Guard factions didn't exempt them from the overall thrust of the Cultural Revolution – previous attempts at respecting the special characteristics of the peoples of the region were labelled 'reactionary'. After Wang was replaced by Long Shujin in 1968 there was no attempt to blunt the force of radical policies. While traditional Han culture was as much a target as that of ethnic minorities, Jiang Qing, Mao's rabidly ideological wife, seems to have had a particular hatred for minorities, whom she described as 'foreign invaders'. In Xinjiang minority customs and beliefs were condemned for being 'backward' and 'feudal'. Mosques were desecrated, Qur'ans were burnt, rural bazaars were closed. Music, dance and popular festivals were forbidden. Uyghur intellectuals were persecuted, such as the linguist Ibrahim Muti'i (who had the three thick volumes of a dictionary he'd worked on dropped onto his head). When I visited the holy tomb of Tughluq Timur, who was the last of the Chaghatai Mongol khans, and who greatly encouraged the spread of Islam in the region, its caretaker told me that the Red Guards had forced the villagers to keep pigs inside it. Similar humiliations appear to have occurred in most parts of Xinjiang. One man in Kashgar who was found to have recited the Qur'an when a friend's baby was born was led around on a donkey with his face blackened, and had to hold a sign reading: 'I must not believe in old ways.' The irony was that the punishment itself was an 'old way' – in the 1930s this was a punishment in some parts of Xinjiang for adulterous couples, who also had their faces blackened, and then were sat naked and facing each other on two donkeys.

Though not able to oppose such attacks on their religion and culture directly, many non-Han peoples found other ways to resist. Religious texts were buried, and some dared to carry on their religious practices in the (theoretical) privacy of their homes. This could involve actual prayers, but there were other, more discreet rituals. Ildikó Bellér-Hann, a historical anthropologist, has written about a number of spiritual practices involved in food preparation, many of them to do with seeking blessings or commemorating the dead. The everyday act of heating oil for cooking could also be a 'private and virtually invisible act of negotiating with the spirit world'.

While Uyghur culture was being suppressed in China, it was being promoted by the Soviets. During the Cultural Revolution a Uyghur-language theatre was opened in Almaty, and in Tashkent a Uyghur ensemble started to play music on Uzbek radio and TV. The latter was partly because the Uzbek vice minister for media was Uyghur, but more because it was a way to attract talent and undermine Chinese policy. It also meant that when relations between the Soviets and China did improve, there were social and cultural links between Uyghur communities in both countries that could be rekindled.

The Cultural Revolution can now be discussed fairly openly in China (albeit within certain limits), but the full story of the persecution of minorities in Xinjiang during that time has yet to be told. However, it seems reasonable to assume that the targeting of non-Han peoples' cultural and religious practices must have seriously harmed relations between them and the authorities. The closest thing to an official apology would come at a meeting in 1978, when the excesses of the period were admitted. It was said that 'the big stick of class struggle' had been wrongfully used to 'persecute many minority national cadres and the masses'. The speech went on to say that this had been an 'extremely bitter experience from which we learnt a lesson' – something that was, alas, untrue.

The chaos of the Cultural Revolution got so out of hand in Xinjiang – there were 1,300 clashes between 1967 and 1968 – that the central government put the running of the region (including the *bingtuan*) under the control of the PLA. The government probably feared that either the Soviets or an indigenous faction might take advantage of the disorder. However, while there were grievances against Communist rule, no significant attacks on the Chinese authorities in Xinjiang took place during the Cultural Revolution. The lack of incident – let alone a mass uprising – suggests either that there weren't high levels of dissatisfaction among Uyghurs and the other Turkic peoples, or that the authorities had successfully driven a wedge between the different ethnic groups. The biggest disturbances in the region took place after the end of the Cultural Revolution, and involved only Han Chinese. Thousands of young people who had been sent from Shanghai to Aksu during the Cultural Revolution wanted to return, but found that their *hukous* had been changed to ones registered in Xinjiang. Thousands of them protested in 1979, and then again in 1980, but few were allowed to leave.

Though the PLA's adoption of control put a stop to serious conflict in the *bingtuan*, it was too late to prevent its collapse. Around 70,000 of its personnel had been declared 'class enemies' or 'demon monsters', and the fighting had destroyed its capacity to function. As in the rest of the country, the Cultural Revolution had destroyed all semblance of normal life, but given the already fragile state of Xinjiang's economy, the damage was proportionally greater. Agriculture failed to grow between 1965 and 1975, despite the 40 per cent increase in population. The dire condition of life in the *bingtuan* led many Han Chinese to leave the region in the mid-1970s: between 1974 and 1975 the Han population fell from 2.3 million to 1.7 million. Finally, in 1975, the XPCC was formally dissolved.

The various bodies that replaced it didn't improve matters. Over the following two years the economy in Xinjiang worsened even further: industrial output declined by two-thirds. More radical reforms, on a nationwide scale, were soon to occur. In December 1978 the new Chinese leader Deng Xiaoping began the *gaige kaifang* – the process of economic 'opening up' that would dismantle most of the key features of Mao's regime. At the beginning this involved the decollectivisation of agriculture, the opening of the country to foreign investment and allowing people to open private businesses, all of which were said to be part of building 'socialism with Chinese characteristics'. As for the apparent contradiction of a communist regime embracing free-market capitalism, this was justified by the reasoning that the transition to pure socialism first required acquiring modern science and technology, so as to develop high levels of productivity.

In Xinjiang, as in the rest of the country, this led to impressive results: its GDP would grow by 10 per cent per year from 1978 to 2000, and in 2000 it would have the highest GDP per capita of any non-coastal province in China. But although the region developed greatly during this time, there were soon doubts about the way in which these new policies were being implemented in the region. There would be awkward questions about the ultimate aim of development – and whether the benefits were being equally shared.

3

'OPENING UP'

In 1984 a small town in south-west Xinjiang was awarded the title of 'Ethnic Unity Model'. The population of Baren, in Akto county, in the Kizilsu Kyrgyz Autonomous Prefecture, was two-thirds Uyghur and slightly less than one-third Kyrgyz, with the remainder Han Chinese, Tajik and Hui. While this kind of ethnic diversity is common in Xinjiang, the authorities seldom miss a chance to stress the value of 'ethnic unity'. The town's apparent stability made the violent incident that took place there six years later an even greater shock for the government – and it is today the event most Western analysts regard as the first major confrontation between Uyghurs and the Chinese authorities in Xinjiang.

According to the Chinese government, on the morning of 5 April an angry mob of several hundred set off from a mosque and then surrounded the compound that housed the local government headquarters. They recited 'sacred war oaths' with the intent 'to create trouble', and some of the protesters are said to have carried a banner predicting the defeat of Marxism–Leninism by religion. A report on the incident on Xinjiang TV would later display documents allegedly found on the protesters calling for jihad and death to 'infidels'.

The situation deteriorated after 300 more people joined the protest later that day. When two officials were sent to negotiate, they were killed by the crowd. In response, armed police were sent in, but were unable to subdue the riot and ended up being held under siege. Though the police came under further fire, they apparently only 'counter-attacked in a restrained manner'. According to some Chinese sources, two carloads of police were killed with axes and knives, and the vehicles were set on fire.

During the night the rioters launched an armed attack on the compound, shooting and throwing explosives. Order wasn't restored until 6 April, when the armed police were reinforced by PLA troops, who claimed they killed ten insurgents. The attack was blamed on a radical organisation called the Islamic Party of East Turkestan, led by Zahideen Yusup, who the authorities said had died during the fighting. There was no suggestion that the riot could have been caused by any local grievances.

While the above account seems to present a cohesive story of what happened, it should be treated with great caution. There's no credible eyewitness testimony or other evidence, such as photos or video footage, with which to corroborate it. A radically different view of events is offered by the WUC, which claims that 'the Chinese government cracked down on peaceful protest by Uyghurs demanding greater democracy and religious freedom […] hundreds of men, women and children have been massacred during the brutal crackdown.'

A similar, if more measured account was put forward by Amnesty International, who said that government forces had dispersed hundreds of Uyghur villagers protesting in front of the local government offices. They cited claims from unofficial sources that 50 protesters died as a result, some of whom were shot while running away, and that there were 'mortar attacks and firing by troops from helicopters'.

These accounts share little beyond an acknowledgement that a crowd gathered outside the Baren government building, and that many were injured and killed in the violence that followed. Many questions remain unanswered, such as whether the protest was planned or spontaneous, or whether the crowd used violence before the authorities intervened.

The closest thing to a report at the time is an article by William Peters, a former British diplomat, who visited Xinjiang in September 1990. Peters notes that the protest took place during Ramadan, and says it was a response to the local authorities blocking the construction of a mosque and madrasa. He also implies that the protesters were both Kyrgyz and Uyghur – not the kind of 'ethnic unity' the government had in mind. He mentions armed patrols and a curfew in Kashgar for several months afterwards, and that the Karakoram Highway was closed that summer. Most intriguingly, Peters claims that a 'reliable source' told him that a different demonstration had been planned by Uyghurs for 12 April, the end of Ramadan, to protest against Han migration to Xinjiang. After the crackdown that followed the Baren incident, this could no longer take place. There is an embarrassment of unsupported rumours in Xinjiang – the inevitable consequence of not having an independent media – but some support for this one comes from a remark made to Enver Tohti (an exiled dissident whose story I tell in Chapter 5). While in Tashkent in the early spring of 1990, Tohti was told to 'Watch the Kyrgyz area in your country, there's something wrong. They are going to do something.'

Though Peters' report is suggestive, it shouldn't be taken as conclusive. Ultimately, whether one decides that Baren was a peaceful protest that reflected ordinary people's grievances or an Islamist separatist rebellion probably depends on one's more general view of the Chinese government, and the reliability of the Chinese media. However, while the veracity of any information broadcast or published under the aegis of the Chinese state (which includes academia) can legitimately be doubted, the presence of a systematic bias doesn't mean that Chinese sources should be dismissed automatically. Despite the presence of a dominant narrative of events, there are still discontinuities in coverage that can be revealing. For example, while many Chinese sources emphasise that the crowd was heavily armed, sources that list the actual numbers of weapons recovered suggest the rioters had far fewer weapons, most of which were crude. These figures undermine the notion that the demonstration was a highly organised and well-financed incident, and instead imply a more impromptu confrontation.

But rejecting the Chinese government's version of the Baren incident doesn't mean we have to accept the WUC's claim that it was a 'massacre'.

There are strong incentives for the WUC and other such organisations to downplay the use of force by Uyghurs: few funders want to be accused of promoting violence. Exaggerating the severity of the Chinese government's response may also be seen as a way to increase attention and sympathy for the WUC's arguments (just as the Chinese government arguably exaggerates the threat of Uyghur terrorism).

The Baren incident was also the first major event in Xinjiang to be covered by foreign media. The international edition of *Newsweek* had a cover story titled 'The other China – restless minorities are testing Beijing', while the *Chicago Tribune* ran a lamentable piece titled 'China's ethnic Turks may wage holy war'. The latter serves as an unhappy reminder that biased and inaccurate coverage of Islam considerably pre-dates the attacks of 11 September 2001.

The Baren incident exemplifies the challenges of attempting to determine the truth about most public disturbances in Xinjiang. Trying to say what happened requires choosing between contradictory accounts put forward by far from impartial sources. In this respect, such incidents recapitulate the general difficulty faced when writing *anything* about the region, including what to call it – even using the name 'Xinjiang' is interpreted by some as a tacit validation of the Chinese government's claim to the territory. As S. Frederick Starr, editor of one of the most influential recent academic books about Xinjiang, put it: 'there is hardly any "fact" concerning Xinjiang that is so solid, no source of information that is so independent, and no analysis based on such overwhelming evidence that someone does not hotly contest its validity or meaning.'

XINJIANG 'OPENS UP'

While it is obviously important to establish what happened in Baren, given the limitations of the available evidence it is perhaps more profitable to examine possible causes. Whether people are peacefully protesting, or leading an armed rebellion, it is often for reasons that stem from the conditions of their daily lives (although this doesn't necessarily justify those actions).

The 1980s were a decade of major political and social changes in China, the principal goal of which was the economic rejuvenation of the country. There was a major gap between the cities and the countryside – in the latter the infant-mortality rate was twice as high as in the cities, only half of all children finished primary school, and around 100 million were perpetually caught between hunger and starvation. In Xinjiang there was a significant difference in rural–urban average life expectancy (69 years in cities compared to 57 in the country). In 1980 Xinjiang had yet to recover from the turmoil of the Cultural Revolution, even in agriculture. It was still reliant on other provinces for grain (and would be until 1985), mainly because Xinjiang's total population had increased to 13 million, much of it driven by state-sponsored immigration from other provinces. The Han Chinese proportion of the population had risen to about 40 per cent – a huge increase, and one that may have been an underestimation, as this figure did not include soldiers and many workers in the state-owned industries and farms whose *hukous* were located in other provinces.

Xinjiang wasn't excluded from the initial phase of economic opening, but it certainly wasn't a priority. Since 1953 China's leaders have presented their policies for the country's development in Five-year Plans (once again aping the Soviet model). Both the Sixth (1981–5) and Seventh (1986–90) Plans focussed on encouraging growth in the south and east of the country; the main requirement of the provinces in the west (which officially includes six provinces and two other autonomous regions besides Xinjiang) was that they supply raw materials to other provinces. The economic rationale for this uneven development was that some regions had to get rich first to set an example to others, allied with which was the idea that the wealth created would then 'trickle down'. Though this misguided belief was widespread in many societies in the 1980s – the wealth usually stayed concentrated at the top – there were opposing voices in China at the time. Some economists presciently argued that increasing the gap between regions could have dire social and political consequences, especially in ethnic-minority regions. Rather than focussing exclusively on development in the east, they argued, there should also be selective targeting of some areas and industries in Xinjiang.

Such ideas were mostly ignored. The main investment in Xinjiang during the 1980s was in infrastructure projects, such as improving transportation within the region and its links to other provinces. The completion of the Karakoram Highway in 1982 also boosted trade between Pakistan and cities in southern Xinjiang. These kinds of major engineering endeavours would remain the linchpin of China's approach to the development of the region.

Though Deng Xiaoping is most commonly associated with the policies of 'opening up', Hu Yaobang, the second most powerful political figure at the time, was instrumental in pushing through Deng's reforms against the objections of Communist Party hardliners. It was Hu who attempted to shift the governance of Xinjiang back to the more permissive approach that had been adopted in the early 1950s. The impetus for this was a riot in 1980 in Aksu over the killing of a Uyghur youth by two Han men. Afterwards Hu initiated a series of inspection tours of Tibet and other minority areas. He proposed that these regions become genuinely autonomous, in part by transferring many Han cadres (consisting of political officers of the Communist Party) to other parts of China. He also advocated that their cultures be encouraged, especially in Xinjiang, which he deemed less of a threat than Tibet, as it lacked an opposition figure with the stature of the Dalai Lama.

These ideas were strongly opposed by the more conservative parts of the Communist Party; one official warned:

> you give them autonomy and they will only turn round and create an East Turkestan. Hu Yaobang also wants to withdraw Han cadres to the interior. That would be surrendering Xinjiang to the Soviet Union and Turkey. Only a traitor would do such a thing.

Hu's proposals weren't fully implemented in Xinjiang: unlike in Tibet, Han cadres weren't transferred out of the region and there wasn't much movement towards real autonomy. It's unclear whether this was because Hu lacked actual commitment to the idea, or, as with Zhang Zhizhong during the Republican era, because his more radical proposals were blocked. (Hu's opponents would oust him from power in 1987.) They nonetheless had a significant impact, according to Ilham Tohti, a professor of economics currently imprisoned on a spurious charge of 'separatism' (see Chapter 8). He argues that during this period there existed relative 'equality among ethnic groups' and a more 'relaxed political atmosphere'.

The most noticeable shift in the new era was a greater tolerance for religion. Xinjiang's Islamic Association was allowed to meet for the first time in 17 years; an Arabic alphabet was reinstated for Uyghur; and thousands of mosques were built or reopened, some with funds from the World Muslim League. Pilgrims were allowed to go on the hadj and there was a surge in religious publications, many of them printed in Pakistan. Muslims were also permitted to study in madrasas abroad.

This new tolerance was partly the result of China's wish to convince potential trading and investment partners from predominantly Muslim countries that Islam was being practised freely in China. A report from Xinhua, the state news agency, spoke hopefully, if not entirely accurately, of Xinjiang's 'long history of close relations with the Muslims of Saudi Arabia, Turkey, Syria, Egypt and Malaysia'.

However, the religious reforms weren't popular with everyone. Some secular Uyghurs in Urumqi argued that religion had been too conservative a force in Uyghur society, and that to encourage it would stifle modernisation. Though this was predominantly the view of a fairly small urban elite, it illustrates one of the potential fault lines that run through Uyghur society.

There was also increasing freedom of expression. Uyghur intellectuals in different cities promoted the work of local writers, many of them from before the Communist era. In the early 1980s the works of Abdukhaliq, a poet from Turpan who wrote under the pen name 'Uyghur' in the 1920s, were republished and there were conferences held about his writing. The revival wasn't a purely literary issue – Abdukhaliq had been executed in 1933 for opposing Sheng Shicai, and was thus considered a martyr. As part of the promotional campaign, a portrait of Abdukhaliq was commissioned, despite the fact there were no photos of him. In desperation, the painter had to resort to exhuming his remains to take cranial measurements.

Another reason intellectuals in Turpan chose to promote Abdukhaliq's work was its nationalistic themes, as this extract from the poem 'Awaken!' shows:

> Hey! Uyghur, it is time to awaken,
> You haven't any possessions,
> You have nothing to fear.
> If you don't rescue yourselves
> From this death,
> Your situation will become very grave.
> Stand up! I say,
> Raise your head and wipe your eyes!
> Cut the heads off your enemies,
> Let the blood flow!

When a large poster of this poem was put up in Kashgar in 1981 the police were so concerned that they launched a search to find the poet, and made people take handwriting tests. Only when they realised that he'd been dead for almost 50 years did they give up.

Writers who had previously been imprisoned, or had their work suppressed, were also permitted to publish. Abdurehim Otkur had been chief editor of the East Turkestan Republic's political newspaper *Altai Gazeti*. In 1949 he had tried to escape China, but was captured and imprisoned until 1958, and then again from 1966 to 1976. After his release he published poems and historical novels set in Hami in the 1920s, which found a large readership. One of his best-known poems, 'Trace', which served as an epigraph to one of these novels, was especially popular.

Our traces are in the deserts and in the valleys,
There are many heroes buried in the desert with no grave.

Don't say they were left without graves,
Their graves covered with flowers in the spring.

Left the crowd, left the scene, they are all faraway,
Wind blows, sand moves, yet our trace never disappears.

The caravan never stops even as our horses become thin,
Our grandchildren or great-grandchildren will one day find those traces.

This poem was reprinted in magazines, put on posters and scrawled on walls. Within the context of a historical novel, this may have seemed innocuous, but when reproduced on its own it could be read as a potent statement about the depth of Uyghur tradition. Most importantly, it seemed to offer a relatively optimistic view of Uyghurs' future – some activists interpreted the use of the future tense at the end as a statement that the struggle for Uyghur independence would one day be successful.

The government also promoted cultural icons from the region, such as Mahmud Kashgari, an eleventh-century scholar who wrote an encyclopaedic dictionary about Eastern Turkic culture (which Ibrahim Muti'i had translated into modern Uyghur after the Cultural Revolution), and Sutuq Bughra Khan, the Karakhanid ruler who converted to Islam in the tenth century. There was even a thousand-page novel written about the latter by Saifudin Aziz, the former regional chairman, which was widely read.

Traditional Uyghur music was also celebrated. Saifudin encouraged the study of *muqam*, the large repertoire of sung stories and poems, instrumental passages and dance tunes. A *muqam* is usually performed by a small ensemble of singers, accompanied by lutes and a drum. The aim of Saifudin's project was to create a formalised canon of 12 *muqam* that would aid their recognition as 'an important treasure in the musical wealth of our multi-national homeland, the People's Republic of China', in the words of the Uyghur scholar Abdushukur Imin. What this initiative shows is that the Chinese government wasn't hostile to Uyghur culture per se – but it had clear ideological reasons for promoting certain aspects over others, in this case to emphasise that while the *muqam* might be a Uyghur tradition, it was primarily a *Chinese* one.

Similar sentiments were expressed at the 1986 National Minority Sports Meeting held in Urumqi. This was something of a misnomer, as there was little competitive element to the displays of skill and athleticism. Banners in the stadium proclaimed: 'To develop the sports of the minority peoples is to further the prosperity of the Motherland.' 'Ethnic unity' was once again emphasised by having teams composed on a regional basis rather than an ethnic one.

The relative liberalisation of culture can be seen as an effort to improve relations between Uyghurs and the authorities after the Aksu riots. But it was also in keeping with the idea that minority culture and identity should be managed by the state, with the ultimate goal of their being subsumed within a national *Chinese* identity. In the short term, activities like the Minority Games or the song-and-dance galas frequently shown on Chinese television aim to foster a benign identity that can be easily managed. As one observer of the games put it: 'The authorities must be hoping to *confine* ethnic consciousness to the realm of folklore.' Minority culture is supposed to be no more than 'colourful reminders of a group's history which do not hinder its integration into the present'.

But the government wasn't going to rely on cultural assimilation to keep control of the region. In 1982 the *bingtuan* were formally reinstated, initially more for their military role than their economic contribution (which was fairly dismal). Wang Zhen argued that the XPCC provided a vital reserve force to back up the PLA: 'These can function as two fists, one in front and another backing it up.' The distribution of *bingtuan* was (and is) determined as much by strategic concerns as by the availability of resources. They encircle most major towns, and are clustered around transport hubs, making it easier to contain any disturbance.

The threat wasn't only perceived to come from internal dissent – tensions between China and the Soviet Union had persisted through the mid- to late 1970s. A 1975 editorial in the *Xinjiang People's Daily* to commemorate the twentieth anniversary of the founding of the XUAR called for action against the 'handful of national splittist elements and counter-revolutionaries under the cloak of religion who throw themselves into the arms of the Soviet revisionists'. Forty years later, one is struck by the remarkable continuity in Communist rhetoric. While the Soviet threat is no longer invoked, the instigators of dissent are still said to be 'hostile foreign forces cloaked in religion'.

The Soviet threat was taken seriously enough for an area bordering Kazakhstan to be put under the control of the PLA in early 1979: China was preparing for border clashes with Vietnam, which was a Soviet client, and feared retaliation. However, relations with the Soviets soon improved, which led to a resumption of trade in the early 1980s, especially via the Horgos border crossing near Yining, which reopened for trade in 1983, and for bus traffic in 1989. This allowed Uyghur families that had been separated since the split in the early 1960s, often with little or no contact, to be reunited finally.

THE WAR IN THE COUNTRYSIDE

While it would be a stretch to say that these were halcyon days in Xinjiang, the new agricultural policies and increased tolerance for religion were certainly welcomed. Contemporary accounts from researchers who visited the area spoke of how, 'Together with the rest of Chinese society, the Uyghurs view the virtual dismantling of economic restrictions, particularly in the countryside, as an opportunity to improve their individual economic status and assert their collective preferences.' Another added that people in Xinjiang 'can now see the shape of the modernisations to come'.

Even in 1996 farmers in south Xinjiang still referred to the reform era as 'the time when the land was given', or, more simply, as 'freedom'. Strictly speaking, the land wasn't given – the state owns all land in China, which in the countryside is administered by village collectives. What villagers were given was the right to *use* certain plots of land. In Xinjiang, as in the rest of the country, the key shift after 1978 was the return of family farms, which allowed farmers to choose the crops they grew (at least in theory). This wasn't initially approved by the state, which at first banned the practice – for many in the party this was a step too close to private ownership. But farmers in many regions, especially in China's rice-growing south, started doing this anyway, often with the collusion of local officials. When this led to a huge increase in harvests, the government quickly relaxed its stance by granting dispensations to remote or geographically difficult locations. By 1982 family farms had become national policy.

Though it may seem surprising that the Chinese government not only allowed this blatant challenge to its authority but also then reversed its own policy, it didn't have much choice. Its ultimate goal was to develop industry, which it couldn't do without improving agriculture. The industrial workforce had to be fed, raw materials were needed for light industry, and without an agricultural surplus to export they'd struggle to earn foreign currency. However ideologically problematic the family farms were for the Communist Party, they were too successful to be stopped.

This didn't mean farmers could do as they pleased. Some officials feared the changes would erode their authority and attempted to prevent farmers from trying to earn money from private trade, which, given the range of enterprises some farmers had at their disposal, was often a quixotic gesture, as this list of activities from Hubei province shows:

Individuals tried raising ducks, keeping bees, putting on theatricals [...] they made bird cages, bean curd, bamboo flutes, and bicycle spokes; they spun wheels of fortune in the street to profit from the seemingly universal urge to gamble and they brought televisions into their court-yards, inviting crowds in to watch for a small fee.

The opening up of agriculture allowed the majority of farmers in China – whatever their ethnicity or location – to increase their incomes and living standards during the first half of the 1980s. But the agricultural gains in Xinjiang were smaller for two main (though connected) reasons. The first was due to environmental constraints: there wasn't much land fit for cultivation, access to water was expensive and many farms were in areas poorly connected to any potential market.

The second was that small farms run by Uyghurs were at a disadvan-tage compared with those of the XPCC, whose larger farms had better access to water, received state subsidies and benefited from economies of scale. This remains true today – in 2012 the XPCC controlled 31 per cent of all arable land. Given that it often also manages water supply, in practical terms it controls far more.

This was certainly unfortunate, probably unfair, but not the result of deliberate discrimination against Uyghurs. At worst, it was because policymakers, or, more realistically, the Xinjiang provincial government, failed to consider the particular challenges faced by Uyghur farmers. If some of the vast sums that the centre was sending to the XPCC had been instead spent on helping Uyghur farmers at this point, there might have been considerable long-term benefits, and not just economic ones.

Nonetheless, living standards did improve greatly in Xinjiang in the early 1980s. If the pace of improvement slowed after 1985 for Uyghur farmers in south Xinjiang (which was where the majority of Uyghurs lived), it was also not due to any particular policy aimed at them. The cause was more general: China was being bankrupted by its farmers. The new policies stipulated that farmers had to supply certain amounts of particular crops, usually grain or cotton, which the state then reimbursed them for. The problem was that the state paid at a much lower rate than the market. The grain price, for example, was fixed at the 1966 rate, which in the early 1980s was only 20 per cent of the market price.

This was understandably unpopular with farmers throughout the country: with a bad harvest, or under different growing conditions, they could end up losing money because the state paid so little. Some farmers dealt with this by growing more lucrative crops, then actually buying the grain on the market and giving it to the state (the cultivation of cash crops saw a 50 per cent increase between 1978 and 1988). But many found a way to exploit the quota system. There were three price categories for grain: basic quota, extra and surplus, the second and third of which were bought at much better prices. What farmers did was find ways to channel more grain into these categories, often by growing the quota crop to the exclusion of all else. There were also ingenious schemes that used the state's incentives against it. If one quota crop (such as cotton) was grown in sufficiently high quantities, then the state might give grain as a reward. If, as was not uncommon, the area also produced grain, the farm might then meet its quota with grain it had grown, and then sell the grain it had got as a reward back to the state at the higher rate. In effect, the farmers were setting the price of grain and the state couldn't afford it. By 1984, 10 per cent of China's annual budget was being used to buy quota crops.

Predictably, the state put a stop to this. After 1985 there was for practical purposes only one price for grain. By 1986 the payments to farmers for grain and cotton had dropped by between 10 and 15 per cent. The response of many farmers was to stop growing grain; the annual yield dropped by 10 per cent. Given that China's population was expanding fast, the authorities had to find a way to restore grain production. In the late 1980s various kinds of sticks and carrots were employed to this effect. The former involved fines, threats, land confiscation and harassment. The *People's Daily* newspaper reported that in some villages in Liaoning province, in the north-east, officials took away farmers' televisions and washing machines, and even hired ensembles to blow wind instruments in the courtyards of farmers who wouldn't cooperate.

The carrot was a set of incentives called the 'three-link' policy that offered farmers cash and coupons for cheap diesel and fertiliser. While in theory this was a good idea – fuel and fertiliser were not easily bought – there were several obstacles. The first, and most general, was that due to a credit problem with the banks at the time there wasn't enough money to pay the cash advances. The other problem was that in some provinces the promised fuel and fertiliser weren't available because corrupt local officials had used the coupons first. This led to major disturbances in some areas: in the summer of 1987 in Hunan province there were over 200 instances of fertiliser warehouses and stores being broken into.

Though China, like all countries, has always had some level of corruption, after 1978 it became rife. With the new opportunities for people to make money came the chance for those in authority to profit, whether in the form of bribes or fines or through the misuse of government money. Some officials may also have been disillusioned by the ideological shift in the country: a lowly official doesn't have many legitimate ways to get rich. The result was that as the 1980s progressed farmers in China were forced to pay an increasing amount in taxes and subsidies to local officials – between 1978 and 1990 the percentage of their income taken by these fees doubled. While some of these taxes were justified, there were also a lot of spurious one-off payments that officials had made up for their personal gain. In the worst cases, farmers were paying up to 67 different fees, some for absurd causes such as 'a tree-seedling deposit' or a 'subsidy for lost working time of students of agricultural radio schools'.

Farmers throughout China would be protesting over these payments well into the next decade, and in such large numbers that many thought it a potential threat to party rule. (By contrast, even after the Baren incident, the authors of an essay in a book summarising major trends in China during the 1990s were able to confidently predict that 'ethnic tensions do not represent a fundamental problem'.) As for the consequences of both these 'taxes' and the shift in the quota system in Xinjiang, once again Uyghur farmers were at a relative disadvantage. Many farms had quotas for both grain and cotton, which together accounted for much of the cultivation in the region. The removal of the higher rates for surplus grain and cotton thus affected a higher proportion of Uyghur farmers' earnings. This didn't plunge such farmers into poverty – but although their incomes and living standards continued to rise, it was at a slower rate than that of city dwellers, the majority of whom were Han.

The result was that the gap began to widen between the country-side and urban centres in Xinjiang. From 1987 to 1994 the GDP of the counties with non-Han majorities declined from 26 per cent to 18 per cent of the provincial total. However, one might again argue that this was part of an overall national trend towards urbanisation – at the time more than a quarter of China's budget was being spent on state-owned enterprises in cities and towns.

A further drain on farmers' resources was the introduction of school fees after the mid-1980s. Though the sums were small, they were a burden that contributed to a rise in the number of Uyghur students dropping out after middle school. By the beginning of the 1990s, Han Chinese were twice as likely to continue studying after the age of 16. This lack of basic – let alone further – education among many Uyghurs from the countryside would contribute to the obstacles many would later face in the altered labour market of the 1990s.

It's unclear to what extent Uyghurs in south Xinjiang in the 1980s were aware of the growing disparity between their economic situation and that of the cities in the region (let alone the economic boom gathering speed on China's east coast). The scholar Linda Benson spoke of the great change in Urumqi, the provincial capital, within only four years:

> When I was there in 1982, the brand new public buses and an occasional donkey cart or bicycle were about the extent of traffic on Urumqi streets. In 1986, one could hardly cross the main streets of the city, the traffic being so heavy and constant.

But apart from a few reports of 'frequent public fights' involving Han and Uyghur youths, for the most part the different ethnic groups lived peacefully, if separately, within Xinjiang's cities. The lack of major protests by farmers during this time suggests that their dissatisfaction with the new policies wasn't yet serious. If anything, it was the interior of rural China that was the 'volatile' and 'restive' region. But when protests involving Uyghurs did break out in Urumqi, and then in Beijing and Shanghai during the mid-1980s, it was over the prospect of policies that would be aimed specifically at them as a minority.

'THE MOST DIFFICULT WORK ON EARTH'

Since its introduction in 1980, the one-child policy has been the most well known, and most misrepresented, of all China's laws. It was introduced to deal with the fast-increasing population: in 1949 there were an estimated 540 million people in the country; by 1976 there were 940 million. This increase was due to a huge decline in infant mortality, and an increase in life expectancy, an achievement that probably isn't acknowledged sufficiently when considering the Communist Party's record. While the popular impression in the West has been that every couple in China was limited to one child, for most of its existence the one-child policy has applied to less than half the population – it prohibits urban residents (those who have an urban *hukou*) from having more than one child. Couples in the countryside are allowed to have two children, though only if the first is female or disabled (an equivalence that speaks volumes).

Given that people in China have traditionally had large families, particularly in the countryside, compliance with the policy was always going to be a problem. The authorities have mainly relied on threats and fines to achieve compliance. Family-planning slogans painted on walls by the roadside have often been both terrifying and unsubtle, such as: 'Kill all your family members if you don't follow the rule!' and: 'We would rather scrape your womb than allow you to have a second child.' There have also been many reports of forced abortions or sterilisation, such as the lawyer Chen Guangcheng's exposure of such practices in eastern China in 2005. Incentives are also provided, such as longer maternity leave and small financial payments to couples who delay childbearing.

In Xinjiang the enforcement of the one-child policy among Han Chinese would cause the Han proportion of the population to drop from 41 to 37 per cent by the end of the 1980s. The return of some *bing-tuan* workers to their home provinces for retirement also contributed to this decline (though it is worth remembering that Han migration from other provinces continued during this period). Concurrently, the Uyghur population grew: family-planning measures for members of minorities weren't brought in until the late 1980s, and weren't enforced until the beginning of the 1990s.

But even the prospect of them sparked protests in Xinjiang. After an official family-planning gazette announced in 1985 that all members of ethnic minorities would be required to limit their family size, around a thousand Uyghur students demonstrated in front of the Regional People's Committee building in Urumqi. They demanded total exemption from family planning, as well as a halt to Han resettlement in the region, the stopping of nuclear testing at Lop Nur in the Taklamakan Desert, and the ending of the transfer of prisoners from other provinces in China to facilities in Xinjiang. The last of these was the modern equivalent of the Qing's policy, and a lucrative business in the 1980s and 1990s, as both the central government and the relevant provincial authority gave the Xinjiang government a one-off payment for every prisoner. By the mid-1990s Xinjiang had accepted an estimated 50,000 of them. For some protesters, it was hard to square the influx of prisoners and Han settlers with the argument that minorities needed to practise family planning because Xinjiang was overpopulated.

Despite further protests by Uyghurs in Beijing and Shanghai, the central government ruled in 1986 that members of ethnic minorities should also be subject to compulsory family-planning policies. In cities, minority families would be allowed two children; in the countryside they would be allowed three. The Chinese government usually presents this policy as evidence of its sensitive approach to dealing with ethnic issues, which at least is an arguable proposition – it might not have been what many non-Han peoples wanted, but they were still getting preferential treatment. What's more contentious is the government's argument that it was the minorities who chose to restrict their birth rate, and that the policy thus reflects their 'free will'. The China Society for Human Rights Studies, an NGO that is both funded by and 'very close' to the Communist Party, claims that in 1949 the population in some minority areas was actually falling, due to a syphilis epidemic among Mongols, Tibetans and other nomadic people. The society claims there was a 48 per cent infection rate among some groups, which seems unlikely, given the national average was between 2 and 3 per cent. It goes on to say that in the early 1980s the increasing environmental impact of population growth 'sparked a discussion about whether ethnic minorities should go in for family planning. Ethnic minority officials were the first to say yes'. Apparently, ethnic minorities 'began to practise birth control on their own', so that the government 'began to change its policies to keep up with such developments'.

The society's article does acknowledge the protest in Urumqi in 1985, though only so as to nullify its significance. It claims that after the protest a Han Chinese doctor gave lectures to Uyghurs in Urumqi on the importance of family planning for economic growth: '"To my surprise, my audiences, mostly Uyghurs, applauded what I talked about," Professor Zhang recalled. "At the end of every lecture people gathered round me, telling me that I was speaking in their interests."'

The true extent to which most Uyghur parents wanted to follow family-planning rules can be seen from the birth-rate figures for 1989. Compared to 82 per cent of Han Chinese, only 40 per cent of Uyghurs had one or two children. Some 15 per cent of Uyghurs had three children, 12 per cent had four, and over 30 per cent had five or more. Uyghurs traditionally have large families for a variety of reasons, most of them religious and cultural, though also because a larger family provides essential agricultural labour. Even after the regulations were introduced, many Uyghurs found ways to have more children than the quota, such as going to different cities to have a child, or getting another female relative to register it as theirs.

However, just because some are able to get round the regulations, that doesn't stop these restrictions being resented. The scale of resistance to family planning among rural Uyghur communities led one official to characterise it as 'the most difficult work on earth'. In recognition of this, officials throughout China are subject to rewards or penalties based on whether they meet population targets set by their administrative region, which in some areas has led officials to be especially strict. This isn't motivated purely by a wish to see the law enforced: some provinces have relied on such fines (now euphemistically known as a 'social support fee') to balance their budgets.

The people this hurt most were those doing poorly paid agricultural work, few of whom could afford to pay fines that sometimes exceeded their annual incomes. In the early 1990s, when family-planning policies began to be enforced among minorities, the majority of Uyghurs in Xinjiang belonged to this category. While the government was arguably to blame for their poor economic situation – caused by the procurement system, the lack of investment in a naturally disadvantaged part of the region and their inability to compete with the *bingtuan* – it's unclear how many Uyghurs in the region thought of themselves as being specifically targeted, that is, whether they thought that their problems were due to ethnic discrimination. But there was soon proof that some Uyghurs were willing to defend a central part of their identity when they thought it was threatened.

NOT ALL (ISLAMIC) PROTESTS ARE CREATED EQUAL

The year 1989 was an excellent one for book-burning and protest. By the end of it, most communist regimes had been toppled by the waves of dissent that swept through Eastern Europe. Earlier in the year crowds in Bradford, Delhi, Lahore and other cities had burnt Salman Rushdie's novel *The Satanic Verses* for its alleged blasphemy. And in the spring and early summer millions of people in Beijing and other cities in China were protesting against government corruption and calling for greater freedoms (which would culminate in the Tiananmen Square crackdown in June).

Amid the turmoil, a smaller march took place in Beijing on 12 May. Around 3,000 members from the Central Academy of Nationalities, most of them Hui or Uyghur, marched through the streets chanting 'Punish China's Rushdie!' The protest was in response to a book called *Sexual Customs* about erotic tastes around the world, which featured a section on the supposed sexual habits of Muslims. The authors were two teachers from Shanxi province; at the time of the protest it had already sold 50,000 copies. For the protesters, the most objectionable parts of the book were claims that Muslims went on the hadj so they could indulge in homosexuality and bestiality (with camels), and that Islamic architectural features such as minarets, domes and tombs were intended to resemble penises or the 'mound of Venus'. The leader of the protest said of the authors: 'These men must be jailed [...] If they disappeared from the face of the earth, we would be happy.'

Many other demonstrations that summer would be dealt with harshly by the authorities, but the timing of the march in Beijing couldn't have been better. The Iranian president, Ali Khamenei, was visiting the country and it would have been diplomatically awkward for China to be accused of preventing Muslims' free speech. If anything, the government went to the other extreme to demonstrate its tolerance. Not only was the march the first demonstration to be granted official approval for three weeks, the authorities even closed off streets, stopped traffic and provided buses to take the marchers home after they'd delivered a petition.

On the same day related protests ignited across north-west China, where the majority of Hui are concentrated. In Lanzhou, capital of Gansu province, 20,000 demonstrators smashed up a government building, burnt a car containing copies of the book and called for the authors' deaths. Though there were clashes with the police, and some arrests, the authorities exercised restraint. All those detained were released soon afterwards. A week later, there was also a protest in Urumqi. Though initially described on public radio as a march in support of the students in Tiananmen Square, it was later described as a hostile incident incited by people opposed to the 'unity of all nationalities' who had misled people 'who did not know the truth [...] to beat, smash, and loot in a big way'. The authorities claimed that 150 police officers and soldiers had been injured, and that 40 vehicles had been destroyed. There are also reports that verses from Abdukhaliq's 'Awaken!' were chanted during the protests, which suggests that some of the protesters were expressing more than religious grievances.

The government response was uncompromising: the three men said to be the ringleaders were sentenced to eight years, 15 years and life imprisonment respectively, while four others received sentences of between one and eight years for offences including damage to personal and private property.

The demonstrations in Lanzhou and Urumqi, though only a week apart and apparently similar in nature, were thus treated very differently by the government. Dru Gladney, one of the most respected scholars of Islam in China, argues that one of the distinguishing features of the (mostly) Hui protest in Lanzhou and Beijing was that it was a protest *to* the government, not *against* it; that is, they were asking the government to intervene in a manner that did not challenge its authority. The fact that their demands were met – the offending book was banned and all copies destroyed – suggests that it's simplistic to think of the Communist Party as inflexibly hostile to all forms of religion.

As for why the demands of a Hui mob were treated differently from the almost identical demands of Uyghur protesters, the usual explanation is that the Hui are judged to be less of a threat. They are certainly more assimilated into (Han) Chinese society. Most Hui physically resemble Han and speak the same language – the Hui were losing their grasp of Persian and Arabic by the sixteenth century. Furthermore, the Hui don't occupy any sensitive regions of the country, and in recent history have shown no signs of wanting greater autonomy (let alone an independent state), which is one explanation for the government's offering them considerable latitude, especially within the Ningxia Hui Autonomous Region in the north-west, whose population is around 35 per cent Hui. There are even reports that one Sufi preacher in Ningxia has over a million followers and a wide network of madrasas and mosques, and met with many fundamentalist clerics while on a visit to Pakistan. The Hui also provide a positive example of the Chinese government's approach to Islam that can be used to reassure investors from predominantly Muslim countries.

The greater integration of Hui into Chinese society is often referred to in a somewhat dismissive manner by many Western scholars (and many Uyghurs). The implication is that their assimilation is a kind of failure, a dilution of identity. Even if this is the case, their assimilation is a comparatively recent phenomenon. Though the history of Uyghurs is often presented as a struggle against various 'Chinese' regimes (one CNN report described Xinjiang as 'a defiant region for 22 centuries'), the history of the Hui in China before 1949 is just as rebellious (if not more). During the nineteenth and early twentieth centuries Hui uprisings broke out throughout western China, including in Yunnan province in the extreme south-west. Tensions between Hui and Han settlers to the region escalated to the point that in 1856 Han and Qing officials in the city of Kunming carried out a three-day massacre of Hui in which over 4,000 people were killed.

A comparison of more recent Hui protests in China with those in Xinjiang is also instructive. While there have been major disturbances in which Hui were involved since the 1980s, they have been presented very differently by the Chinese authorities. In October 2004, the *New York Times* reported that violent clashes between Hui and Han in Henan province in central China had left nearly 150 people dead and forced authorities to declare martial law. In 2009, and then in 2012, the demolition of a mosque caused major protests in Hui communities. None of these events were characterised as 'terrorist' incidents, either at the time or since (which, as I shall argue later, contrasts sharply with the framing of dissent in Xinjiang after 2001).

Another notable feature of the Chinese government's version of these events is that, unlike such incidents in Xinjiang, it's not claimed that the Hui protests are inspired either by political motives or any form of religious extremism. In this respect their portrayal is the mirror image of how Xinjiang protests have generally been presented, especially since Baren. Although, as I have argued, there were many other reasons for the villagers of Baren to be dissatisfied with the authorities – agricultural policies, the presence of the *bingtuan*, the introduction of family-planning restrictions – none of these were acknowledged as potential causes. It was simply the work of a handful of extremists. In May 1990 Tomur Dawamat, the chairman of the Xinjiang People's Congress, argued that 'the main danger to Xinjiang's stability is the domestic and overseas national separatists waving a banner of an independent East Turkestan'.

THE RESPONSE TO BAREN

Twenty-five years later, there's still uncertainty about the causes of the Baren incident. But there was nothing ambiguous about the authorities' response. Though the incident was not explicitly labelled as Islamic terrorism, the tightening of religious policies in Xinjiang was a clear signal that they thought religious extremism was a major cause. In the following months the authorities targeted 'illegal religious activities', halted mosque construction, closed schools of religious instruction and increased state monitoring of Islamic clergy. Imams were required to undergo political education and some 10 per cent of the roughly 250,000 clergy the authorities examined were defrocked. It was also reported that 8,000 Communist officials had been dispatched in work teams to the countryside, so as 'to stabilise the border regions and strengthen political organisations'. The function of these teams was to 'reform' the existing practices of the authorities, with a particular emphasis on their ideology.

On 16 September 1990 the Xinjiang authorities issued new regulations stating that 'religious professionals' in Xinjiang must 'support the leadership of the Communist Party [...] and oppose national separatism'. The *Xinjiang Daily* reported that all religious leaders must be licensed by officially recognised 'patriotic religious organisations' and their credentials must be reviewed yearly and could be cancelled by local Religious Affairs Departments. The regulations also banned the teaching of religion and the distribution of religious material outside the premises of officially registered organisations (that is, in people's homes or any other private setting). Collectively, these regulations thus amounted to a clear statement of intent that there would be no aspect of Islamic practice that the government did not plan to oversee. Though many of these regulations applied equally to other religions in China, this fact probably would have been of little comfort to Muslims in Xinjiang. The following year, Xinjiang's party secretary, Wang Lequan, was explicit about the government's intentions regarding religion. He said the 'major task' facing the authorities in Xinjiang was to 'manage religion and guide it in being subordinate to [...] the central task of economic construction, the unification of the motherland, and the objective of national unity'.

Religion wasn't the only sphere the government began monitoring more closely. In 1991 Turgun Almas, a 68-year-old Uyghur historian and researcher at the Xinjiang Academy of Social Sciences in Urumqi, was placed under house arrest for his book *The Uyghurs*. Though the book had been approved for publication in 1989, in the strained political climate after Baren its version of history was judged to be a 'nationalistic' view that supported 'independence and separatism'. This wasn't entirely unfounded: Almas had used the discovery of several two- to six-thousand-year-old mummified Caucasian bodies in the Tarim Desert to support the claim that Xinjiang was Uyghurs' true homeland. He went so far as to argue that if the Jews could be given back their homeland after 2,000 years, then so could the Uyghurs. One problem with this is that while the mummies weren't Chinese, they also couldn't be some kind of Uyghur ancestor. According to Elizabeth Barber, an expert on prehistoric textiles, the bodies and facial forms associated with Turks and Mongols don't appear in the region until a thousand years after the mummies lived: the more likely explanation was that they were migrants from central Europe. Almas' case rested on the shaky logic that because there were signs of shamanic practices in the burial sites, and because Uyghurs had originally practised shamanism, the bodies were therefore Uyghur.

Academics, teachers and other intellectuals throughout Xinjiang were strongly urged to criticise Almas' writings at political meetings. Between July and October 1991 the *Xinjiang Daily* published four articles that attacked the author and sought to discredit his work, one of which listed a hundred errors in his books. His books were banned and those confiscated were burnt, but such drastic measures only served to increase interest in his work. During the rest of the decade Almas remained under house arrest; he died in 2001.

To try to counter this version of history, the state commissioned a series of books on Xinjiang that emphasised its long-standing role as a region *within* China. These were aimed at students of all levels, from high school to university; knowledge of their contents was assessed by exam. Greater scrutiny of Uyghur-language publications was also introduced, and the staff of several magazines were replaced.

Both the campaign against Almas and the religious restrictions can be viewed as the start of a campaign against Uyghurs, and for the most part these *were* a response to events in Baren. There were undoubtedly officials who blamed Baren and other incidents on the relative slackening of state control over religion and culture in the 1980s. But it's worth remembering that the social and political climate in China had become much less permissive since the Tiananmen crackdown the previous year. After 1989 the state took tighter control of the media and education, and greatly increased the amount it spent on internal security, especially the People's Armed Police. Whether this political shift merely facilitated the strict policies of the Xinjiang authorities or actually encouraged them to go further than they might have otherwise is unclear.

DOES 'RELIGIOUS EXTREMISM' EXIST IN XINJIANG?

Neither the political climate nor the many other reasons for dissatisfaction among Uyghurs precludes the possibility that the Chinese government was responding to a legitimate threat: that there was growing support for 'separatist' ideas among Uyghurs and that these were being fuelled by 'religious extremism'.

The degree of support for 'separatist' ideas among Uyghurs is perhaps the biggest unanswered question about the problems in Xinjiang, and is likely to remain that way. In China, the subject has always been too sensitive for public discussion, including on the internet – forums, message boards and social media have been monitored since the internet became available in China in the mid-1990s. When Uyghurs do speak about such topics, it is usually in private, and there have certainly always been some who express their dislike of the government and a wish for independence.

But there is (or should be) a huge gap between reporting the opinions of individuals, or even a social circle, and making a judgement about what most Uyghurs in Xinjiang want. For the most part, the Western media hasn't been cautious enough in its discussion of the issue, and has often spoken of 'independence movements' or 'separatist groups' without having had much, if any, contact with people involved in either. The spouting of anti-Han prejudice is usually treated as if it were equivalent to support for independence, but this ignores the potentially vast gap between people's spoken attitudes and their actual beliefs. When I first went to Xinjiang in 2000 I was struck by how quick many Uyghurs were to make prejudicial remarks about the Han (generally consisting of jokes or comments about them being ugly, weak or cowardly), usually during our first meeting. But some of these were only made for my benefit, and in that sense were partly 'for show'. Over the course of a year I realised that these kinds of comments certainly weren't a reliable guide to whether or not the person advocated any form of separatism.

It's been rare for journalists to be as open about our lack of knowledge on this question as Nicholas Kristof, a *New York Times* correspondent, who in 1993 wrote:

> It is difficult to gauge whether the ethnic unrest is simply like the racial tensions found all over the world, including in the United States, or whether they are so profound that they threaten Chinese rule in the region. So little is known about the public mood that it is not even clear that most people favor independence.

More recently, a 2013 *Washington Post* article had the good sense to answer its own bad question – 'What do Uighurs in Xinjiang want?' – honestly: 'You can't lump all Uighurs together. Different factions want different things – from more equitable treatment to outright secession from China.'

If we can't gauge support for Uyghur independence, what about the notion that the way in which some Uyghurs practise Islam in Xinjiang requires stricter supervision than the form of Islam practised among Hui communities? Religion has played a central role in relations between Uyghurs and the Chinese state since the Baren protests (and even more so after 9/11), both in terms of how Uyghurs define themselves in opposition to the Chinese government (as we shall see in Chapter 4) and in terms of how the Chinese government has characterised dissent in the region.

Yet the supposed target of the Chinese government's crackdown after Baren (and many times since) wasn't religion, that is, Islam, per se, but 'religious extremism'. According to Abudulrekep Tumniaz, dean of the Xinjiang Islamic Institute:

Religious extremism is a political issue rather than a religious one. As a border region with people from various ethnic groups following different religions, many social problems in Xinjiang are intertwined with religious and ethnic issues. That's why terrorists and separatists use religious extremism to brainwash people and instigate hatred to achieve their political goals.

The Chinese government has seldom offered much explanation of what constitutes 'religious extremism', though the term is generally taken to refer to Islamic beliefs that derive from Wahhabism, the conservative branch of Islam that originated in Saudi Arabia. In an article in the *China Daily* in April 2014, a Xinjiang official in charge of religious and ethnic affairs was quoted as saying that 'a majority of terrorist attackers have watched videos of religious extremism, and some have shouted extreme slogans out loudly during attacks. They have lost the basic humanity and rational thoughts.' The article went on: 'Nuer Bekri [the top official in Xinjiang] said that extremists forbid believers to watch TV, listen to radios, read newspapers or even "laugh during weddings or cry during funerals"'.

Though there's no tradition of fundamentalism in Xinjiang – as testified by the negative reaction to Ya'qub Beg's attempt to impose similar ideas – there's broad agreement that some elements of Wahhabism did gain acceptance in Xinjiang from the 1980s, mainly in the south. This manifested itself in more women wearing veils, an increased interest in studying Arabic and greater attendance at Friday prayers. One cause of this was the influx of Pakistani traders and religious items into south Xinjiang, and the ability of Uyghurs to visit Pakistan for trade and religious education. However, the caveat needs to be made that these shifts in religious observance might not have been caused by a shift to Wahhabism itself, but by a general increase in devoutness.

There was also some resistance to the introduction of such ideas. In the late 1980s Abdul Hamid, the imam of a mosque in Kashgar, launched a programme of religious reform that tried to introduce elements from the Saudi form of Islam (the Hanbali school of Islamic jurisprudence). This had a strong streak of egalitarianism that appealed to many young people, though it was unpopular with the religious elite of Kashgar, who branded his ideas 'Wahhabi'. When in 1997 the government fired Abdul Hamid from his position, it was probably at the behest of, or at least with the support of, most of the religious establishment.

Yet even if some elements of 'religious extremism' did get introduced into Xinjiang in the 1980s, this doesn't mean they were the cause of the Baren incident or any subsequent confrontations between Uyghurs and the authorities. Though a protest may have a religious element – such as the chanting of slogans or the use of religious iconography – and also draw legitimacy from ideas of 'justice', there may be many other factors causing dissent. As Gardner Bovingdon argues: 'Uyghurs have often used religion as a vehicle to express wide grievances or have made the state's repression of religiosity examples of broader repression.'

To say that the Baren protest was caused by the protesters' religious beliefs – whether 'extreme' or not – ignores other aspects of Uyghur identities: their very different linguistic, cultural and historical experiences from those of Han Chinese (something the Western media is arguably guilty of when it characterises Uyghurs primarily, or solely, by their faith). Given that Uyghur and Kyrgyz farmers in Baren already had economic grievances against the state, the closure of the mosque may just have been the gripe that tipped the scales.

Another reason to be cautious in linking religion and protest in Xinjiang, at least during the 1980s, is that the Uyghur intellectuals promoting nationalism were mostly secular. As discussed earlier, culture has been just as much a vehicle for dissent as religion. It's therefore inadvisable to generalise about the causes of Uyghur protest in Xinjiang as a whole during this period. The different incidents in Xinjiang in the 1980s can instead be seen as separate responses to overlapping grievances and concerns among Uyghurs.

Most, if not all, of these issues would continue to be sources of contention during the 1990s, but with several crucial differences. One was that the gap between the poor and affluent would widen considerably, and in most places the majority of the disadvantaged were Uyghurs, often for reasons that were clearly due to government policy. Another difference was that the break-up of the Soviet Union and subsequent formation of new, ethnic-majority states would encourage some Uyghurs to aspire towards greater self-determination, while also strengthening their sense of a shared ethnic identity. This growing sense of injustice, combined with many Uyghurs' frustrated aspirations for greater social and cultural freedoms, would cause relations between Han and Uyghurs to deteriorate further.

4

STRIKING HARD: THE 1990s

In May 1993 the Chinese media reported that a crowd of 10,000 had 'stormed the district and township governments and schools, beat up cadres and teachers, smashed public and private property'. When the police responded with tear gas, some were taken hostage in retaliation. The crowd also set police cars on fire and vandalised the homes of local leaders.

It could have been a scene from Urumqi in 1989 or Baren in 1990. But the riot didn't happen in Xinjiang, and the protesters weren't Uyghur. They were Han farmers from Renshou county in Sichuan province. They were angry at the many taxes being levied on them, in some cases up to 17.5 per cent of their income (the legal limit was 5 per cent). One resident explained the protest by saying: 'We tolerate it when officials embezzle state funds, now they embezzle from us common folks. How can we tolerate that?'

The state response to this major challenge to authority was also revealing. Despite being attacked with rocks and bricks, there were only a few arrests, and those were for property damage. The dispute was resolved when the deputy governor ordered that the taxes be repaid to the peasants with interest.

There was nothing exceptional about Renshou. It was a poor, agricultural county whose farmers had typical grievances: heavy taxation, the crop-quota system and the growing exodus of its labour force. Young and middle-aged people were leaving their villages to find better-paid jobs in the cities, which meant that there were fewer hands to work the family plots. The fact that the rioters were dealt with leniently, as the

Hui protests had been in 1989, suggests that in many instances it hasn't been the causes of dissent (whether economic or religious in nature) that have led the Xinjiang authorities to respond severely, that is, with mass arrests and often lethal force.

A key element of this strategy has been how such incidents are framed. After the student demonstrations in Urumqi in 1985, officials ruled that the primary threat to Xinjiang's stability came from minority 'splittism at home and abroad', which became the stock explanation for any mass incident. Since then, many events with apparently similar causes to protests in other parts of China have been portrayed by the authorities as 'separatist' or 'terrorist' attacks. Though one can't entirely discount the possibility that some were precisely that, it raises the question of why the Chinese government has been so reluctant to acknowledge other potential causes of protest, given that in some instances these appear to have been the same as those of other 'mass incidents' in China.

One possible reason is that Xinjiang's strategic value has made the authorities more security-conscious. A prolonged period of instability would provide any neighbouring hostile force with a good opportunity to cause further disruption. But while this might have been a factor after the Sino-Soviet split in the 1960s, there haven't been serious threats to China's territorial integrity since the fall of the Soviet Union. This is reflected in the low numbers of PLA troops stationed in Xinjiang after the 1990s – the military centre for China's north-west isn't even in the region, but in Lanzhou in neighbouring Gansu province.

A more likely cause stems from the ideological basis for Chinese policy in Xinjiang. Since 1949, the government has claimed that its main goal is to develop the region for the benefit of all its peoples, as recently articulated in a 2009 white paper on 'development and progress in Xinjiang':

Since 1949, particularly after China's reform and opening-up in the late 1970s, Xinjiang has entered an era of rapid economic and social progress and enhanced comprehensive strength, *with the local residents enjoying the most tangible benefits*. Proceeding from the state development strategy and the fundamental interests of the people of various ethnic groups, the Chinese government has paid great attention to the development and construction of Xinjiang. It has made it a national basic policy to help the frontier areas develop their economy *for the common good and wealth* [my italics].

Such sentiments constitute a promise to *all* the peoples of Xinjiang, and perhaps especially to non-Han peoples, who have so frequently been told that they lag behind the Han. The state is required to promote the common prosperity of all ethnic groups by both the Constitution of the People's Republic of China and the Law on Regional Ethnic Autonomy. For the Chinese government to acknowledge that its policies in Xinjiang have not promoted equal development among the different peoples would greatly undermine its legitimacy.

Yet in the early 1990s there *were* signs that the government was finally starting to focus on Xinjiang's economic development. The Eighth Five-year Plan (for 1991–5) specified more investment in the region, mainly due to the discovery of a new oilfield in the Tarim Basin. China National Petroleum Corporation, a state-owned enterprise, sent 10,000 workers to Xinjiang to develop the oilfields at Karamay and Korla, and there were new railways and roads constructed, one of the main ones being from north to south. While these oilfields would soon be producing large revenues, because the companies that owned them were state-owned, the greater share of their profits went to the central government. The other main economic hub in the region, Urumqi, also continued developing fast.

The main economic opportunity for Uyghurs at the time was created by the removal of many restrictions on trade, especially with other countries. In 1992 the government announced that Xinjiang was 'opening strategic passes and pulling down fences'. Banners in the streets proclaimed: 'Let Xinjiang understand the world; let the world understand Xinjiang.' The main target of this initiative was the new Central Asian states formed after the break-up of the Soviet Union. The hope was that trade, tourism and joint investment would provide a major boost for Xinjiang's economy.

Initially this was a great success. In 1992 there was $220 million in border trade, a 350 per cent increase on the previous year. This also benefited many Uyghurs, who had the cultural and linguistic skills to act as middlemen for trade with these countries. Though direct trade between Central Asian states and factories in other parts of China would soon greatly reduce such opportunities for Uyghurs, this period was important because it helped strengthen the Uyghur middle class in many cities, and made a few millionaires, such as Rebiya Kadeer, who by the mid-1990s was one of the wealthiest people in China.

The cross-border trade also allowed Uyghurs in Xinjiang to establish (or renew) ties with relatives, friends and business partners in these countries, giving them the chance to see what life was like for Uyghurs in the new republics. There's no doubt that the establishment of these new ethnic-majority states, so close to Xinjiang, boosted the desire among Uyghurs for either greater autonomy or the formation of an independent 'Uyghuristan'. In the 1990s a plethora of organisations dedicated to promoting Uyghur nationalism and human rights was established in the new states, especially in Kazakhstan and Kyrgyzstan, most of which were secular in orientation. A few of these, such as the Eastern Turkestan United Revolutionary Front, advocated a more militant approach to dealing with the Chinese state, but there's no evidence that this or any other such organisation played a role in any of the scattered confrontations between Uyghurs and the state during this period. The main function of these Uyghur nationalist groups was to offer support and raise the international profile of Uyghur concerns.

Yet in contrast to the greater investment in infrastructure, little was done to help agriculture in south Xinjiang. The quota system was just as onerous, with many farmers having to grow cotton despite it yielding little, if any, profit. For many families there was insufficient land to generate enough crops to sell as surplus, making it hard to acquire cash. Most had to resort to small-scale trade in crafts or other goods, which were sold at weekly markets. They were also required to contribute a considerable number of days of free labour on 'communal projects' like digging trenches and mending roads. The overall poverty of the region was remarked on by Uyghurs who returned to Xinjiang after decades spent in Kazakhstan, as shown in Sean Roberts' 1997 documentary *Waiting for Uyghuristan* (which also offers an invaluable record of what Kashgar, Urumqi and Yining looked like in the mid-1990s).

Despite the hardships for farmers in south Xinjiang there weren't any major protests in this region in the early to mid-1990s, certainly none on the scale of that in Renshou. This doesn't mean there weren't grievances among these communities; what's more likely is that the increased surveillance after the Baren incident prevented any serious disturbances. Instead farmers in south Xinjiang showed their opposition to the agricultural policies by using the same kinds of tactics that have been used by peasants throughout China, the so-called 'weapons of the weak': faking production reports, working slowly and conspiring against officials. In one village in south Xinjiang in 1995 farmers were allocated a quota of silk to produce and then sell to the state, work that was labour intensive and that they had little previous training in. The farmers intentionally made such a terrible job of growing silk that they were given no quota for it the following year.

The measure of any policy depends on its implementation. In the mid-1990s the situation of Uyghur farmers in eastern Xinjiang was very different to that of those in the south. In Hami farmers had far more latitude about what crops and agricultural techniques they used, and were required to do much less communal work, only 3–5 days a year. Though no specific reasons were given for this much looser application of policy, eastern Xinjiang has long been culturally (and sometimes militarily) more closely aligned with the authorities in China. Hami gave troops and provisions to the Qing armies marching towards the Zhungar forces, and in the late seventeenth century became a protectorate of the Qing (an event celebrated in official histories as a model for modern Uyghurs' subordination to the Chinese state). More saliently, Hami has a higher proportion of Han than south Xinjiang, and many more Uyghurs there speak Chinese. One explanation for the fact that the same policies were applied differently in south and east Xinjiang is thus that the authorities were playing favourites – the farmers in Hami were being rewarded for being more integrated. Another is that eastern Xinjiang is a less politically sensitive area than the south as it has no external border.

What can be said with certainty is that eastern Xinjiang has been both more prosperous and more stable than the south. The Turpan region has experienced very few violent incidents since 'opening up'. The main crops of the Turpan oasis – grapes and other fruit – have generated more wealth for farmers than the wheat, maize and cotton that have been the mainstays of the south. In the mid-1980s, it was so economically successful it attracted migrants from inner China, some of whom came to do menial jobs like digging canals and collecting and repairing old shoes. These workers were part of China's massive 'floating population', those who move between cities in search of work and usually end up doing temporary, badly paid jobs, often in construction. Their living conditions are usually poor, and they lack access to welfare and medical care, as their *hukous* are registered elsewhere. These migrants were thus very far from the stereotype of the Han coloniser, which makes it unsurprising that most were on good terms with local Uyghurs. Some Han even opted to hold their weddings at halal restaurants so their Uyghur colleagues could attend. This relative ethnic harmony has meant that the authorities have taken a much gentler approach to policing the region. In April 2010, when many cities in Xinjiang still had a large and conspicuous security presence after the Urumqi riots the previous year, Turpan had few, if any, police or army patrols.

The economic situation in Turpan and Hami demonstrates the need for caution when making generalisations about Uyghurs' grievances in Xinjiang. Though there are some policies that affect all Uyghurs (and other non-Han peoples) in Xinjiang, such as in education and family planning, for others regional differences lead to very different outcomes. This is even true for policies that 'manage' religion – in recent years, a stricter approach has been taken in Kashgar and other southern towns than in Urumqi.

THE BREAKING OF THE IRON RICE BOWL

But in the mid-1990s the greatest contrasts in living conditions weren't those between different Uyghur communities. Throughout China, the economic boom driven by the factories on the east coast was quickly widening the gap between the town and the countryside. By 1995 the average rural annual income was less than a quarter of what was earned in cities. In Xinjiang the rural–urban income difference was higher than the national average, and greatest in the Uyghur-dominated south-west. Uyghurs accounted for over 90 per cent of the population in 13 of the 20 official areas of extreme poverty in Xinjiang. The death rate in Kashgar was six times worse than in Karamay (a city built on oil revenues with a mainly Han population), due to inferior medical facilities.

This rural–urban inequality was partly the result of the government's push to increase urbanisation throughout China (a trend that continues, the rationale now, as then, being that the more people living in cities, the better for the economy). But the special circumstances of Xinjiang, where so much more investment had gone into the cities, coupled with the tendency of new Han settlers to live in these cities, meant that Xinjiang's urbanisation rate was just over 50 per cent, a level that China as a whole wouldn't reach for more than a decade. This no doubt widened the gap between the largely Uyghur countryside and the mostly Han-dominated cities, but there were additional factors that led to many Uyghurs' impoverishment, both absolute and relative.

One factor was the renewed vigour of the XPCC, whose ranks started to increase again in the 1990s. Increased migration from inner China caused Xinjiang's population to grow by almost a third over the course of the decade, the fastest growth of any province in the country. There were, however, several ways in which this new influx differed from previous migratory waves. In the 1990s the migrants were coming of their own volition, albeit in many cases in response to incentives offered by the state, such as a two-year exemption from land rent. Another difference was that the XPCC began to expand further into south Xinjiang, adding to its growing environmental problems, principally desertification and a shortage of water (the Tarim river, one of the main rivers in the south, was already gravely depleted by the expansion of irrigation required to grow cotton). Despite the unpopularity of this with local farmers, there were plans to bring even more people to south Xinjiang. In 1992 the government announced that 100,000 people whose land was due to be flooded by the gargantuan Three Gorges Dam project were going to be resettled in Kashgar. The scheme was only cancelled after major domestic and foreign opposition.

The resurgence of the XPCC was the result of policies specific to Xinjiang – at best, their negative effects on Uyghur farmers' livelihoods can be attributed to a lack of foresight by the provincial authorities. The other major factor that would particularly impoverish Uyghurs and other non-Han looks at first sight less culpable, in that it stemmed from national policy. In the Maoist era most Chinese citizens relied on the state to meet their housing, employment and health needs, an arrangement known as the 'iron rice bowl'. People lived in a *danwei* ('work unit') that provided all these facilities. In many respects this was a microcosm of Chinese society, in that it reproduced its basic political hierarchy: whether the *danwei* was a school, hospital or factory, Communist Party officials were always the top leaders.

In the freer economic climate of the 1980s, working for a state-owned enterprise (SOE) was no way to get rich, but at least it offered a secure income, or so people thought. The problem was that most SOEs were too inefficient to compete with the new private businesses. By 1994 many were suffering such huge losses that the only option was to close them. According to China's Ministry of Labour and Social Security, 21 million workers were laid off over the next decade. This was probably a massive underestimation, due to the political sensitivity of the issue – the closures led to protests throughout the country – but even if one accepts it, the scale of the change this wrought on Chinese society was still immense. The percentage of the workforce employed in SOEs dropped by more than 50 per cent during this period – between 1995 and 2000, 600,000 jobs were lost in the state sector in Xinjiang alone. At the same time, the private sector expanded. In 1996, 17 per cent of jobs in Chinese industry were in privately owned companies; by 2001 the equivalent figure was 44 per cent.

The general demise of the state sector, and the resulting unemployment, led to social and economic problems for communities throughout China. But in Xinjiang this caused greatest harm to non-Han peoples, who were more heavily represented in the public sphere. This was due to preferential policies that made it easier for them to get work in certain industries, most of which also had minimum quotas for minority employees. Until the late 1990s higher education was an almost guaranteed path to a job for life for Uyghurs. This kind of affirmative action certainly helped to lessen the income gap between Han and minorities (though arguably at the cost of endorsing paternalistic notions of the Han as the more 'advanced' ethnicity helping the 'backward' minorities). At the same time, it also meant that proportionally more Uyghurs ended up being laid off as a result of the SOE closures.

What further exacerbated this trend, somewhat counter-intuitively, was that in Xinjiang reform of SOEs didn't actually go as far as in other provinces. Many industries were exempted from market forces, in particular mining and other extractive businesses. While it's understandable that the state chose to keep its monopoly – these had become the most lucrative part of Xinjiang's economy – commercial factors were not involved in the decision to retain the structure of the XPCC. In many respects, this was the biggest SOE of all in the region, and, from a purely economic point of view, was ripe for breaking up into smaller units, as had happened for agricultural communes in other parts of China: the XPCC was so inefficient that 80 per cent of its funds came from government subsidies. As had long been the case, the true value of the XPCC was judged to be its role in promoting 'stability' (though arguably by this point its dominance of Xinjiang's natural resources, while failing to provide employment for Uyghurs, was having the reverse effect). However, the XPCC wasn't entirely exempt from the reforms. From 1995 to 2000 around 140,000 of its workers were made redundant.

The most notable feature of both the *bingtuan* and the extractive industries in Xinjiang in the 1990s was that despite being state-owned they did not have quotas for minority employment. The XPCC was at least 90 per cent Han Chinese. Even the 600,000 seasonal labourers it hired to pick cotton every year generally came from outside Xinjiang. In the oil sector the situation was no better: of the 20,000 oil workers in the Tarim Basin, very few were not Han. Thus in Xinjiang the state preserved its monopoly in the agricultural and industrial sectors, while Uyghurs and members of other minorities were almost completely excluded from both.

The only options left to many Uyghurs were to find work in the private sphere or to go into business themselves. The private sphere unfortunately had no preferential hiring policies, which meant that the (mostly Han) employers were under no obligation to hire members of minorities who often couldn't speak good Chinese, and in some cases were less qualified, owing to their difficulties in accessing education. Another thing most Uyghurs lacked was the *guanxi* ('social connections') that help with pretty much *everything* in China, whether it be a business deal, obtaining medical treatment or getting one's child into a good school. Those from minorities who did get jobs tended to be over-represented in manual, poorly paid jobs, while Han were over-represented in skilled and well-paid managerial positions.

Some Uyghurs were forced to go and work in Kazakhstan (Roberts' documentary *Waiting for Uyghuristan* features interviews with several such workers). It's worth contrasting the difficulties Uyghurs faced with the easier situation of most laid-off *bingtuan* workers, many of whom found work in private firms or started their own businesses – by 2000, 13 per cent of the *bingtuan* labour force were self-employed.

There were, however, Uyghurs for whom language wasn't a barrier. Since the 1980s there had been two parallel educational systems, one where the classes were in Mandarin, and another where they were in the main minority language of the area. Most Uyghurs and other non-Han students went to the minority-language school (these students were known as *min kao min*), but there were some students, especially in Han-majority cities like Urumqi, whose parents presciently recognised the advantages of fluency in Chinese and sent their children to a Chinese-language school (these were known as *min kao han* students). A further incentive for minority parents to send their children to a Chinese school was that *min kao min* students needed to do an extra year of study at university to raise their Chinese level for most subjects. In 1990, when average tuition fees were 120 yuan per year, this added cost wasn't necessarily prohibitive, but once education became subject to market forces, and fees rose sharply (to an average of 4,500 yuan by 2000), the price of an extra year was too steep for many Uyghur parents.

While the greater unemployment among Uyghurs fostered a sense of unfairness, the blurring of the line between the state and private business only increased the perception of discrimination. Both cadres and the armed forces were encouraged to pursue private business, which created considerable scope for corruption. Usually this involved using the authority (and resources) of the state to gain an unfair business advantage, often via expensive meals, heavy drinking and visits to karaoke parlours and brothels – activities that are an integral part of social relations among the wealthy and powerful in China.

There were also more flagrant cases of corruption. In 1996 officials in Shawan county, in north-west Xinjiang, were found to have confiscated 530 hectares of land from Kazakh herders to use as farm-land for their own gain, and – as if that were not enough – had also, as government employees, been given privileged access to seeds, fertiliser and irrigation equipment.

There's no doubt that the reform of the SOEs was economically necessary, but it is hard to believe that the provincial or central government didn't consider that this might be disproportionately harmful to those from minorities, given that their relative disadvantage was already recognised in the form of preferential policies in employment and other spheres. Legislation that required private companies to practise some form of preferential hiring policies would at least have recognised the problem. Instead, nothing was done, and from the mid-1990s unemployment rose sharply in Uyghur communities in both north and south Xinjiang.

While on paper Xinjiang's economy continued to improve through-out the 1990s, so that by 2000 it had the highest GDP of any non-coastal province, even official statistics showed that this apparently rosy picture obscured the vast gaps in prosperity between different regions. Areas with high GDP per capita – Urumqi, Korla and Karamay – all had a clear Han majority. The number of people from minorities in any given area was inversely proportional to its prosperity. At this juncture, the authorities might have done well to recall the warnings of some Chinese economists in the 1980s about the risks to stability of pursuing uneven development.

That Uyghurs and other minorities were getting relatively poorer while the proceeds from the exploitation of Xinjiang's natural resources were fuelling the development of infrastructure and Han-majority cities in the north (or going back to the central government) was a clear violation of the promise that the region would be developed for the good of all. Unsurprisingly, this didn't help relations between Han and Uyghurs. Though there's a tendency to present relations between these communities as unrelentingly dire – yet another case of the 'ancient ethnic hatreds' argument that has often been invoked since the

Yugoslav wars of the 1990s – in some regions of Xinjiang there have been phases of rapprochement. In addition to the reports of socialising between Han and Uyghur in Turpan in the 1980s, some Uyghurs in Urumqi apparently visited their Han colleagues during the Chinese New Year period.

The decline in relations between Han and Uyghurs in the 1990s should thus be seen as the result of the shift in policies that boosted inequality in Xinjiang, something that had been worsened by the continuing influx of settlers from inner China. The scholar Michael Dillon has argued that this decline led to a surge in political violence that 'became more severe and more organised' as the decade progressed. In support of this assertion, he provides a list of incidents in different locations, including a spate of bombings in early 1992 and assassination attempts in the summer of 1993. When one reads this litany of gunfights, explosions and shootings, one can be forgiven for thinking that Xinjiang was certainly a 'restive' and 'volatile' region during that period. Obviously, these serious disruptions of public security were of great concern to the authorities. What's unclear is whether there was any connection between these episodes, in terms of either motive or those involved in their planning. Unless this can be demonstrated, it's hard to see how one can argue that they represent an escalation in political violence, unless the fact that they all took place in Xinjiang is sufficient proof in itself. What little is known about these incidents comes from less than impartial sources such as Uyghur émigré organisations, the Chinese state or Hong Kong newspapers with a strong anti-China bias. Dubious accounts do not become more plausible by being collated.

It's also difficult to use single, extremist acts as indicators of ethnic relations in general, at least not without making all kinds of assumptions about the motivations and grievances of both the perpetrators and the wider Uyghur community. Perhaps a better approach is to examine the patterns of daily life in Xinjiang at that time, and the kinds of attitudes that many Uyghurs expressed.

SEPARATE WORLDS

For most visitors to Xinjiang in the 1990s, what was immediately obvious was the degree of segregation between Han and Uyghurs. At its most basic, this was spatial: in almost every town or city the two groups lived in separate neighbourhoods. Predominantly Han areas usually had modern residential buildings, generally four- or five-storey blocks of flats, whereas in mainly Uyghur neighbourhoods families tended to live in single-storey brick or adobe houses built around a walled courtyard. These different neighbourhoods had their own shops, markets and restaurants, which were mainly frequented by the local residents. Transitioning between these different communities, with their very distinct linguistic and cultural qualities, could be an abrupt, sometimes disorienting experience, like stepping between worlds.

To some extent, this separation was a consequence of the fact that most Han were relatively recent arrivals for whom new accommodation had to be built. The dietary restrictions of Uyghurs and other Muslims also prevented them from eating in non-halal restaurants or Chinese people's homes, a division that was replicated in schools and universities in Xinjiang. Han and Uyghurs had no problems living in the same apartment building, as was the case in the accommodation provided by state institutions like schools, hospitals and universities.

The real sign that ethnic relations had worsened was the social separation of the communities in many cities. Young people from different ethnic groups rarely dated, let alone married each other. Even in Urumqi, at one time the most ethnically integrated city in the region, the consequences could be more serious than mere disapproval. One Uyghur girl with a Han boyfriend told her interviewer:

> It's really hard for us to even go out anywhere. If other Uyghurs see us together in public, they give us trouble. If Uyghur men see us together on a public bus, they swear at us and hit us. Uyghur women aren't so bad, but they still make comments.

Relationships were not the only boundary some Uyghurs in Urumqi sought to defend. Food acquired an added significance as a cultural marker, one that went beyond the existing requirement that it be halal. For some Uyghurs, the notion of what food was 'clean' shifted to emphasise not only whether it had been prepared in the approved manner, but also whether the food had come into contact with any Han. This led some Uyghurs to start avoiding Hui-run restaurants, even though they were halal, either because they sometimes had Han customers, or because the Hui were more likely to do business with Han. Some Uyghurs refer to Hui dismissively as 'watermelons' – green (Muslim) on the outside but red (Communist) on the inside.

There were also rumours about Han trying to contaminate Uyghurs' food, or even that they were putting pork fat into the water. Brick tea became the focus of a major boycott by Uyghurs after a businessman claimed to have gone to where the tea was made in China and 'discovered that they let pigs walk over the tea leaves and that the place was very dirty', causing many to switch to tea from India. This story, and the avoidance of Hui restaurants, can be seen as attempts by some Uyghurs to highlight the differences between themselves and Han Chinese. To this end, many Uyghurs began to stress their use of Xinjiang time as a way to reject Chinese rule and emphasise the boundaries between themselves and the Han, most of whom use Beijing time in their personal lives (this is less true for Han who have been living in Xinjiang for a long period).

The importance of religious faith to Uyghurs versus the supposed atheism of the Han was another point of difference frequently stressed. In many places in Xinjiang this led to an upsurge in mosque attendance, and a greater emphasis on the importance of fasting during Ramadan and abstaining from alcohol. It also encouraged men to grow beards and wear skullcaps. The wearing of another kind of hat, a stiffened cloth cap known as a *doppa*, also became a way for Uyghurs to assert their identity, both ethnic and regional (there are different *doppas* for Yining, Hotan and Kashgar).

Speaking Uyghur also became an increasingly important way to express one's identity, especially in view of the growing marginalisation of the language in employment and higher education. The reduced fluency of some *min kao han* Uyghurs (especially with reading and writing) became a contentious issue. Some Uyghurs started sarcastically describing *min kao han* students as 'the fourteenth minority', the implication being that their poor grasp of the language meant that they didn't deserve to belong to their actual ethnic group. Some *min kao han* students thus ended up isolated, as they were accepted by neither Han nor other Uyghurs.

The bolstering of Uyghur identity also heightened the existing divisions within many communities. Stressing the centrality of faith, language and diet as defining characteristics of being Uyghur meant that any Uyghurs who failed to conform to these standards also had to be censured. In Yining in the early 2000s there were clear social divisions between Uyghurs who considered themselves 'good Muslims' and those who were not. The former often refused to go to weddings of 'bad Muslims' because they said there would be alcohol and dancing.

By separating themselves from the Han, and drawing unfavourable comparisons, some Uyghurs were trying to reinforce what it meant to them to 'be Uyghur'. But the separation between Han and Uyghur wasn't absolute. In the early and mid-1990s there were still parts of daily life in which people from these communities could interact, such as by playing pool against each other or visiting the same dance halls. Work was the main sphere in which the boundaries were weaker. Many Uyghurs still worked for the state, including within the police, the judiciary and other parts of the security services. There was also a degree of cooperation among entrepreneurs. In many cities, including Urumqi, it was common for Uyghur kebab sellers to set up their stands outside Han-owned restaurants (which thus weren't 'clean'), which they encouraged people to attend. In return, the Han management of the restaurant allowed its customers to order kebabs and have them brought inside.

One way to interpret this is that Uyghurs were willing to be flexible on matters of principle when it was to their advantage. But people's sense of who they are is more diverse than just their ethnic membership. It includes their sex, age, occupation, social class and where they're from, all of which can influence behaviour in any given situation. In this case, it was less important that the people were from different ethnic groups than that they were trying to earn a living by similar means. There's also ethnographic evidence that suggests that many Uyghurs' sense of identity was still primarily rooted in a sense of local community, rather than in any ethno-national identification. Justin Jon Rudelson's *Oasis Identities: Uyghur Nationalism along China's Silk Road* (1987) provides a rich portrait of life in Turpan, while Jay Dautcher's *Down a Narrow Road: Identity and Masculinity in a Uyghur Community in Xinjiang China* (2009), which is about life in Yining, is probably the best book to read to get a sense of what ordinary life was like for many Uyghurs at that time. The long-standing rivalry between oases (usually expressed through jokes and teasing) is just as evident in Xinjiang today as it was in 1996 when Dautcher heard this insult in Yining for people in Kashgar:

> Kashgarian you dolt
> It has become springtime
> Throw away your leather sandals
> Make yourself a drum.

Uyghurs' hostility towards Han was most evident in the widespread use of negative stereotypes (and the use of the derogatory word *xitay*). These managed to encompass virtually every aspect of their physical and mental character, whether it be their bodies, faces and supposed lack of strength, or their supposed cowardice, treachery, parasitical nature and lack of culture. (Many Han expressed similarly unflattering opinions about Uyghurs.) In 2001, when I worked in Yining as an English teacher, I found that many Uyghurs were so keen to stress these differences that they often brought them into conversation apropos of nothing. After I was introduced to two Uyghur men who sold leather goods in the bazaar, one said: 'Many Han people make a noise when they eat,' to which the other laughed and replied, 'That's just them speaking!' On another occasion a teenage girl in a village answered my question as to whether there were any Han living in the vicinity by saying: 'No, you would be able to smell them.' When I asked what they smelt of she said: 'Spices, mostly chilli,' presumably in reference to the greater amount of chilli pepper used in some kinds of Chinese food.

Even during formal written exercises, Uyghur students would write things like: 'Not all Chinese people have small eyes, small noses but it's very common. You can find beautiful Chinese people, but few, and you must pay attention.' This negative stereotyping allowed some Uyghurs to feel a sense of agency in a situation where they had little power. It also provided an outlet for frustration and hostility without serious risk.

PROTEST SONGS

There were similar opportunities in the cultural sphere, especially through music, which was much harder to regulate than print or broadcast media. In part this was due to the authorities' difficulties in understanding the songs' potential interpretations, but also because the main form of transmission – the music cassette – was so easily shared. Some of these songs used traditional folk-musical styles but with contemporary lyrics, while others used pop and rock styles. According to Rachel Harris, an ethnomusicologist at the School of Oriental and African Studies in London, many of these pop songs were influenced by different musical cultures, such as those of Turkey, Central Asian states, India and Spain, and as such are evidence of the rich, globally oriented music scene in Xinjiang.

But it was perhaps the folk songs that had the greatest impact. What made them especially influential was that they didn't require any degree of literacy to be understood – they spoke just as much to farmers in south Xinjiang as they did to intellectuals in Urumqi. These songs were a far cry from those of state-approved Uyghur musicians in Xinjiang, many of whom sang in Chinese. Songs like 'Our Xinjiang is the most beautiful place', 'Please taste a piece of Hami melon', and 'Lamb kebabs oh so fragrant!' promoted the idea of Xinjiang as a safe and colourful place with abundant resources. The new folk songs rarely made direct political statements, preferring allegory and ambiguity.

This didn't mean that the authorities took a lax approach. Kurash Kusan, one of the best-known singers in Xinjiang in the 1980s and early 1990s, had his music banned after releasing a song called 'Do not sell your land'. He was subsequently jailed for nine months, and eventually had to flee the country. Some Uyghur musicians with equally provocative lyrics, like Askar ('Grey Wolf'), were able to evade a similar fate by moving to Beijing and other cities outside Xinjiang, where the local authorities were less concerned about the content of their work. This was possible until 1995, after which Uyghur-language music could only be released by state-owned recording companies, which kept a much closer eye on the lyrical content.

Despite the increased scrutiny, there was still a thriving under-the-counter trade in bootleg music cassettes. One of the most popular was a compilation by Omarjan Alim, from Yining. The first verse of his song 'Mehman Bashlidim' ('I brought home a guest') was interpreted by many Uyghurs as a critique of the dispossession brought about by Han settlement:

> I brought a guest back to my home
> And at the back, lay down a cushion
> Now I cannot enter
> The house I built with my own hands.

Subsequent verses talk of 'still more guests': 'they filled that place / then lopped off the entire branch / and took the fruits away'. The song concludes by speaking of how the guest 'jumped into the seat of honour / and boss became to us / and boss became to us'.

Alim's songs had other potential messages than just critiquing Chinese policy. Some also appeared to take aim at Uyghur officials for collaborating or being corrupt. The idea that some Uyghurs were perceived as 'traitors' for being too pro-government does explain the killing of a number of government officials in May 1996, and the murder of the imam of Kashgar's main mosque in the same month (something that would happen again in 2014). However, given that no one claimed responsibility for either incident, this shouldn't be considered a definitive explanation. Officials in China, whether secular or religious, are liable to be unpopular for a wide variety of reasons that may have nothing to do with their ethnicity or political views.

Another song laments the apathy and infighting among Uyghurs that has apparently fostered their decline:

> No room for us to tread one wide road
> We hurry down our narrow lanes
> Building traps for one another
> To cause each other's fall.

This type of self-criticism is still common among Uyghur intellectuals, some of whom blame conservative (that is, religious) elements in Uyghur society for hindering its development – implicit in which is the idea that a more developed, unified region might have avoided being conquered by either the Qing or the Communists.

To the extent that the deliberate separation and frequent prejudice did help unite Uyghurs, it did so at great cost. The misunderstanding and mutual ignorance that already existed between many Han and Uyghur communities in Xinjiang was strengthened, and in some cases led to violence. In Hotan in 1995 a crowd spilling out from a mosque after prayers blocked traffic. When the police tried to clear the street, some in the crowd misunderstood their actions as an attempt to arrest the imam of the mosque. A riot broke out and there were numerous casualties. Video footage of the scene shows a crowd of people in the street, some of them throwing stones. The Chinese government now characterise this incident as a 'terrorist' attack, though there's no evidence that it was premeditated.

The long-term consequence of the animosity between Han and Uyghur has been even worse: the blurring of the line between hatred of the authorities and hatred of Han Chinese. Throughout the 1980s and 1990s, most violent incidents were directed against the state and its representatives, but it was only a matter of time before ordinary Chinese civilians also became a target (as they would in the Urumqi riots in 2009).

The promotion of Uyghur identity also stoked the desire for independence in the 1990s, especially among young people (though it's unclear what proportion of Uyghurs desired this). It was common to hear Uyghurs express the hope that an external agency would attack and defeat China and thus allow their people to be free. Before 1997, the main candidate was Britain, which some Uyghurs thought was bound to fight China in order to retain sovereignty over Hong Kong, which was due to be handed back that year. After the 9/11 attacks, some Uyghurs in Yining told me that they hoped China was responsible so that the United States would then invade. While it's easy to dismiss such hopes as ludicrous, they show the sense of desperation felt by many.

SEEKING ESCAPE

The widespread unemployment and poverty among young Uyghur men caused many to start drinking heavily and using drugs. The problem was worst in secular northern cities like Urumqi and Yining; in southern Xinjiang the religious prohibitions on alcohol and drugs limited their use. In Yining in the early 1990s many men gathered once a week or more for binge-drinking parties at which jokes, stories, poetry and music were shared until all were drunk. Opium and hashish may also have been part of some of these evenings. The availability of heroin in China had increased greatly after 'opening up' – especially across the border between Burma and Yunnan province, and also from Afghanistan. There were certainly opiates on sale in the centre of Urumqi in 1993 – young men were selling it in the evenings in the vicinity of Rebiya Kadeer's department store.

At that time there were few options for treatment for either drug or alcohol use. Though Chinese law provided for the 'rehabilitation' of drug users, this amounted to little more than being locked up. Medical treatment in such places was almost non-existent. In addition to having to go through withdrawal without assistance (methadone wasn't available in state clinics until 2004) the detainees had to perform unpaid work, referred to as 're-education through labour', for up to 18 hours a day, sometimes in terrible conditions.

Private clinics did exist in Xinjiang – some advertised on billboards on the road between Urumqi and Yining – but were little better. These charged very high prices and their methods relied on addicts going cold turkey. An added deterrent was that such clinics often had to provide the police with a list of their patients. While this didn't automatically lead to criminal charges, there was a risk of ending up on the *zhongdian renkou*, a 'special population' register for criminals, prostitutes and dissidents. Being on this list could make it harder to find work or housing and lead to restrictions on freedom of movement.

Given the limitations of the private sector, Uyghur communities had little choice but to try to tackle the drug problem themselves. In 1994 a group of young intellectuals and religious students in Yining revived the *mashrap*, an old form of social gathering that aimed to transmit social, moral and cultural education from older to younger generations. Though popular in the area in the 1940s and 1950s, by the 1970s such 'backward' customs were prohibited. A typical *mashrap* lasted about four hours, the first of which involved eating and talking informally. The second was dedicated to sharing information about the problems of alcohol and drugs, during which there would often be a 'judgement' scene in which one of the participants would be confronted with some recent 'crime'. Sean Roberts, a social anthropologist, describes an episode in which Abdull, a young man, is accused of drinking vodka at a birthday party the previous week:

> Abdull looked visibly embarrassed as he tried vainly to get sympathy with excuses about peer pressure. The *qazibäg* [judge] explained that drinking alcohol was harmful to one's health and was a waste of the money that was needed to feed and clothe one's family. Furthermore, it was *haram* [forbidden] and partaking in such activity was contrary to a Muslim's act of submission to God.

Such 'crimes' were met with humorous punishments. Abdull's was to 'go fishing in the lake', which required him to remove sweets from a basin of water using only his mouth while kneeling with his hands behind his back. Roberts describes how 'he fell face first into the water, and all the men in the room erupted into laughter'. Each time, Abdull's face was wiped and he was asked if he wanted vodka now. Other punishments included 'taking a photo', in which the man was made to stand against a wall with his arms outstretched, and then a bucket of water was thrown at him, leaving his outline against it. A slap on both cheeks was called 'giving a baked dumpling', in reference to the method by which uncooked dough was slapped against the walls of clay ovens. The aim of such embarrassment was to make the 'guilty' renounce their transgression and promise to behave better, and dissuade others from committing similar 'crimes'. But in keeping with the light-hearted nature of the 'punishments', a *mashrap* was also often a forum for riddles, joke-telling, poetry recitation and music, which took up the remaining two hours.

By the summer of 1995, the revived *mashraps* had become very popular, with around 10,000 young men taking part, and had spread as far as Urumqi, Kashgar and Almaty in Kazakhstan. Though not all Uyghurs may have approved of the religious content of the *mashraps*, there was certainly widespread support for their attempts to deal with a dire social problem. Initially, the *mashraps* also met with the agreement

103

of the city authorities. They were supported by several cultural institutions in the city, who donated materials for a library in Kepekyuzi, one of the villages surrounding Yining.

What seems to have changed their minds was the campaign organised by a number of *mashraps* in Yining to boycott shops selling alcohol. This proved very effective – some local shops stopped selling it for fear of reprisals. When the *mashraps* in the Ili region subsequently elected a leader – Abdulhelil, a 28-year-old businessman with three children – the authorities quickly summoned him for questioning along with several others. In July 1995 the government denounced *mashraps* as a breeding ground for separatist ideas and 'illegal religious activities', and banned them. This would surely have happened even without the religious element: the Chinese government hasn't been shy about stifling manifestations of civil society that it deems a threat, whether they be environmental NGOs, legal-reform campaigners or labour-rights organisations. The authorities would also have distrusted the *mashraps*' strengthening of ethnic boundaries, and their promotion of a sense of kinship among young Uyghurs (not the kind of 'ethnic unity' they generally favour).

At first the ban was not heavily enforced, except through small fines. Though this made some *mashraps* go underground, it was not enough to discourage some from organising the 'First Annual Football Contest of Mashrap Youth' in mid-August 1995. Football is popular in Xinjiang – many *mashraps* had already formed teams to encourage young men to have a healthier form of leisure activity. But when the organisers went to ask for permission from the authorities (which is required for any large gathering of people in China) they were asked to provide a huge administration fee: 50,000 yuan. Though the organisers managed to collect this, they were subsequently asked for an additional, larger fee. The organisers couldn't pay this, but said they could raise it through ticket sales, to which the authorities responded by refusing permission entirely. They even went so far as to remove the goals from the main football pitch and from local schools, and then, just to make absolutely sure, placed tanks on the pitch on the day the event had been planned for.

This show of force successfully stopped the football contest from occurring, but provoked further opposition. Two days later about a thousand Uyghurs gathered in the main square in Yining to protest, but the authorities had been tipped off already and were well prepared. Snipers were posted on the roofs of the surrounding buildings, and many streets were blocked with barbed wire. Soldiers patrolled with assault weapons and in armoured vehicles. Though many such confrontations have ended badly in Xinjiang, on that occasion the protest dissolved with only a few arrests.

The *mashraps* continued in secret, and were needed even more after the government launched its 'Strike Hard, Maximum Pressure' campaign against crime. This drastically reduced the amount of heroin available, causing many users to switch from smoking the drug to the more effective method of injection. Given that needle sharing was common, HIV spread rapidly throughout Xinjiang's drug users, 85 per cent of whom were Uyghur men aged between 20 and 40. According to the Chinese Centre for Disease Control, the highest rates of HIV infection among intravenous drug users were in Urumqi (40 per cent) and Yining (85 per cent). This soon began to spread into the non-drug-using population via prostitution, especially due to the lack of sexual-health education. Even in this sphere there were marked ethnic inequalities. In Aksu the local government only gave foreign sexual-health workers educational leaflets printed in Chinese, not Uyghur, and advised the workers to avoid brothels in Uyghur areas because they were apparently not safe.

By 2000 Xinjiang would account for 10 per cent of China's HIV cases, a hugely disproportionate share, given its small population. This was perhaps the starkest illustration yet that the position of Uyghurs in Xinjiang was becoming untenable. A radical reassessment of policy was obviously required, not just in economic and health terms, but also in education and religious management.

Unfortunately, the government had other priorities.

A TWO-FACED STRATEGY

Since 'opening up', the Chinese government's approach to Xinjiang has been Janus-faced. On the one hand, it has offered the carrot of economic development, often with the explicit rationale that this growth will automatically promote social stability. This isn't a bad assumption: a state that is able to provide jobs and sufficient access to education and health care for the majority of its citizens usually doesn't face substantial opposition, even if other 'freedoms' are curtailed (the Chinese government being the case par excellence). Yet even if this goal had been achieved to the equal benefit of all the peoples of Xinjiang, there would still have been dissent. As the Chinese scholar Cao Huhua argues: 'Economic growth cannot guarantee vulnerable populations the freedom to exploit their abilities, or to achieve social and political rights regardless of their identity or place in society.'

The other face of Chinese policy in Xinjiang, especially after 1990, has been a focus on 'security'. In one respect, this is understandable – Xinjiang *does* have long, porous borders with a number of countries that have experienced considerable periods of instability in recent years, such as Afghanistan, Tajikistan and Pakistan. The development of both military and police capacity in the region is certainly justified on these grounds. What has been far more problematic is the state's approach to perceived threats to 'internal security'. The resentment these policies have provoked among Uyghurs means that the problems in Xinjiang cannot be reduced to purely economic issues.

In March 1996 the state's objectives were clearly stated during a meeting of the seven most powerful men in China, the Standing Committee of the Communist Party's Politburo. A special session had been convened to discuss Xinjiang, the record of which was sent to the regional authorities, in effect giving them their orders. Like most of the workings of the Politburo, such instructions are usually highly secret, but in this rare instance they were leaked. The main aim of 'Document No. 7', as it was catchily titled, was to 'foresee possible dangers', and 'dam the river before the floods come'. Some of its general directives sounded eminently sensible:

> When resolving problems that occur between ethnic groups or within an ethnic group, adhere to the principle of seeking truth from the facts and resolve it accordingly. Do not resolve everything unselectively as an ethnic problem. Prevent conflicts between people from becoming an ethnic conflict.

The specifics of the document revealed a more uncompromising approach to the governance of Xinjiang, especially with regard to religion:

> Severely control the building of new mosques [...] Relocate or replace quickly people who are hesitant or support ethnic separatism. Give leadership positions in mosques and religious organisations to dependable, talented people who love the motherland. Stop illegal organisations such as underground religious schools and Qur'an studies meetings.

It also made clear that south Xinjiang needed to be the focus of attention to ensure 'security':

> While performing the task of maintaining the stability of southern Xinjiang well as a major point, take great effort to strengthen the economic development of the region. With the money of the central government and the help of the locals, quickly complete the southern Xinjiang railway, push the development of cotton production and petroleum as well as the petrol-chemical industry *in order to change the region's poor and backward face* [my italics].

The main aim here seems to be to create at least the *appearance* of prosperity in the region. The improvement of the livelihoods of 'the locals' was not listed as a priority; though Uyghurs in south Xinjiang were part of cotton production, this activity was so unrewarding it only impoverished them further. The document instead placed more emphasis on the need for surveillance of 'the locals', instructing the authorities to 'establish a sensitive information net and manage to get information on a deep level which can covertly alert beforehand. Establish individual files; maintain supervision and vigilance.'

Despite being a classified memo, Document No. 7's overall message was thus really no different from the official line. Religion was seen as a potential threat, as it could be used by separatists; so long as Xinjiang's GDP increased, everything would be fine.

This correspondence raises the thorny question of whether the Politburo, or the Xinjiang authorities, actually believed this to be the case, and if so, on what basis. There's certainly a long history in China of minor officials only telling their distant superiors what they think they want to hear (especially during the Mao era). But even assuming that the authorities have been aware of the systematic inequalities experienced by non-Han peoples in Xinjiang, it's possible that within the government discussion and reform of its policies in Xinjiang (and other minority areas) has been just as hampered as it is in public. The Chinese Communist Party is not a monolithic entity. The party has always had different factions, which can crudely be characterised as hardliners and reformers. Since 1989 the former have been in the ascendancy, and have resisted any major slackening of political control. To some degree, the party may thus be trapped in its own rhetoric, so that there's only one politically acceptable way to conceptualise the situation in Xinjiang. This narrowing of the terms of discussion can be seen as analogous to the way in which many Uyghurs in Xinjiang in the late 1990s blamed all their problems on the Chinese government; the irreconcilable narratives currently offered by the Chinese government and the WUC illustrate how little progress has been made since then.

The Xinjiang authorities responded quickly to Document No. 7. The following month the 'Strike Hard' campaign was launched, which had existed in other provinces since 1983 as an annual crackdown on crime. But in Xinjiang in 1996 it was given an explicitly ideological rationale. The Xinjiang government claimed that:

> There is every indication that national separatists are working in collusion with all kinds of criminal and violent elements. Their reactionary and sabotage activities are increasingly rampant and have seriously threatened the safety of people's lives and property, as well as social stability.

By lumping ordinary crime and social and political dissent together in this fashion, the authorities sought to tarnish the legitimacy of the latter. In subsequent years this tactic would be taken to its logical conclusion, in the form of mass-sentencing rallies where murderers, rapists and 'separatists' were given death sentences in front of a crowd of thousands.

It's rare for a prominent government initiative in China not to be swiftly trumpeted as a major success by its media. True to form, the *Xinjiang Daily* reported several months later that there had been 2,500 arrests, and that 6,000 pounds of explosives had been seized, along with 31,000 rounds of ammo (the listing of redundant statistics is a lamentably pervasive feature of both Chinese government prose and most of its school textbooks). Though such figures, for all their precision, are impossible to verify, there were certainly mass arrests throughout Xinjiang. The 'Strike Hard' campaign made the Yining authorities arrest young Uyghur men suspected of taking part in the *mashraps*, or of criticising the government. A number of these arrests were due to informers within Uyghur communities (in accordance with Document No. 7's prescription about creating a 'sensitive information net'). Many of these arrests happened in the middle of the night, and relatives were not told where the detained were being held (many were taken to so-called 'black jails', detention centres that do not officially exist). To all intents and purposes these young men 'disappeared'; however, there were rumours that some of the detained were subsequently found dead in the countryside. Whether or not this was true, the rumour was indicative of (and also worsened) relations between Uyghur communities in Yining and the authorities.

The government also sought to disrupt cooperation between Uyghurs in Xinjiang and the Uyghur organisations in the new Central Asian republics. In 1996 China formed an intergovernmental organisation known as the 'Shanghai Five' (whose members were China, Kazakhstan, Kyrgyzstan, Tajikistan and Russia), which aimed to promote stability in the region. Though China's main interest was 'security', for the other members China's economic cooperation was of greater value. Previously, most of these republics had been relatively safe bases for the diverse Uyghur organisations, but by 1995 this had already begun to change. In that year President Nazarbayev agreed that Kazakh security services would monitor Uyghurs in the country and share the information with China. The following year, just before the Shanghai Five met for the first time, Kazakhstan's foreign minister told Uyghurs not to promote any form of separatism in China, an activity he described as the 'political AIDS' of the era.

After the formation of the Shanghai Five many Uyghur groups would be banned and their members subjected to harassment from local security forces. Many groups were forced to relocate to countries that didn't have extradition agreements with China, in particular Germany and the United States – the story of these groups and their leaders will be told in Chapter 5. In 1999 Kazakhstan extradited two Uyghurs with Chinese citizenship who were accused of separatism even though they were at risk of execution. In 2001 the Shanghai Five was renamed the Shanghai Cooperation Organisation (SCO), following the inclusion of Uzbekistan.

'NOTHING FROM THE GOVERNMENT'

Even by Xinjiang's standards, Yining is remote. In 1997 it had no railway station, and was a seven-hour car ride from Urumqi, or 14 hours by bus. Admittedly, it had a miniature airport that received one, sometimes two flights a day from Urumqi, but this was beyond the budget of most except officials or businessmen. The majority of people (and goods) headed to Yining had no choice but to travel the long road through a desolate landscape in which any buildings seemed misplaced. After many hours, hills rise on either side of the road, soon growing taller, and then nearer, until any vehicle has to snake its way between them. Then suddenly the hills fall back and a vast lake of brilliant blue or blankest white (depending on the season) extends to the horizon. From there the road turns careful hairpins down through alpine scenery, until it reaches the floor of the Ili valley.

At the beginning of 1997 there were many ways in which Yining was noteworthy. It was famous for the apples grown in orchards around the city. It was known for its kind climate, its frequent blue skies, its birch and poplar trees. As an almost border town (the actual one with Kazakhstan was a short bus ride away) it had a frontier feeling. There were Uzbek, Kazakh and Russian goods in the bazaar, and still some nomadic herders driving sheep through the hills. It was also of histori-cal interest, as the former capital of both the second East Turkestan Republic, and the Qing's military centre (the garrison buildings of which could be seen in the nearby town of Huiyuan). Yining had the additional distinction of being the only city in northern Xinjiang with a Uyghur majority (the population of 330,000 was about 48 per cent Uyghur and 36 per cent Han, with the remainder being mostly Kazakh and Hui). On the negative side, it also had some of the highest rates of alcoholism, drug use, HIV infection and unemployment in the region. It should also have been notorious for the uranium mine in nearby Kunas township, where convicts worked, and which had a death rate of 10–20 per cent per year, but its existence was a state secret.

But ever since 1997 Yining has been best known for the violence that consumed the town in early February. Like the demonstration in Baren in 1990, the event is now seen as one of the milestones in Xinjiang's recent history, and as such is fiercely contested by the Chinese govern-ment and Uyghur activists. What's different about the Yining protests is that the event and its causes are better understood. While the area was closed to the foreign media, there's still a considerable amount of eyewitness testimony and even some film footage.

On the night of 4 February 1997 the police arrested around 200 people at mosques and private-study groups. On the morning of 5 February, 500 young Uyghur men staged a peaceful protest against the arrests and the banning of the *mashraps*. They marched through the town carrying a religious banner and shouting slogans, reports of which differ greatly. Some are said to have been secular ('Don't pay taxes'; 'We want nothing from the government'), though others were religious. After several hours riot police attacked the protesters and used dogs against them. The police ended the demonstration by firing into the crowd and arresting hundreds of people. Later that afternoon a second protest took place, which included many relatives of the arrested. This too was brutally put down using riot police, water cannon and tear gas; there were further arrests. There are claims that some of the arrested were held outside, despite the freezing conditions, causing many severe cases of frostbite. So many were arrested that the prison facilities of the *bingtuan*'s 4th Division, located in Yining, are said to have become full, requiring the others to be taken to black jails outside the city. Many of the arrested were held without charge for weeks or even months.

Over the next two days unrest spread into the suburbs. Cars were set on fire, and there was destruction of property. Some retaliation against the police seems to have occurred, and there are unconfirmed reports that several Han civilians were attacked. Exactly how many died during the unrest is unclear. Some Western scholars suggest at least 300, but far higher numbers have been cited by many Uyghur activists, who often refer to the event as 'the Ghulja massacre'.

While the scale of the protest may have initially overwhelmed the authorities, troops were quickly brought in from Urumqi and Lanzhou. During the following weeks a full-scale curfew was imposed in Yining. Paramilitary (from the XPCC) and army soldiers patrolled the streets.

Extensive house-to-house searches were reported, plus large-scale arbitrary arrests. According to Amnesty International, between 3,000 and 5,000 people were detained.

The government's immediate response was to downplay the seriousness of the incident, arguing that there was no political cause. It was 'just an act of beating, smashing and looting by some drug addicts, looters and "social garbage"'. To emphasise that all was fine, on 8 February state media also reported that 'tens of thousands of Muslims of all ethnic groups left their homes in great delight and went to their mosques in the city' to celebrate the start of Eid (the festival that marks the end of Ramadan).

The official version of what happened in Yining would change radically over the next several years. In 2002 it would be redefined as 'a serious riot during which the terrorists shouted slogans calling for the establishment of an "Islamic kingdom"'. The riot was blamed on an organisation called the 'Eastern Turkestan Islamic Party of Allah', a group that had not been mentioned before, and has not been blamed for anything since. The lack of detail about this organisation in anything other than official Chinese accounts has led many scholars to question its existence.

Many Western journalists emphasised the protests' political nature; few, if any, described it as terrorism. An Associated Press report described the events as 'a Muslim march demanding independence'; CNN called it a 'protest against Beijing rule'. Though there was surely some truth in these accounts, the 'separatist' elements of the incident seem to have been less important than the local grievances. Obviously, 'separatist', 'religious' and 'human-rights' concerns are not mutually exclusive. The Uyghurs who took part in the Yining protests, and those elsewhere, may have been protesting for some or all of these reasons. As a Uyghur friend of mine in Yining put it: 'Some came because they hated the Chinese or the government, some because they were angry about not having jobs, some because their imams told them to, some because they like fighting.'

Any attempt to smooth the complexity of motivations of those involved into a single explanation, as frequently occurs in the Western media's reporting and official Chinese accounts, is extremely questionable: often what it reveals is the speaker's preferred version of events. What compounds the problem is that journalists or scholars rarely find people willing to be interviewed about their participation in protests in Xinjiang (and almost never anyone responsible for more violent actions). This is entirely understandable, given the severity with which the authorities treat such matters – in Xinjiang just talking to a foreign journalist can get a person detained. It does mean, however, that there is a tendency to apply stock explanations when trying to make sense of these incidents.

Though the Baren episode received some international coverage, the Yining protests did far more to raise the profile of Uyghurs. One Saudi Arabian newspaper cautioned China about the 'suffering of Muslims whose human rights are violated'. The US Congress responded by passing a bill approving Uyghur as one of the broadcasting languages of Radio Free Asia, the US-funded organisation that claims to promote freedom of information and human rights. The following year Congress also included Uyghurs on a list of peoples facing religious persecution. Turkey was more explicit in its condemnation of the handling of the Yining protests, which were also criticised by the European Union. In April 1997 the European Union expressed concern at 'the arbitrary arrest and execution of a number of Uighurs in Eastern Turkestan and condemned China's policy aimed at eliminating the culture of the Uighur people, most of whom are Muslim'. The European Parliament called on the Chinese authorities to 'stop oppressing the Uighur and to launch political talks with all the parties involved in the issue of Eastern Turkestan'. This statement is also noteworthy for its use of the term 'Eastern Turkestan', something normally avoided by states or supra-state bodies, as it calls into question the legitimacy of China's claim to the territory. Whether this was intentional, due to carelessness, or the result of lobbying by one of the numerous Uyghur activist organisations operating at the time is unclear.

The Yining protests led to an increased police and military presence throughout the region. The *South China Morning Post*, a newspaper based in Hong Kong, reported that an estimated 100,000 additional troops had been moved into Xinjiang. Despite this, three bombs exploded on public buses in Urumqi on 25 February, killing nine people and injuring 28 others. The date was most likely chosen because the memorial for the recently deceased Deng Xiaoping was happening in Beijing on the same day. This was clearly an organised act of terrorism (in that it involved the deliberate killing of civilians for apparently political aims). Given that the bombings took place within several weeks of the Yining protests, it's not unreasonable to assume some connection between the two events, though it's not known who was responsible. In response the authorities placed soldiers with machine guns at the bus stops on the main bus routes, while soldiers in trucks patrolled the city streets.

When there were further bus bombings on 7 and 8 March in Beijing, the immediate assumption was that they were connected to those in Urumqi. This notion was certainly taken seriously by many – some Uyghurs reported that many hotels in Beijing refused to let them stay and that taxis wouldn't stop for them. Such discrimination has remained routine, though there have been peaks after major incidents such as the riots in Urumqi in 2009, the Tiananmen explosion in 2013 and the Kunming attacks the following year.

But the bombings in Beijing in 1997 may have had nothing to do with Xinjiang. China's main legislative body, the National People's Congress (NPC), was holding its annual meeting in the city, and there were many people in the country with grievances against the state. Beijing receives thousands of people every year who come to petition various government departments, often about local injustices and corruption. Few of these cases get a proper hearing. The failure to respond to citizens' complaints is one of the main causes of mass incidents like

Renshou. Some petitioners are driven to more extreme acts. During the late 1990s there were a number of bus bombings in other parts of China that had no plausible link with Xinjiang. (Explosives aren't that hard to obtain in China, as they are frequently used for demolition. I've even seen farmers using dynamite for fishing.) Another problem with linking the Beijing bombings to those in Urumqi is that no one claimed responsibility for either; even Abdulahat Abdurishit, the chairman of Xinjiang, denied there was any connection.

As with the Baren incident, the authorities responded with mass detentions and increased surveillance. In mid-April there were trials for those arrested during the protests, the majority of which were just for show. The sentencing of 30 of them took place at a rally in Yining city stadium that was attended by about 5,000 people (most of whom were likely soldiers or state employees). Three men were sentenced to death on charges of 'causing injury, arson, hooliganism, smashing property and looting'. The others who had received prison sentences were driven through the city streets in a convoy of open trucks and buses. When a crowd of mostly relatives and friends approached the trucks, the police escort opened fire, reportedly killing three people and injuring ten others. A report in the *Ili Evening News* of 1 May 1997 described the civilians as 'rioters'. The report also claimed that the armed police had first fired warning shots into the air.

More arrests occurred over the following months. On 22 May, the *Ili Evening News* reported that police raids had been carried out in the area as part of a 'Strike Hard' action against 'violent criminals'. By June, the authorities had begun explicitly to link separatist activities with religion. The *Xinjiang Daily* reported that a crackdown on underground religious activities had resulted in an official banning of the construction or renovation of 133 mosques. There were also demolitions of existing mosques – at least 70 were destroyed in the Ili area between 1995 and 1999, while in Urumqi in 1998 alone 20 were destroyed. The rationale for this in some cases was that they were too near schools or universities, and thus might influence children.

Students of any age were already restricted from mosque attend-ance, but after 1997 this began to be enforced more seriously. That year posters were put up at a university in Hotan announcing that six students had been expelled and arrested for taking part in an illegal Qur'an study class. The Xinjiang government claimed to have broken up more than 100 such classes. A report boasted that 'illegal religious activities were cleaned up [...] district by district, village by village, and hamlet by hamlet'. In July 1997, Amudun Niyaz, chairman of the Xinjiang People's Congress, publicly called for the 'waging of a people's war against separatists and illegal religious activities'. Although he was careful to add that the issue was 'neither an ethnic nor a religious problem', the fact that it was only Uyghurs being arrested would not have been lost on many.

In Yining, and to a lesser degree Urumqi, the effect of the crackdown was the opposite of what had (presumably) been intended. Some of the most devout Uyghurs I knew in Yining – those who prayed five times a day and never drank, and whose idea of fun was watching DVDs about the hadj – admitted to me that they had been 'very bad Muslims' before 1997, and had often drunk alcohol and smoked, and rarely gone to the mosque. It would be simplistic to say that their change of ways was purely an act of defiance against the state, though it was most likely a symbolic act of protest for many of them. The authorities' strict response to protest in Yining and other cities in Xinjiang meant that for many Uyghurs this became the only viable method of opposition. However, the religious resurgence can also be seen as a response to the social and economic problems that many Uyghur communities faced. Like the *mashraps*, religious participation offered many Uyghurs an alternative to the sense of hopelessness engendered by their economic situation, one that offered the possibility of personal, and even national, salvation.

Given the many social and cultural benefits of the *mashraps*, it was unsurprising that after the Yining crackdown they were revived in Almaty in Kazakhstan in late 1997. The geographical proximity of the city to Yining, coupled with its large Uyghur population (an estimated

100,000), meant that it was (briefly) a place in which Uyghur cultural and national issues could be freely discussed.

The harsh response to the Yining protests also worsened relations between Han and Uyghur communities, causing a greater social separation. During the year I spent in Yining I only once attended a social gathering in someone's home at which both Han and Uyghurs were present, and on that occasion the Han woman was a visiting scholar from outside Xinjiang. As for weddings and any meals in restaurants, these were Han or Uyghur only. The only instance I can recall of Han, Uyghur, Kazakh and Hui people enjoying something together, of their own volition, was a grisly set of cockfights in the countryside. And this increased separation wasn't just an expression of the poor relations between Han and Uyghur in Yining; it also reinforced it.

Mass arrests and executions continued in Xinjiang over the next two years. Between 1997 and 1999, Amnesty International recorded 210 death sentences and 190 executions, mostly of Uyghurs convicted of subversive or terrorist activities after only cursory trials. During this period the ratio of death sentences to population size was several times higher in Xinjiang than in any other part of China.

This intensification of the crackdown on Uyghurs had been aided by legal changes that made it easier to detain (and convict) anyone on arbitrary grounds. In 1998 China's NPC modified the old legal category of 'counter-revolutionary' crimes to one called 'crimes against the state'. Many of these offences carried a heavy prison sentence or even a death sentence. The new category included 'ethnic discrimination' or 'inciting anti-ethnic feeling', the criteria for which were so vague that almost any act of dissent in Xinjiang (such as saying that Uyghurs were disenfranchised) could be punishable. The law has rarely offered protection to citizens of the People's Republic of China, whatever their ethnicity – those with political power have always controlled the judiciary. Even wealth has offered no defence: in 1999 the government sent the richest woman in China to prison.

5

EXILES

Rebiya Kadeer inspires strong reactions. In 1995 a Chinese magazine article rhapsodised about her 'eyes of wisdom' and 'brilliant business mind'. As the richest woman in China at that time, and the seventh-richest person in the country, such high praise was not unwarranted. But the tone of the state's comments soon shifted. In 2000 it imprisoned her for eight years for 'disclosing state secrets', and only released her in 2005 on medical grounds. Today the Chinese government regards her as a separatist in league with terrorist forces, and brands her 'a regular liar and a bald-faced one at that'.

Her leadership since 2006 of the World Uyghur Congress (WUC), an umbrella organisation for a number of Uyghur activist groups, is the main cause of their ire. Kadeer's work in this role has evoked equally strong positive reactions from some politicians, human-rights activists and (even) journalists. A gushing profile of her in the *Washington Post* in July 2009 called her 'The mother of the Uighur movement', while, in the same month, the British *Independent* newspaper claimed that 'to the West and her own people, she is a heroic freedom fighter'. She has twice been nominated for the Nobel Peace Prize, and since her release from prison has met a number of world leaders and senior political figures, particularly in the United States (including President George W. Bush). A documentary about her entitled *The 10 Conditions of Love* appeared in 2009, the same year that her autobiography, *Dragon Fighter*, was published in English.

Kadeer was born in 1949 in the north-western Altai region of Xinjiang to moderately prosperous parents, who had much of their property confiscated when she was young. In 1961 they were forced to move south to Aksu, where she married a man who worked in the local bank. She had eight children with him, then divorced him in 1976. After that she opened a laundry; then she started selling sheepskins, gold and other commodities, which was illegal at the time. She then remarried, to a man named Sidiq Rouzi, who had been imprisoned for conflict with the authorities. In the early 1980s she moved her business and family to Urumqi. There she expanded into real estate and, later, the import and export of goods between China and the Central Asian states. Her wealth brought her into contact with Xinjiang officials, who appointed her as a delegate to the Xinjiang People's Congress in 1987. Her status was enhanced by being appointed as a delegate to the NPC in Beijing. By 1994 she was the richest woman in China and the subject of a profile on the cover of the *Wall Street Journal*. The following year she was a member of China's delegation to the UN Conference on Women in Beijing, where she was introduced to Hillary Clinton, at that time the First Lady. During the same year she showed up to a government meeting wearing 21 pieces of jewellery worth 50,000 yuan ($8,000), which she explained by saying it was how Uyghur women responded to an important occasion.

In 1996 her husband left China and sought asylum in the United States, where he began working as a journalist for Radio Free Asia. In 1999 Kadeer was arrested for stealing state secrets and sentenced to eight years in prison. According to the *Urumqi Evening News*, she had been posting Rouzi local newspapers, which, though freely available, weren't intended for international readership. The US Congress called for her release on numerous occasions, and in March 2005 she was released on medical grounds, which may have been a quid pro quo for the United States' not pursuing a resolution on China's human-rights violations at the UN that year, as it had done previously. She flew to the United States and was reunited with her husband and some of her children. But in 2006, after she became head of the WUC, four of her children who were still in Xinjiang were arrested and given long jail sentences for non-political crimes like tax evasion.

Under Kadeer's leadership the WUC has helped raise consciousness of Uyghurs' problems in Xinjiang (though the increased media attention since the Urumqi protests in 2009 has also played a role). In her autobiography she says: 'I want to be the mother of all Uyghurs, the medicine for their ills, the cloth with which they dry their tears, and the cloak to protect them from the rain.' Though a noble (if somewhat over-cooked) sentiment, it doesn't exempt her from an issue any exiled leader faces – by what right can she claim to represent all Uyghurs? To object that she wasn't elected (except by the WUC) is of course absurd, but there remains the more serious question of whether her views, as expressed by the WUC, accurately reflect the plural grievances and aspirations of Uyghurs, both in Xinjiang and outside.

Given the widespread censorship and limits to reporting in Xinjiang, this question is almost impossible to answer. But as Kristian Petersen, an assistant professor at the University of Nebraska, argues: 'The "silence" of the native community has allowed the diasporic community to create an image that reflects their particular goals.' There are unquestionably many Uyghurs who respect, even revere Kadeer, but there are also many other Uyghurs outside Xinjiang who don't agree with the agenda she has pursued. Until 2009 it was unlikely that many Uyghurs outside of Urumqi had even heard of her, but after the Urumqi riots the Chinese media was in such a frenzy to demonise Kadeer that it raised her profile considerably.

The question of who has the right to speak for Uyghurs is certainly not new. The history of activism among the Uyghur diaspora can be seen as a 50-year debate over this and other issues, particularly since the 1990s. A series of similarly named organisations in a variety of locations have disagreed over such questions as whether to advocate full independence or genuine autonomy for Uyghurs, the role of violence in the struggle to achieve nationhood, and the need to include other non-Han minorities in Xinjiang in any future state.

The restrictions on the media (and later on the internet) in Xinjiang have meant that the audience for most of the Uyghur activist groups has been the 500,000 Uyghurs living in the diaspora. The first of these groups was started by Mehmet Emin Bugra and Isa Yusef Alptekin after they fled from Xinjiang to Turkey in the early 1950s. There they conducted political activism by traditional methods – printing journals and newspapers and attending conferences. During the 1950s and 1960s Bugra and Alptekin sought to make alliances with decolonisation movements and international Islamic organisations. Though some of these passed resolutions, no state ever implemented any resolution about Xinjiang. After Bugra died in 1965, Alptekin remained the key figure in Uyghur activism until his death in 1995. He received plenty of support from the Turkish government, as the idea of giving aid to the international Turkic community had domestic political currency. The Uyghur and Tibetan movements were also aided by the establishment in 1991 of the Unrepresented Nations and Peoples Organisation (UNPO), which was co-founded by Isa's son, Erkin Alptekin, and whose aim is to promote the voices of unrepresented and marginalised nations and peoples.

Turkey remained the centre of Uyghur activism until the break-up of the Soviet Union. But with the easing of restrictions on people's movements and the media, it was unsurprising that the demographic superiority of Uyghurs in the former Soviet Central Asian states gave them prominence. Kazakhstan and Kyrgyzstan together account for more than half the Uyghur diaspora. Soon after Kazakh independence two Uyghur organisations were established in the country. The Uyghuristan Liberation Organisation (ULO) was broadly similar in goals and methods to Alptekin's Turkish groups, in that it tried to raise international awareness of Uyghur issues and sent printed materials and cassettes into Xinjiang. The other group, the Eastern Turkestan United National Revolutionary Front (UNRF), professed a more radical agenda. Its founder Yusupbek Mukhlisi claimed to have an underground army of 30,000 and to be responsible for a wide range of violent incidents in Xinjiang. In 1997 his son would claim responsibility for the Urumqi bus bombings. However, there's no evidence for the involvement of either son or father in any major incident in Xinjiang, which has unfortunately not stopped some analysts from reproducing their claims when arguing that Xinjiang is beset on all sides by Islamist terrorists (a subject I discuss in Chapter 6).

During the 1990s there were two attempts to unite the Turkish and Central Asian Uyghur groups into a single organisation, first in 1992, and then in 1998. Both failed due to financial problems and disputes over goals. The one outcome of this process was the founding of the Eastern Turkestan National Centre (ETNC) in Istanbul in 1998, which, although not the government in exile that some had hoped for, did offer cultural and humanitarian support to Uyghurs. There were also signs that the US government was starting to pay attention to events in Xinjiang. In 1998 Uyghur-language broadcasts were added to Radio Free Asia, the US-funded network whose mission statement is to promote free expression in repressive states (its motives and impartiality remain a subject of debate).

However, by the end of the decade both Turkey and the Central Asian states became precarious places for Uyghur organisations to operate from. China began putting pressure on Turkey from the mid-1990s. In 1995 there was a proposal to name a park in Istanbul after the recently deceased Isa Alptekin, to which the Chinese ambassador strongly objected, accusing Turkey of meddling in China's internal affairs. Though the proposal was carried through, some kind of compromise may have been reached, as the following year Qiao Shi, the chairman of the NPC, one of China's main legislative bodies, thanked Turkey for its policy of non-interference. In 1998 Turkish officials told Uyghur leaders not to demonstrate against the Turkish foreign minister's visit to China; in 1999 the Turkish president told Li Peng, then chairman of the NPC Standing Committee, that he was against any separatist elements that targeted China.

In the Central Asian states there were more stringent restrictions on Uyghur activist groups following the establishment of the Shanghai Five organisation in 1996. As well as the extraditions detailed in Chapter 4, there were also restrictions on many Uyghur cultural organisations. In early 1998 the *mashraps* in Almaty were banned.

From 1999 there was a westward exodus of Uyghur groups, first to Europe, then to the United States. Though there wasn't a large Uyghur population in these countries, as places with legally guaranteed freedom of speech, where China had less leverage, they were good bases from which to operate. At a large gathering of Uyghur groups in Munich in 1999 (which Mukhlisi refused to attend because of its prior commitment to the use of non-violent methods) there was a further attempt to form an umbrella organisation. Despite disagreement over leadership and other issues, the different groups did succeed in this aim, though not without choosing one of the most absurdly unwieldy names any activist group has ever inflicted on itself – the Eastern Turkestan (Uyghurstan) National Congress (even its acronym is woeful – ET(U)NC).

Despite the handicap of its name, the organisation stayed intact and also raised its profile – its meeting in October 2001 took place in the European Parliament. The importance of the internet as a means for the group to organise and promote its agenda during this period cannot be overstated: it allowed the ET(U)NC to engage with and mobilise the Uyghur diaspora and thus become a genuinely transnational organisation. China's increasingly strident rhetoric after the 11 September attacks about being a victim of Islamic terrorism in Xinjiang (see Chapter 6) is also likely to have added an urgency to Uyghur groups' efforts to highlight what they perceived to be the real causes of dissent in the region.

In what seemed a further sign of unity, in April 2004 ET(U)NC merged with the World Uyghur Youth Congress to become the World Uyghur Congress (WUC). Its leaders were chosen from the various Uyghur groups that composed it, and included Erkin Alptekin (as president), Alim Seytoff (from the Uyghur American Association) and Mehmet Tohti (from the Uyghur Canadian Association). Unfortunately their legitimacy was almost immediately called into question by the formation of a self-proclaimed 'East Turkestan Government in Exile' (ETGIE) in September 2004, which described itself as 'the sole organ of the ETR authorised to protect the rights of the people of Eastern Turkestan Republic'.

The presence of two organisations, each claiming to be the sole representative of Uyghurs, could have easily degenerated into Pythonesque farce. The WUC prevented this by using the (in theory) higher status of the ETGIE against it, arguing that it would only cooperate with the rival organisation if the United States officially recognised the ETGIE as a legitimate governing body. When the United States refused to do so it undermined the already dubious legitimacy of the group, and since then the ETGIE has been almost invisible (it is almost never quoted in media reports).

It was a shrewd move on the part of the WUC, as the United States – or to be precise, a bipartisan political organisation called the National Endowment for Democracy (NED), which was funded by the US Congress – was moving towards funding part of the WUC already. In late 2002 Omer Kanat and Alim Seytoff, who were based in the United States, had applied for NED funding for the Uyghur American Association. When the NED awarded them funding in 2004, and again the following year, it was an endorsement of another key difference between the WUC and ETGIE. Whereas the ETGIE was clear about its desire for Xinjiang's independence, the WUC has been more guarded on this matter, and has certainly given greater prominence to human-rights concerns.

KADEER'S LEADERSHIP OF THE WUC

After her release in 2005, Kadeer assumed the leadership of the Uyghur American Association, and then in 2006 was elected leader of the WUC. In many respects, she was a logical choice – as an imprisoned dissident who had been the subject of reports and campaigns by Human Rights Watch and Amnesty International, she brought the WUC both kudos and greater exposure. In financial terms, the WUC and its organisations acquired greater resources and security. From 2004 to 2011 the NED gave large grants not only to the WUC, but also to the Uyghur American Association ($1.7 million), the International Uyghur Human

Rights and Democracy Foundation ($850,000) and the Uyghur PEN Club ($300,000). As Yu-Wen Chen, author of a recent book on Uyghur organisations, remarks, the WUC 'has successfully created a survival niche that is attractive to grant-givers'. In her media appearances Kadeer is usually an impassioned, effective speaker able to communicate her message quickly. She seems like a leader.

The circumstances of Kadeer's life before assuming the leadership of the WUC were far from easy, and her remarkable success in business is worthy of respect. She also doesn't get enough credit for overcoming the considerable gender prejudice she faced in Uyghur society – few, if any, Uyghur women have achieved comparable success in any other field, whether it be music, literature or politics. Yet her achievements also raise awkward questions for someone presenting herself as an opponent of Chinese policies in Xinjiang, especially her membership of the Xinjiang People's Congress and then the NPC. Though the Chinese government exaggerates when it claims that her success was entirely attributable to their support for her – she had a large fortune before joining the Xinjiang People's Congress – it certainly wouldn't have hurt to have so many political contacts.

Kadeer's answers to the questions of why she sought to build a business empire, and agreed to work with what she regarded as an occupying regime, are most fully set out in her autobiography *Dragon Fighter*. In it she presents herself as being dedicated to the welfare of Uyghurs from a very early age, often with the barely concealed suggestion that God has chosen her for the role. The implication that she is 'special' in some way runs throughout the book. She claims that after she was born her father dug a hole to bury the sheets on which the birth had taken place (a custom in some parts of Xinjiang). In the hole he apparently found a huge deposit of gold that saved the family from poverty. Later she says she was told by one of her relatives: 'You don't belong to us, you belong to the people.' There's a general lack of humility throughout her description of her childhood. She writes: 'I was always ready to step in where I could to provide solace or protection for others,' and later boasts that 'every girl wanted to be my best friend, and even the older ladies were eager to talk to me. When I was out and about, I could feel people looking at me admiringly.'

At times she implies that she has saintly powers. Kadeer claims: 'If any of our relatives fell ill, my siblings would look at me as if there was more I could do.' At her wedding to Rouzi, his family are said to have believed that 'an angel had descended from heaven to visit their home'. There are other episodes in which divine intervention is implied. When she and Rouzi are rescued after being trapped by fallen logs, it is said to be 'like a little miracle'. Even the choice of site for her business in Urumqi is blessed: she recalls: 'It seemed to me that God had led me to this little pile of rubble.'

While this kind of auto-hagiography will seem overdone to many readers, it can be understood as an attempt to present herself as *the* legitimate spokesperson for Uyghurs. As Jeff Daniels, the director of *The 10 Conditions of Love*, argued in an interview with me: 'She's unabashedly advocating a cause that she needs to be a symbol of. She feels it's important to push that narrative, to a point where it's clearly at odds with her own story. I think she doesn't care. The whole point is that she's trying to advocate a cause.'

Portraying herself as a person whose chief motivation is to help her people may be an attempt to deflect criticism of her business empire and membership of the political elite. Kadeer claims her epiphany over the liberating power of money came in 1971, after bribing a Red Guard to stop the beating of a Uyghur writer: 'A cold shudder passed through my body. *I actually held the power to make a difference with my money.*' Later in her business career she tells her children: 'It wouldn't be enough if I earned money only to support you and myself. I already have that amount. What I need is to earn more money for our people too.' The construction of a department store in Urumqi is presented as the culmination of this process: 'The building introduced me to Uyghur people in the way that I had always hoped it would. It embodied my strength and my spirit of resistance against opponents.'

Though one might be suspicious about Kadeer's claims that her motive for getting rich was to help her people, she did carry out philanthropic activities in the mid- to late 1990s in Urumqi. One of the main strands of this was the 'Thousand Mothers' movement, an investment collective whose profits were supposed to fund community projects like schools and cultural events. This was soon closed down by local officials, no doubt partly because the government generally mistrusts most civil-society organisations, though it may also have been due to rumours about her hiring university students to give Uyghurs history lessons in the store (which for the authorities would be a political issue).

While she presents this as an example of the Chinese government's determination not to allow anyone to help Uyghurs, there is certainly at least one exception. Since 1996 the Nurtay Haji Orphan School has provided a home and education to Uyghur and Kazakh children in Yining. The school is located in a peaceful area close to the Ili river, and is funded by Nurtay Haji Iskander, a wealthy Uyghur CEO of the China Xinjiang Western Nur Group, a manufacturing and transportation conglomerate. Despite the name, not all of the children are orphans: many have parents with drink or drug problems, or who are in prison. (This is a good example of how the waves of mass arrests in Xinjiang cast a long shadow over Uyghur communities. Even with the orphanage, in 2001 there was still a very high number of Uyghur children living on the streets in Yining.)

The local authorities did not provide any financing for the school but did monitor the content of classes; it was reportedly stressed that there could be 'nothing religious or harmful to social and ethnic unity'. When I visited the orphanage in 2002, both Nurtay Haji and the teachers seemed caring and dedicated. In 2006 the government awarded him the title 'Charity Star'.

KADEER'S POLITICAL CAREER

Another problematic issue is Kadeer's explanation for taking part in the NPC. She claims that 'in those days I held a false belief that the officials governing our homeland were well intentioned but simply did not understand the true problems of our people'. While a belief in the virtuous ignorance of the central government about local corruption and poor governance isn't unknown in China, it does contradict her earlier admission that as a child she realised that 'those in the government generally thought that the only way they could live in peace and quiet was if all of us regional natives were exiled or murdered'.

Some might also question Kadeer's account of her role at the NPC meetings. She presents herself as a crusading presence who dared speak truth to power. She says she asked Wang Lequan, the top official in Xinjiang at that time: 'Are you eager to see our blood flow?' and warned him: 'Don't force the common people to rise up'. At the NPC meeting in Beijing she says she gave a speech that contained the sentence 'To murder one of our people has become almost as commonplace as shooting a bird', and adds: 'At this point, I noticed that several delegates were wiping their eyes'. The idea that Kadeer was repeatedly allowed to speak so bluntly goes against everything that's known about politics and freedom of expression in China, especially on a subject as sensitive as ethnic relations.

Like many of her speeches, the book also contains numerous assertions that few, if any, scholars would support, such as claims that there are 20 million Uyghurs worldwide, and that the reason HIV infection is so high in Xinjiang is because the government sends all the Han people with HIV from elsewhere in China to the region. In a similar vein, she claimed in an interview in 2010 with the *On Islam* website that

> before 1987 [the] sex trade was never known in East Turkistan. Religion and traditions of Uyghurs have always been standing against this; we never heard about it before then [...] Uyghurs also have not heard before then about drugs. Drugs came from mainland China.

While prostitution and drug use did increase in Xinjiang (and throughout China) after the 'opening up' period, the assertion that neither existed beforehand is contradicted by travellers' accounts and the testimonies of Uyghurs, many of whom attest to the common use of hashish, often at a *gulkhan*, a 'house with four big rooms where they sold meat and tea and people smoked hashish'. Kadeer's aim in invoking the idea of a 'pure' Uyghur society is perhaps to heap further blame on the Chinese government, but by doing so she obscures the economic and social conditions that led Uyghurs to abuse drugs and alcohol. When she discusses the 1997 Yining protests in her book, although the *mashraps* are referred to, there is virtually no mention of what prompted their revival.

To some degree, the problems with Kadeer's own personal story are arguably akin to the issues with the nationalist version of history that the WUC offers. In both instances a simplifying, unitary narrative has been imposed onto messy and conflicting information, with the aim of telling a story where issues of blame, virtue and victimhood are cast in black and white. According to Jeff Daniels, the reason is most likely that Kadeer 'feels that the misinformation that China feeds the world gives her licence to do the same to promote her own agenda'.

Both Kadeer and the WUC unquestionably play a vital role in raising consciousness of the situation of Uyghurs in Xinjiang. Some of the groups beneath the WUC umbrella, like the Uyghur Human Rights Project, do take a more rigorous approach than their parent organisation, and provide well-researched reports. But the frequent insistence of Kadeer and the WUC on a binary narrative about Xinjiang is regrettable and unnecessary. Given that Kadeer's position as leader is unlikely to be contested, and that the WUC has achieved what all the previous Uyghur organisations failed to do – unified different groups around a common manifesto, attracted sufficient funding to have a wider impact, and created headquarters in multiple stable locations (such as Munich and Washington) – it can afford to present a more careful account of the issues in Xinjiang. There's no need for exaggeration: in all likelihood, the truth is bad enough.

FALLOUT

One of China's most wanted men drives a London bus. Enver Tohti drives the No. 254 bus route, which I used to take from Lower Clapton to Stamford Hill. I must have seen him many times, but on each occasion the most I would have done, after swiping my Oyster card, was say hello to him in an automatic way. I certainly didn't wonder where he was from (let alone think he might be Uyghur). If his face or shaved head made any impression, it wasn't a lasting one.

When I met him properly it was in November 2013 in a cafe near Euston station. Enver had contacted me about getting my book about the 1997 Yining protests translated into Uyghur. We spoke for an hour about the social, religious and economic problems facing Uyghurs in Xinjiang, and about the recent car explosion in Beijing that the government had blamed on Uyghur 'terrorists'. At no point did he seem familiar. Only near the end of our meeting did I ask Enver what he did for a living and how he had first come to London. He said he'd been a doctor in Urumqi, the capital of Xinjiang, but that he now drove a bus. He added, very matter-of-factly, that he could never go back to China without being arrested. In 1998 he had worked on a documentary for Channel 4 about the deaths caused by Chinese nuclear weapons testing in Xinjiang. After the programme aired there was an international outcry, and Tohti had to seek asylum.

China conducted its nuclear tests in the Taklamakan Desert in south Xinjiang. Though the nearest cities – Urumqi, Turpan, Korla and Hami – were all between 200 and 300 kilometres away, this isn't far enough for safety: the wind can blow radioactive particles for thousands of kilometres. The first test took place in 1964. Over the next 32 years there were 45 more tests, some of them underground, some in the atmosphere. The tests were not a secret: the Chinese government made a propaganda film in the 1960s that stressed their safety. Though people in Xinjiang saw signs of the testing – Enver remembers dust from the explosions falling from the sky – there was no discussion about the possible impact on the public's health. In 1985 several hundred Uyghur students pro-tested in Beijing about the testing. There was renewed concern from Uyghur organisations in Kyrgyzstan and Kazakhstan in the early 1990s, which led to the issue being raised by the Kazakh president. In 1991 it was estimated by the International Physicians for the Prevention of Nuclear War that the total amount of plutonium released by the testing into the atmosphere was about 48 kilograms in weight – what might seem a small number until you consider that one millionth of a gram of plutonium-239 can cause cancer if inhaled. In July 1996 the Chinese government announced that testing was going to stop.

This might have been the end of the story, had it not been for the documentary, in which Tohti's participation was crucial – he stole the secret reports that confirmed the cancer epidemic in Xinjiang. It was subsequently estimated by Jun Takada, a Japanese physicist, that given the population density around the test sites, around 200,000 people could have died from acute radiation exposure, and that another mil-lion are likely to have received doses sufficient to cause birth defects and cancer.

In some respects Enver was luckier than other recent Uyghur dis-sidents. Ilham Tohti (no relation), a Uyghur scholar, was jailed for life in September 2014, while Rebiya Kadeer was imprisoned for eight years for 'endangering national security'. But Kadeer received financial sup-port from the United States and Uyghur diaspora organisations after her release, and was thus more fortunate than most political refugees, who have few resources and little support. When Enver came to the UK in 1999 he had $5 in his pocket. Unable to work as a doctor, he found employment as a porter, a hotel clerk, a nightwatchman, and, since 2010, as a bus driver. Taking part in the documentary cost him his profes-sion and his family, and meant that he could never go back to China.

In her autobiography, Rebiya Kadeer claims that from an early age she knew it was her 'duty to liberate the Uyghur nation from its occupiers'. But there was nothing inevitable about Enver's decision to oppose the Chinese government. His childhood and early life was one of modest privilege. He was born in 1963 in Hami in eastern Xinjiang; one of his earliest memories is of travelling frequently on the train, as both his parents worked for the Urumqi Railway Bureau. His father was in charge of the conductors, and his mother was a ticket inspector. Soon after his birth they moved to Urumqi. They lived in an area where there were few Uyghurs, so Enver went to a Chinese nursery, and after that a Chinese school. He told me he was the only Uyghur in a school of 300 pupils. He didn't even have any Uyghur friends when he was growing up. As a result, his spoken Chinese is better than his Uyghur.

I asked him what it had been like to be in a minority of one at school. We were sitting in his flat in Hackney, drinking single-malt whisky and eating *polo*, a dish of rice, carrots and succulent lamb. He put his glass down and said:

'You feel you are a stranger to this people. But if you are very confident you feel that they are the strangers. Because it was my hometown, and they had come from outside. So my classmates liked me and respected me. I was the class monitor.'

This is an important position in any Chinese classroom, one that usually signals a degree of political trust (Rebiya Kadeer had also been class monitor). But there were less pleasant reminders that he was different. When he was seven one of his classmates invited him for dinner, which was the first time he'd been to a Chinese home:

'His mother offered us pork, which was very generous, because meat was a big luxury. She had good intentions but I said: "We don't eat pork." My classmate said: "Really? Why not?" His father said: "Because pigs are the ancestors of Uyghurs." Then my whole body was shaking because I used to be proud that Uyghurs are the descendants of the dragon. And suddenly I am the descendant of the pig.'

It was so rare to see another Uyghur in his neighbourhood that whenever his grandparents came to visit they stuck out so much they got arrested. According to Enver, this was because they didn't have an Urumqi *hukou*. The local militia came to check these almost every night, because the station was a sensitive area: 'They took my grandparents away and then next morning my parents would have to go and get them,' he said and then laughed at the stupidity of it.

Though Han–Uyghur relations in Xinjiang have often been strained, there have certainly been phases when some communities were closer than they are today. Enver remembered that at Chinese New Year in 1974 his mother came home one day with a family of Han Chinese. They had travelled from Henan province, but their relatives didn't come to the station to meet them. They had nowhere else to go, and it was –25°C, so his mother had brought them home: 'They ended up staying for two weeks!' Enver recalled. 'After that their relatives came to pick them up. Every New Year we receive a present from them.'

Xinjiang wasn't spared the chaos of the Cultural Revolution, but the Tohti family nonetheless prospered during the 1970s. Enver's mother gave birth to three more boys, and his father was promoted in 1978 to assistant head of the department. They also got to travel for free on the trains (something Enver would also do when he became a surgeon in the railway hospital).

I asked Enver when he first knew he wanted to be a doctor. I assumed he'd had a strong passion for medicine, given the risks he'd taken to expose the health costs of the nuclear tests. But Enver had wanted an entirely different career:

'During the Vietnam War, although we were senior middle-school students [between 16 and 18], we were all mobilised. We formed a civil militia corps of 120 students. We had two months' weapon training. We were given strategic defence tasks; we were told that our school was on the third defensive line in case of a Soviet invasion. As the monitor I had the semi-automatic rifle the army used in the Korean War, and I had three bullets. The rest had empty guns. We were patrolling at night and I was so proud, because I had been trusted, and all the Chinese were taking orders from me, a Uyghur.'

As a child, he liked guns and could usually tell what kind of plane was flying overhead. His maternal uncle was the vice director of the state bookshop, and so was able to feed Enver's interest in all things military:

'There was a book about Mao's Long March which contradicted what our teacher said. Our teacher said they were fighting the Japanese, but the book said the Communists were just escaping. If I knew I would be here now, I would have kept all those books.'

He sighed, and it might have been a poignant moment if Angela, Enver's Moldovan wife, whom he met in London, hadn't called out to him:

'Enver, I have a problem with my Skype!' she shouted from the next room.

'No, no, no, I am in the middle of an interview!' he yelled back.

'You should go,' I said, and he stood. While he was gone I looked around the room. On a high shelf, above a huge TV, there was a photo of his two children, a girl and a boy. In the photo they were teenagers, but I had met her on my way in. She was in her mid-twenties, with a long face and large eyes; Enver told me proudly that she was going to do a master's at UCL. How she came to be in London, given the restrictions usually placed on dissidents' families, wasn't clear to me.

When Enver came back he poured us both a double. He explained that he ended up being a doctor, and not a soldier, because of a mistake on his part. Though he had applied to Xinjiang military school, he had done so during one of the alternate years when they weren't accepting Uyghurs or recruits from other minorities. (This is a trade-off for the preferential admissions system that makes it easier for people from minorities to gain places in some years.) By the time Enver realised his mistake it was too late – all his other choices were full. He was told that he would instead be going to medical school. He didn't like it, but thought he had no choice: 'Because we had been conditioned in that way,' he said. 'We thought our future was given by leaders somewhere. We had no freedom to choose. It wasn't a deliberate thought, it was a lazy thought – we don't care, this is the way, all I have to do is learn and pass the exam.'

And so, with great reluctance, in 1980 he went to study medicine in Shihezi, a predominantly Han Chinese new town close to Urumqi. The college was two miles from the centre and, as Enver remembers, not much fun: 'Around there it was just fields. There was nothing to do except get drunk.' He did, however, have one fond memory, albeit a ghoulish one:

'A road passed from the college to the hospital, and it was downhill. It was winter, just after it snowed. The road was very slippery. That day the teacher said to me and my classmate: "Go to the anatomy store and get 20 heads and bring them to the classroom." In each bucket, we had five heads. On the way my friend fell and ten heads rolled down towards the hospital gate. I saw all the people screaming and trying to run away. We tried to collect them, but there were only nine! One was still missing.'

I asked him how they obtained 20 human heads. His hand brushed the question aside:

'We had plenty! Hundreds! In Shihezi so many executions are carried out around there. Nobody wants the bodies if they are political prisoners. Even if they are relatives, they keep their distance, so the corpses go to the university.'

For many years, China has had one of the highest execution rates in the world; in 2009 the Chinese government admitted that executions were the main source of transplanted organs. But according to Enver, there was a grisly silver lining to this:

'Medical students in China are much better at anatomy than their Western contemporaries who only use models. We have a real corpse.'

He stopped talking as his daughter came in, and I wondered if she'd heard. But if she had, she didn't seem bothered. She took her phone charger and left.

After Enver graduated in 1985 he moved back to Urumqi and worked as a resident in the Central Hospital of the Railway Bureau – the hospital for railway staff. In 1988 his mother pressured him into marrying the daughter of one of her old classmates. His mother had gone from being a ticket inspector to vice prosecutor of her city district, and was clearly used to being obeyed. She said to him: 'You are the oldest son: if you don't do what I say, how can I control the rest?' Unsurprisingly, the marriage didn't last long. After his daughter was born in 1990, he got divorced. The following year he became a specialist in oncology. In 1993, his parents arranged another marriage, this time to the daughter of one of his father's classmates. The outcome was the same, except that this time he had a son before his divorce in 1994.

Enver enjoyed the status and attention of being a doctor in a top hospital. But he still wasn't happy: 'I didn't feel it was a respectable job. The salary was less than [that of] one of my friends who drove a coal truck.'

I pointed out that he had probably had few expenses, given that his rent and all other bills were paid for by his work unit. Enver shook his head: 'My trouble starts from here. As a physician, I was entitled to a two-bedroom flat, but I was only living in a one-bedroom flat. After I became a physician I started applying for it, but I never got it even though I applied four times. When a widow, a very pretty Chinese woman who had come to our hospital only three years before got a three-bedroom apartment, this blew my mind. As minority staff, we thought we were privileged, but after everything happened I understood who is privileged.'

His colleagues frequently brought up the ways that Enver, as a Uyghur, was different from them, such as that Uyghurs don't eat pork. Enver recalled an occasion when he was in the department office with eight other Chinese doctors: 'A nurse came and asked a question, which only I knew the answer to. Then the nurse said, "Wow! I didn't know that a sheep-brain-eating man is that clever!"' He responded in kind by saying: 'Listen, pig brain or sheep brain, which is cleverer?' His colleagues then accused him of being prejudiced.

Yet without one of these petty remarks he would probably never have investigated the cancer rates in Xinjiang. In 1994 the chief of the cancer ward joked: 'Oh, Dr Enver! You are always so proud of your Uyghur people's health – look at our department. We only have 40 beds and ten are occupied by your Uyghurs.' Enver didn't like him much anyway (he suspected the chief was trying to seduce his wife), which meant this poor joke had an even greater effect: 'After he said this, because I really didn't like him, it made me wake up.'

Given that Urumqi Railway Bureau had 160,000 workers, and only 5,000 were from ethnic minorities, the latter were vastly over-represented on the cancer ward. Enver started trying to find out why, beginning with the patients' records. Initially the archives refused to give him access to them; he had to pretend he was writing a paper to get permission from the chief of surgery. The records showed that the most common types of cancer were leukaemia, lung cancer and malignant lymphoma. The shared cause for these is radiation exposure. His suspicions were further confirmed by a survey his hospital commissioned on cancer rates along the railway line, which also showed very high figures (which weren't included in the published version of the report).

This was a bleak time in Enver's life. He had just got divorced again and was still being refused the two-bedroom flat. Ironically, it was these personal and professional frustrations, rather than a principled decision to expose the cancer epidemic, that made him leave China. In December 1996 he managed to get permission to study Uzbek in Tashkent for a year. There he was offered a job in a hospital after demonstrating his proficiency at using an electric knife for breast removal, a technique few local doctors were skilled at (it cauterises bleeding fast, but with a risk of burning). But after the job fell through, he had to start doing acupuncture to earn a living.

He might have been there a long time if he hadn't run into a friend of his first ex-wife. She told Enver that his ex-wife was now in Istanbul and was interested in getting back together with him. When he agreed, his ex-wife got the ETNC, a Uyghur political and cultural organisation, to send him an invitation to come to Turkey to study. He arrived in Istanbul in December 1997. At this point Enver could have still returned to China, though he did not plan to:

'I thought I was going to start my new life in this country. I started learning Turkish at Istanbul University, which was paid for by the Turkish government. I started visiting the ETNC, and got in touch with new issues about East Turkestan.'

Though it was ultimately Enver's choice to take part in the film, it was the ETNC who put him in a position where he had to make it. Knowing that he was an oncologist, they introduced him to Richard Hering and Stuart Tanner, two British film-makers who had previously made a news segment about the Yining riots in 1997. Their plan was to pose as tourists and film undercover using hidden cameras, a technique still in its infancy: Hering recalls that he had to get a Russian man who ran a shop that sold electronic goods on Tottenham Court Road in London to make the equipment. Hering and Tanner planned to investigate birth defects in the cities near the test sites while Enver obtained classified information from the Central Hospital of the Railway Bureau in Urumqi.

There's a shot in the film that shows Enver, then with receding black hair, on a ferry on the Bosphorus, apparently relaxed. But while the worst that would happen to the film crew was deportation, for him getting caught would mean 20 years in prison: 'I knew this was spying, and I knew the consequences of it, and I said yes straight away. But I could feel a chill on the back of my neck.'

Enver admits that he also enjoyed the attention: 'Back then, when a foreigner was interested in Uyghurs we were excited. We thought they were like gods, like saviours to us.'

In the villages around the test sites the film crew met many young people with twisted limbs, cleft palates and other birth defects. In the hospitals doctors spoke anonymously of the high rates of malignant lymphoma, leukaemia and lung cancer. Though they attracted suspicion, the film crew was never detained, but the threat of this was always present. When I spoke to Stuart Tanner in October 2014, he recalled the feeling of being 'at risk at any time, for asking too many questions, for asking questions of the wrong person and being reported on and picked up. Every day we were worried that was going to happen.'

During this time Enver was scared, but a part of him also liked it: 'Sometimes you enjoy having a secret,' he told me.

The biggest problem they encountered was that the medical library which had the documents Enver needed was closed for the holidays:

'We thought we were really fucked. I said: "Let me make a visit to that library." I went and showed them my ID card and told them that I needed to consult some materials. The librarian was a very ordinary Chinese guy. He said that if I bought him dinner, he would give me access. So I took this guy to a restaurant where there were prostitutes. I called two, one Kazakh, one Chinese, and I gave them 100 dollars each. At that time this was a huge amount of money. I told them, "This is a good man. If you make him really happy, you will get 100 more." He went away with them. Next morning when I arrived at the library he gave me a spare key.'

The documents Enver obtained showed that the rate of cancer in the villages around the test sites was 30 times the national average. When the documentary was broadcast in October 1998, the Chinese government did not respond. According to Enver: 'If they denied it, it would be like a confession. And I didn't say anything political, I just talked about victims. I put a knife to their weak point.'

When Enver returned to Istanbul he started working in a hospital. I asked him how the ETNC had treated him, given the film had been their idea. Enver said that all they did was buy him a meal. A greater concern was how the authorities would treat his relatives in Xinjiang: in China the spouses and relatives of many dissidents are often harassed or incarcerated. Four of Rebiya Kadeer's children were jailed in 2006, in obvious retaliation for her activism. But Enver's family weren't visited by the secret police until 2004, when they adopted a soft approach. Enver said they told his mother: 'Your son just made a mistake. He didn't do anything bad. We also have made some mistakes. We do apologise. If he accepts our apology we welcome him to come back. His position in the hospital is still there. We will even promote him.' In addition, they offered him the large flat he had always wanted, and regularly brought his mother gifts on Islamic holidays, including, on one occasion, an entire sheep.

Such tactics aim to make relatives put pressure on exiles to return. There can be a degree of performance to such a process, whereby there are rewards for relatives who pretend to cooperate. In 2005 Enver told his mother to agree with whatever they said about him, and believes that it was because of this that his daughter was allowed to come to the UK in 2007. The only problem was that his mother got carried away with playing her part. 'She started trying to persuade me to go home because the police had told her to do that. I said: "Are you mad?" She said: "You told us to accept what they said!"'

Though Enver had planned to stay in Istanbul, his position there soon became unsafe. In 1999 Li Peng, the Chinese prime minister, was due to come to Turkey to sign an extradition treaty. Enver knew he had to flee, and chose the UK, as this was where the film-makers came from. He arrived in the UK in March 1999 and claimed asylum. At first he stayed with a Turkish doctor, and then after a short time met up with the documentary crew. Enver expected them to offer some financial help, and the fact that it wasn't forthcoming obviously disappointed him. But the film-makers were in no position to do so. Hering recalls that when he came back from filming in Xinjiang he was broke, had no job and was suffering from a tropical disease.

Over the next decade Enver moved from job to job. For a while he cleaned a theatre in Aldwych; he remembers finding £80 and a Gucci watch under the seats on his first night (a watch his wife still wears). He met Angela when they were both working in a hotel. In 2005 he tried to go back to Turkey to work in a private hospital but on arrival was detained for five hours, then sent back to the UK. Although UK nationals can get a visa on arrival at the airport, Enver was told he had to apply for one beforehand.

In some respects, Enver has been leading two lives since he came to the UK. Apart from his friends in London's small Uyghur community, no one else in the city knows his history; none of the other bus drivers even knows he used to be a doctor in China. It's only in recent years, with the growing popularity in China of social-media apps like WeChat and WhatsApp, that his articles are being circulated there: 'My mum says to me: "What did you write?" and I say: "I didn't write anything," and she says: "Yes you did!" and I say: "That was ten years ago!"'

However, although the immense harm to public health caused by nuclear testing in Xinjiang is a continuing problem – the Chinese government has yet to acknowledge it, let alone offer compensation – the issue currently receives little media or scholarly attention. Enver partly blames the WUC for this: 'I don't think they are promoting this issue. They can't avoid this issue. But there's no updated information. I even translated the Channel 4 documentary into Chinese myself. But the film is not available in Uyghur. It would be very easy for them to do this.'

It's unlikely that Enver will practise medicine again. He wants to give up driving a bus and open a Central Asian restaurant, but can't find a business partner. When I asked him how he felt about that now, his smile was rueful: 'If I said I didn't have regrets, that would be a lie. I gave up that good life. But I would do it again. What happened is something unacceptable.'

Though Enver and Rebiya Kadeer became dissidents for very different reasons, both paid a heavy price for denouncing Chinese-government policy in Xinjiang. As Stuart Tanner puts it: 'It takes some very brave individuals who take the risks of exposing these things in order to show the world what's going on.' Their very different stories demonstrate the government's long-standing determination to prevent open discussion of the social and economic problems that Uyghurs and people from other minorities face in Xinjiang, an approach that hinders any attempt to solve these issues. Instead, the government has launched one grand initiative after another, each of which it has subsequently proclaimed a success. At the end of the 1990s, and in the wake of the many issues raised by the Yining protests, the government unveiled its latest great plan for Xinjiang.

6

THE PEACOCK FLIES WEST

The new millennium began with a promise for the people of western China: finally, they would share the wealth with which the coastal regions had been blessed. In November 1999 the campaign for a 'Great Development of the West' (also known as 'Open Up the West') had been announced by Jiang Zemin, then Chinese president. It was intended to 'reduce regional disparities and eventually materialise common prosperity'.

Like many grandiose state campaigns in China, it was heavier on rhetoric than actual policy details. Initially it wasn't even clear what constituted 'the west'. Geographically western regions like Xinjiang, Qinghai, Sichuan, Tibet and Gansu were included, but there were also three small subdivisions of provinces in the centre of the country (in Hunan and Hubei) and in the north-east (in Jilin province). Though there weren't defining criteria for membership of the plan (neither geographical nor in terms of GDP), the existence of significant minority populations in these three areas (as well as most of the geographically western areas) might have been taken as a tacit admission that there were still major inequalities not only between regions, but also between ethnic groups. The fact that the initiative was framed as a way to promote social stability on a national level could also be read as an acknowledgement that such inequalities had the potential to cause 'mass incidents'.

The need for the economic focus to shift away from the south and east at some point had been articulated during the early phases of 'opening up'. But it was Deng Xiaoping who put a timetable on this, promising in 1992 that the government would 'definitely resolve the problem of disparities between the rich coast and the poor interior gradually and smoothly' by the end of the millennium. The person most responsible for keeping the idea on the agenda was Hu Angang, a highly influential academic, who repeatedly warned that the central government had to take an active role in the economy, as otherwise the gap between the poorer and more affluent regions would keep increasing.

Though Jiang Zemin, despite being Deng's successor, was in no way required to keep his promises, the timing was opportune. After 13 years of negotiations, China was about to join the World Trade Organisation, which meant that Chinese domestic markets would soon be open to international trade. Chinese companies would thus face competition from foreign companies, something that was likely to hurt inland provinces more. The investment provided to the Open Up the West campaign was meant to compensate for this, and also intended to attract foreign investment, as Hu Angang stressed in an interview in 2000. When it was suggested to him that the heavy regulation of the internet in China might put off foreign investors, he responded: 'The government is afraid by [*sic*] number of pornographic sites that are available on internet […] But I don't think that the foreigners spend their time putting on-line pornographic shows. So, let them come and do their business!'

The initial signs, however, suggested that foreign investors were hesitant for less prurient reasons. After 70 Hong Kong CEOs made a ten-day tour of the west of the country, they were only willing to invest $30 million. As the head of the British Chamber of Commerce put it: 'Specifics are needed as the hinterland is a big place.'

The Open Up the West campaign was for the most part an amorphous policy conspicuously lacking in measurable targets. At best, it had general aims, such as shifting the migration of labour away from the south and east, and, as a member of the State Council (China's main administrative body) put it, in gratuitously poetic terms, instead to 'make the peacock fly west'. While this wouldn't start happening in the rest of China until the end of the decade, in Xinjiang it had of course been going on since the 1950s with the successive waves of Han migrants who joined the XPCC. According to Nicholas Bequelin, a senior researcher at Human Rights Watch, for this and other reasons the Open Up the West campaign shouldn't be seen as any great shift in Beijing's policies for Xinjiang. Instead, they are best regarded as a consolidation of the previous decade.

This was certainly true of the areas in which investment primarily occurred. Of the initial 900 billion yuan (at that time, around $100 billion) that was pledged over the next decade, 70 per cent went to northern Xinjiang, mainly for building infrastructure and expanding the energy sector. These funds were supplemented in the Tenth Five-year Plan by the promise of a further 420 billion yuan (then $51 billion), almost twice what had been given in the Ninth Five-year Plan.

Within Xinjiang, the importance of the XPCC for promoting stability was again emphasised. Ma Dazheng, a scholar and policy adviser, called for an expanded role for the XPCC, and in an internal memo explicitly stated that it was the ethnicity of its members (rather than their business or military roles) that made them important. Ma was of the opinion that 'Hans are the most reliable force for stability in Xinjiang', and advocated that Han settlement in south Xinjiang be encouraged so as to encircle predominantly Uyghur areas (a notion that arguably parallels Israeli settlement policy in the occupied Palestinian territories). Having a large Han population was thus seen as a way to turn a peripheral, frontier part of China into a region that more resembled the centre.

However, while the aims of the XPCC may have remained broadly the same, its methods were changing. Since 'opening up', the XPCC had been gradually shifting away from the military–agricultural model to something more corporate (albeit state-owned). In 1998 the XPCC was renamed as a corporation, given further legal autonomy (*bingtuan* have their own courts) and placed under the control of the central government. From then on the only role for the PLA and the People's Armed Police was in providing military training for a small number of its members. Thomas Cliff, a researcher at the Australian National

University, argues that this shift reflected a belief that 'economic power was accepted as a legitimate form of control […] in a way that military force was not.'

While no one could say the central government was unwilling to invest in Xinjiang, the main sectors chosen were the same as those that had been the focus of previous investment. On a national scale, it made excellent sense. China's energy needs were continuing to increase fast, and Xinjiang had a huge concentration of natural resources – in 2000 it was already producing around 11 per cent of the country's crude oil and 13 per cent of its natural gas – as well as being close to possible energy sources in Central Asia. The construction of a 4,200-kilometre pipeline for natural gas from the Tarim Basin to Shanghai, a project run by state-owned PetroChina, and which was completed in 2004, was an important step in the process of integrating Xinjiang with the rest of the country. The importance of Xinjiang to China's overall economic strategy was further underlined by the promotion of Wang Lequan, Xinjiang's party secretary, to the Politburo in 2002.

The investment in northern industries and infrastructure did create jobs and improve material conditions, but the beneficiaries were predominantly urban Han Chinese. In 2000 the rural–urban income gap in Xinjiang was 30 per cent higher than the national average – with the largest disparities in southern Xinjiang, which was still primarily agricultural. Though the south had 47 per cent of Xinjiang's population, it accounted for only 20 per cent of the urban population.

The Open Up the West campaign's emphasis on transferring natural resources out of Xinjiang, while providing few substantial benefits for Uyghurs in the region, led many observers to label it a colonial scheme. The question of whether it is appropriate to view Xinjiang as an internal colony of China has been the subject of much debate, with the answer often depending on one's views about wider historical questions and the legitimacy of Communist rule in the region, and one's definition of a colonial relationship. It's probably true that the idea of Xinjiang as a colony is used without due care, but it doesn't seem too much of a stretch to say that there were colonial *aspects* to the campaign. Xinjiang's oil and gas weren't easy to remove and transport, and the Xinjiang government did receive some tax income, but the bulk of the profit nonetheless left the region.

It wasn't necessary to subscribe to the narrative of a Han government pillaging a Uyghur homeland to find fault with the Open Up the West campaign. Some Chinese commentators saw it as an aggressive strategy by the economically and politically stronger coastal provinces. A researcher from the Sichuan Academy of Social Sciences summed up the campaign as 'western exploitation, eastern development'.

One of the strongest concerns was the environmental cost of development, especially in water-scarce regions prone to desertification such as Xinjiang. While ecological protection was repeatedly emphasised as a priority by officials, the fact that the State Environmental Protection Administration wasn't part of the core group leading the plan suggested otherwise. The main environmental commitment was a series of campaigns to tackle water pollution and illegal logging and to promote afforestation. The prognosis for these attempts was gloomy. The poor planning, implementation and legal enforcement of previous similar campaigns caused Elizabeth Economy, author of *The River Runs Black: The Environmental Challenge to China's Future* (2004), to predict in an article that they had 'little chance to address the problems in a meaningful manner'.

There was also a colonial flavour to comments made by Li Dezhu of the State Ethnic Affairs Commission, who once again stressed the inferiority of the minorities and their need to learn from the Han. For Li, there was nothing problematic about such sentiments – in his view, the different ethnic groups of China were all part of one vast, extended family.

Funnelling investment into the northern part of Xinjiang was presented as a way to reduce inequality. The guiding assumption, as in the 1990s, was that the prosperity generated from investment in the northern industries would trickle down. Some Chinese economists pointed out that this logic, which had also been employed at the start of the 'opening up' period, had already been proved wrong on a national level (hence the need for the Open Up the West campaign). As one expert suggested in 2001: 'the government may have to sacrifice economic efficiency in their investment and industrial location decisions', in other words, start encouraging industry in southern Xinjiang.

While this advice wasn't heeded, there was finally an admission that the loss of the preferential employment policies had had a greater impact on minorities. In 2001 the study group of Xinjiang's Communist Party concluded that 'the difficulties of finding a job for the minority labourers have become bigger and bigger, especially in contracted farm work and non-public industrial work'. The group concluded that the same issues existed for professional work, arguing that 'compared to Han graduates, it is harder for minority graduates to find work'. However, the official explanations for this did not acknowledge the extent of prejudice against Uyghurs within the labour market (both informal and institutional), or their virtual exclusion from some of the largest sectors of the economy. Apparently the real thing keeping Uyghurs back was that they didn't speak Chinese.

'BILINGUAL' EDUCATION

The problem wasn't that Uyghur students didn't learn Chinese. Since 1984 all Uyghur students had been taught Chinese during preschool classes; before that Chinese had begun in the first year of middle school. The cause of the Chinese government's concern was apparently that Uyghurs weren't learning it well enough, and, as they saw it, the reason was that they weren't learning *in* Chinese.

Up until the late 1990s, education in Xinjiang had been mostly segregated on ethno-linguistic lines. Han students had their own schools where they were taught in Chinese, while those from ethnic minorities were taught in their own languages in separate schools. Though some ethnic minorities did attend Chinese-language schools (the *min kao han*), this was always a small proportion, around 6 per cent of minority students, and almost exclusively in cities. While there were obvious advantages for Uyghur students to learn in Chinese in a place where the Han were the majority, such as in Urumqi, in most of south Xinjiang, where less Chinese was spoken because there were fewer Han, it made just as much sense to have children taught in Uyghur. But it wasn't only a question of practicalities: even in places like Urumqi, some Uyghur parents with two children (as was their right) opted to send one to a Chinese-language school and the other to a Uyghur-language school. Having their child taught in his or her own language, while surrounded by his or her peers, was seen by many parents as a vital part of their child's social and moral development, and a way to ensure his or her connection to Uyghur culture.

Yet at the start of the 2000s there were obviously major problems with the minority-education system. Only 35 per cent of minority students went from junior middle school to senior middle school (for ages 16–18) in Xinjiang, compared to 87 per cent of Han Chinese. In Kashgar the figure was as low as 18 per cent, and in Hotan, only 10 per cent. Many Chinese experts, such as the social anthropologist Ma Rong, put this down to 'the historical failure to develop high-quality minority education in Xinjiang'. This was not meant as a critique of Chinese educational policy in Xinjiang since 1949, but more as a reference to the supposed 'backwardness' of the region. Ma's comment was not entirely unfounded: before the Qing reconquest of Xinjiang, education was limited to Islamic instruction. The Qing did introduce reforms, but these were principally neo-Confucian schools for the children of the Turkic elites. After the fall of the Qing, modern schools were introduced, though few from minorities opted to attend.

But as Eric Schluessel, a Central Eurasian scholar, convincingly argues, the next few decades in Xinjiang saw widespread innovation in minority education under the dual influence of Jadidism and pan-Turkic ideas. Jadidism was an educational-reform movement (*jadid* means 'new' in Arabic) whose influence was concentrated in north

Xinjiang. It advocated that Islam should occupy a secondary, moral role in education; the primary goal should instead be to prepare Muslims to participate and prosper in modern society. Pan-Turkism's approach was broadly similar, and stronger in south Xinjiang, as many intellectuals from there had been schooled in the Ottoman Empire.

For Ma to speak of 'historical failure' was thus somewhat disingenuous. While education has improved greatly in Xinjiang since 1949 – especially in the promotion of literacy and levels of student enrolment – many of the problems with the current system have a more contemporary origin. In one district of Kashgar 68 per cent of students dropped out for financial reasons. Although tuition fees would be abolished in 2006, there are still many other expenses involved in sending a child to school. Even if Uyghur parents could afford to pay, many with low incomes may not have seen the point in sending their children to school if they thought it made no difference to their chances of finding a job.

The 'backwardness' of minority education wasn't just a pedagogical issue. According to Wang Lequan, the fundamental problem was the Uyghur language itself. He claimed that 'the languages of the minority nationalities have very small capacities and do not contain many of the expressions in modern science and technology'. The remedy for this was to switch from Uyghur to Chinese as the main language of instruction, preferably for all subjects, to ensure that 'the quality of the Uyghur youth will not be poorer than that of their Han peers'.

As with Ma's assertion about minority education, there was some basis for Wang's claim. Modern Uyghur isn't as well endowed with technical and scientific vocabulary as Chinese, but this is not, as Wang implied, due to any intrinsic shortcoming of the language. The inadequacies of modern Uyghur have far more to do with linguistic policies in Xinjiang since 1949, many of which have been motivated by political concerns.

Before 1949 Uyghur was written in an Arabic script and contained many loan words from Russian. After 'liberation', the minority languages were under the authority of the Xinjiang Language and Script

Committee, who first switched Uyghur to a Cyrillic script, as was used in the Soviet Union, but then, after the Sino-Soviet split, introduced a Latin script, so as to impair communication between minorities in Xinjiang and the Soviet republics. (By contrast Tibetan, which didn't have such sensitive borders, was allowed to keep the writing system it had been using since the seventh century.) The effective suspension of education during the Cultural Revolution only added to the linguistic confusion, which was compounded by the prejudice against any form of minority culture. An Arabic script wasn't reintroduced until 'opening up'. Traces of both previous systems can still be seen on older buildings in many cities in Xinjiang.

The Committee had less interest in helping Uyghur to modernise. Russian loan words were discouraged in favour of ones from Chinese, even though Russian ones would have been easier for Uyghurs to learn (due both to prior knowledge and to the fact that both are stress-based languages, whereas Chinese is tonal). New Uyghur vocabulary for science and technology could also have been coined, something that Kazakhstan was able to do with the Kazakh language after independence.

That the Xinjiang authorities made no effort to do so, and instead preferred to stop Uyghurs learning in their own language, spoke volumes about the low regard in which they held Uyghur culture. However, China's constitution and many of its laws do guarantee a place for minority languages in education and culture. Article 12, for example, states that 'educational institutions which mainly consist of students from minority nationalities may use in education the language of the respective nationality'. For this reason, the government described the introduction of Chinese as a language of instruction for minorities as a switch to 'bilingual education'. The roots of this went back to the late 1980s, when there had been a working group about the possibility of establishing some trial schools. By the early 1990s there were around 50 trial bilingual classes in Xinjiang. In these Chinese was only used in a few classes, mainly science and maths, so at this point 'bilingual' was a fair description of the teaching methods.

The *min kao han/min kao min* system was preserved until the mid-2000s, but the direction that the educational system was going to take had already been signalled by the announcement in September 2002 that university courses would no longer be taught in Uyghur. Higher education had been a subject of equal concern for policy advisers like Ma Rong, who bemoaned that Chinese-taught and Uyghur-taught subjects were 'virtually isolated from each other even though they occur on the same campus'. This was true, and also compounded by Han and minority students requiring separate dining halls (for halal and non-halal food) and often living in separate dormitories. Though there were problems with this system – having little social contact certainly didn't help the divisions between Han and Uyghurs – for Ma the real problem was that it meant that these minority students 'can hardly communicate with people who do not speak their native language in study and work'. In effect, Ma was arguing that the most important language for Uyghurs to speak in the Xinjiang *Uyghur* Autonomous Region was Chinese. As for the idea that privileging Chinese over Uyghurs' native language might have detrimental effects on their ability to communicate in their own language, let alone social and cultural consequences, this was something he did not acknowledge (even though the experience of *min kao han* students already proved otherwise).

There was also no official suggestion that Han Chinese, who were (and are) officially not the majority ethnic group in an autonomous region with a titular majority, should learn a minority language. Only a very small number of Han in Xinjiang can speak more than a few words of any minority language, even those that grew up in the region; the exceptions tend to be elderly people who came to Xinjiang in the 1950s or 1960s, when there were far fewer Han Chinese. Before 1978, Russian had been the main foreign language studied, but in some schools in Xinjiang Han students had been taught Uyghur from the third year. But after 'opening up' English became the most important foreign language in education. In 2006, a teacher in Aksu, a city on the northern edge of the Tarim Basin, recalled that before the 1980s, Chinese schools offered Uyghur lessons to Han students from Year 3, so Han students could speak Uyghur language and Han and Uyghur children would play together. It was good for them to have this language exchange and mutual understanding. It is different now. After the open and reform policy, Han parents are only interested in their children learning English and schools have replaced Uyghur language lessons by English lessons.

One of the least enforced regulations in Xinjiang is the injunction that political 'cadres of Han nationality should learn the spoken and written languages of the local minority nationalities'. There are few attempts to encourage this outside of well-meaning, if risible, initiatives like a TV programme in 2004 called *One Sentence a Week* that offered the same sentence repeated, in Chinese and Uyghur, for ten minutes. However, to Ma Rong's credit, he did propose that some Han should learn Uyghur or another minority language instead of English at school if they didn't plan to use English in their careers.

Throughout the 2000s the Xinjiang educational authorities aggressively sought to increase the amount of bilingual teaching in minority schools. In 2004, when around 20 per cent of minority classes were said to be 'bilingual' (though to varying degrees), the authorities announced their 'Decision to Vigorously Promote Bilingual Teaching', one of the implications of which was that Uyghur teachers had either to retrain to teach in Chinese or to retire. For many Uyghur teachers, especially the older generation, retraining wasn't a possibility owing to their poor command of Chinese. The regulations about using Chinese in class were especially strict – any teacher caught using Uyghur to supplement their Chinese explanation could be fined. Non-Han teachers also had to prove their fluency by taking an exam – fake certificates for these were soon selling for between 2,000 and 3,000 yuan.

By the end of the decade all senior high-school classes in Urumqi were being taught exclusively in Chinese; the goal was that 85 per cent of preschool classes would be taught almost exclusively in Chinese by

2012. The only subject prescribed as a Uyghur-taught class was one on the Uyghur language itself – thus the only course in which teachers could speak Uyghur was one that treated the students' native language as if it were a foreign language or some archaic tongue. This guarantee that minority students would be able to hear their own language in school for two hours a week allowed the authorities to perpetuate the misnomer of 'bilingual education'.

Further justification for the obviously unequal ratio of Chinese to Uyghur instruction was provided in 2005 by the introduction of the idea of 'language harmony'. Earlier that year President Hu Jintao had put forth the concept of the 'harmonious society', which offered a pleasantly vague vision of a China in the not-so-distant future where every part of society worked for the betterment of the whole. 'Language harmony', as expounded by Zhou Qingsheng, a Chinese academic, merged this neo-Confucian ethic with a twist of capitalism, arguing that it should be up to free-market forces to determine the value of a language. This meant every language had its place in society, depending on said value. A 'harmonious' relationship between the languages in society would be where a less valued language (such as Uyghur, Tibetan or any other minority language) yielded to another of greater 'value' (with the most valuable always being Chinese). The influence of this unpleasantly utilitarian notion could be seen in a speech in 2007 by Nuer Bekri, chairman of the Xinjiang government, who said that 'the social function of each language differs greatly according to the history, geography, and distribution of its population'.

For the Xinjiang authorities, the benefits for minority students learning in Chinese were exemplified by a programme that since 2000 had been sending minority students from poor, rural areas in Xinjiang to top schools in major cities in inner China. This 'Xinjiang Class' was a four-year boarding school that was essentially a *min kao han* school taken to its logical conclusion. The minority students of the Xinjiang Class weren't just learning in Chinese, with Han Chinese peers, they were also doing it outside of their native-language environment. For the first five years there were only a thousand students sent each year, but after that the numbers increased rapidly – the projected number of students for 2014 was around 10,000. The authorities have been at pains to stress that these schools are not, as some argue, an attempt to sever any sense of ethnic identification in these students, and in their defence point to the provision of halal canteens and the observation of cultural festivals (albeit mostly their secular components). These attempts at cultural sensitivity have occasionally backfired, as one teacher reported:

> We are very sensitively dealing with these students because we are not familiar with their ethnic customs. Once, some Uyghur boys dyed their hair yellow, and some Uyghur girls colored their fingernails. We thought these behaviors were their ethnic habits and let them be.

Nonetheless, the ideological aims of the Xinjiang Class aren't disguised. The schools' priorities include 'strengthening support for the Chinese Communist Party, love for the socialist motherland, upholding the unity of China's nationalist education' and promoting 'education of the unity of peoples – i.e. Han are inseparable from ethnic minorities, ethnic minorities are inseparable from Han, and every ethnic minority is inseparable from each other.'

This kind of propaganda was also heavily present in the new textbooks Uyghur students had to use in bilingual education. The first lesson in one of them is a crash course in patriotism:

Lesson One: We are Chinese
Sentence Pattern: We are Chinese. We love our motherland.
Dialogue:
JIA: I am Chinese.
YI: I am also Chinese.
JIA: We are all Chinese.
YI: We love our motherland.
JIA: The capital city of our motherland is Beijing.
YI: We love Beijing, the capital city of our motherland.

There were few, if any, attempts to provide Chinese-language materials for minority students that acknowledged the different social and cultural conditions in which they were learning. As one teacher in south Xinjiang put it:

> Most lessons are not relevant to the life of students who don't use Chinese outside the classroom. For example, I taught them to use Chinese to buy vegetables but when they go to the market, they only need to speak Uyghur.

One might argue that this focus on a broader Chinese context was precisely the point. The promotion of national identity, rather than any sense of local belonging, was the aim of the new bilingual education. There's nothing unusual about a state using education to try to instil a sense of citizenship in students, through both covert and overt methods, but the bilingual policy was trying to go a step further. Given that any kind of non-Han ethnic identity is viewed by the Communist Party as an obstacle to social development, one aim of promoting 'bilingual' education in Xinjiang was surely to foster the loss of cultural and linguistic identity among Uyghurs.

However, the experience of some Uyghurs in the Xinjiang Class suggests that even this most immersive kind of 'bilingual' (that is, virtually monolingual) education may not reliably produce the kind of assimilated Uyghur young people the government is hoping for. Timothy Grose, who has been studying the Xinjiang Class since 2006, argues that many Uyghurs in the programme maintain a social distance from their Han classmates. Among the students he interviewed, all expressed a strong identification with Uyghur cultural and religious traditions. This raises the question of whether 'bilingual' education in Xinjiang, while certainly a threat to the Uyghur language, may also produce a very different generation of Uyghur youth, whose sense of identity isn't just 'Chinese' or 'Uyghur'. Of perhaps equal, if not greater, importance may also be the influence of global youth culture spread via music and the internet. According to Joanne Smith Finley, who researches Uyghur identity and youth culture, the result may be a more 'pluralistic "internationalist" identity'. If this is accompanied by 'a heightened degree of tolerance from the rest of the Uyghur community', then these students may come to serve as a bridge between Han and Uyghur communities.

Ultimately, the real problem with bilingual education was that Uyghurs weren't consulted about a radical shift in policy that was likely to have huge implications for their language and culture. In the past major changes to policy had often been met with demonstrations, such as with the family-planning protests in Urumqi in the 1980s. The centrality of language to Uyghur identity and culture, as typified by the frequent disapproval of *min kao han* students, made some reaction to the imposition of the bilingual-education policies seem almost inevitable.

But in sharp contrast with the vigorous protests against 'bilingual' education that would take place in Qinghai and Tibet in 2010, in Xinjiang there was no great show of opposition. One reason was that there were definitely Uyghur parents who wanted their children to acquire good Chinese, so as to help their prospects (evidence that many Uyghurs don't unconditionally reject all forms of Chinese governance). As for the likelihood that this would come at some cost to their children's fluency in their native language, some parents downplayed this as a possibility, arguing that home education could stop this happening. However, given that very few had been willingly sending their children to *min kao han* schools, there were clearly other reasons why Uyghurs didn't protest more strongly.

If you'd asked the authorities to explain the lack of visible opposition, they might have said, as Wang Lequan did on 2 September 2001, that it was because conditions in Xinjiang were 'better than ever in history'. Wang went on to add that society was stable because 'people are living and working in peace and contentment'. But although the social and political climate in Xinjiang during the 2000s was certainly not conducive to expressing dissent, it wasn't because conditions were 'better than ever'.

CHINA JOINS THE WAR ON TERROR

One of the main problems with trying to write about violent episodes in Xinjiang is attempting to establish their frequency – working out who did what and why relies on first knowing that something actually happened. For every incident in Xinjiang the authorities have had to decide whether to try to prevent discussion of it, or to publicise it. Both strategies have advantages, and both have accompanying risks. Public disturbances can make the authorities look weak (especially the local government in the area in which the episode occurred) and encourage people in other areas to give vent to their grievances. But trying to pretend an episode didn't happen allows other parties to control the narrative of the event (even if only in the form of rumour, which can be especially potent in Xinjiang). From another perspective, public disturbances present the authorities with an opportunity to promote a particular agenda. This can be either an existing policy or a shift in policy direction – but an almost entirely state-controlled media has allowed the authorities to present a mostly consistent message.

Given the often scant details that exist for many of the episodes that are known to have taken place in Xinjiang from 1949 to 2000, one might conclude that during this period the authorities often took the more conservative option of trying to suppress information about overt acts of resistance to state power. From the founding myth of the 'peaceful liberation' of Xinjiang to the contention that there was no opposition to disastrous campaigns like the Great Leap Forward or the excesses of the Cultural Revolution, the prevailing tendency of the state in Xinjiang was to try to present a positive view of life in the region that emphasised the social progress being made. When episodes did occur that were too big to cover up, they were often presented as the work of criminals with no ideological agenda. Thus the Yining riots were initially presented as the work of a 'small number of criminals' who carried out 'beating, rioting and looting'.

I was living in Yining when two planes crashed into the twin towers of the World Trade Center in New York on 11 September 2001. Though the event was covered by Chinese news – within days a DVD compilation of footage of the attacks was on sale – the news that it was being blamed on Islamic terrorists did not inspire any particular foreboding among the Uyghurs I knew. Almost all of them condemned the attacks, though one man doubted that al-Qaeda was responsible. His hope was that the Chinese government was to blame. He said that, then, 'the Americans will fight the Chinese. They will win and we will be free.'

When the Chinese government announced in October 2001 that it, too, was a 'victim of international terrorism', it shouldn't have been a surprise. At first glance, they had all the ingredients necessary to make such a claim: a string of violent incidents linked to a Muslim ethnic group concentrated in a region close to Pakistan and Afghanistan. There was an air of confidence in their expressed hope that 'efforts to fight against East Turkestan terrorist forces should become a part of the international efforts and should also win support and understanding'.

Within China, this announcement was the start of a shift in how Xinjiang (and Uyghurs) were perceived. Wen Bo, a researcher from Beijing who took a trip to Xinjiang in October, spoke of hearing many

> war rumours and stories of danger in Xinjiang. The rumours led
> some of my friends to admire me for taking such a trip at that time
> to Xinjiang, an Islamic region of China. Others were more concerned
> about my safety.

In November 2001 the government made the link between the US Global War on Terror and its own concerns explicit. On 14 November a Foreign Ministry spokesman gave a press briefing on Uyghur separatism. It was claimed that some Xinjiang separatists had received training in Afghanistan before being sent to China, and that an organisation known as the East Turkestan Islamic Movement (ETIM) was supported and directed by Osama Bin Laden. Apparently Hasan Mahsum, the leader of

ETIM, had met Bin Laden in 1999 and 2001, and received promises of 'an enormous sum of money'. Over 300 Uyghurs were said to be fighting with the Taliban. Bin Laden's aim was apparently to launch a 'holy war', with the aim of setting up a theocratic Islamic state in Xinjiang. While the Chinese government didn't provide much proof of these assertions, it was hard to discount the announcement by the United States that their forces had captured 22 Uyghurs suspected of being al-Qaeda fighters in Pakistan and Afghanistan. These men were interrogated for several months, then flown to Guantánamo Bay in early 2002.

A white paper published in January 2002 offered an expanded version of China's argument that it was the target of international terrorists. The document was entitled 'East Turkestan terrorist forces cannot escape with impunity' and provided an explanation for the origin, causes and crimes committed by terrorists against China. It argued that 'in the beginning of the twentieth century, a handful of fanatical Xinjiang separatists and extremist religious elements fabricated the myth of "East Turkestan" in light of the sophistries and fallacies created by the old colonialists'. The document went on to state that between 1990 and 2001 over 200 terrorist incidents had taken place in Xinjiang, resulting in the deaths of 162 people of all ethnic groups, including officials and religious personnel. It blamed a series of riots, explosions, assassinations and arson attacks on ETIM and a number of different organisations. The Baren incident became the responsibility of the 'East Turkestan Islamic Party', while the Yining protests were blamed on the 'East Turkestan Islamic Party of Allah'. At no point was it suggested that ethnicity had played any role in the incidents. When Uyghurs were mentioned in the document, it was only as victims of the terrorists. The point was emphasised by the statement that terrorism in Xinjiang 'has been firmly opposed by people of all ethnic groups in China, including the Uygur [*sic*] people'.

There were many reasons to be sceptical of the white paper's claims, not least their timing. It was too convenient that the Chinese government had suddenly decided to admit its apparently long history of terrorism.

The paper also contained many inconsistencies and questionable assertions. Sometimes 'East Turkestan terrorist forces' were blamed for an incident, but in other instances a specific group was named. Though some of these groups had been mentioned by China before, like ETIM (albeit only very recently), others like the 'Islamic Holy Warriors', the 'Shock Brigade of the Islamist Reformist Party' and the 'East Turkestan Islamic Party of Allah' were previously unknown. The absence of any other information about these groups made some observers wonder if they existed at all. As for the scale of the terrorist threat, the assertion that there had been 'over 200 incidents' looked to be an exaggeration. Obviously, it all depended on how 'terrorism' was defined. While there isn't an internationally accepted definition, for most experts a terrorist act is a politically motivated, planned attack on civilians with the intent of making a public statement and creating widespread fear. Few would agree with the white paper's classification of 'crop burnings' and 'robberies' as terrorist attacks.

The myriad problems with the white paper did not prevent the US government from endorsing China's claims. In September 2002 the United States placed ETIM on one of its lists of terrorist groups – not, as is sometimes erroneously stated, the US Foreign Terrorist Organizations List, but the Terrorist Exclusion List, which calls for far weaker (mostly financial) measures to be taken against those listed. Though ETIM hadn't been explicitly blamed for many of the 'over 200 incidents', the United States mistakenly (presumably) attributed all these incidents to this group. By doing so it established the narrative about ETIM being China's al-Qaeda equivalent; even now the Chinese government and the Western media give ETIM prominence when discussing terrorism in China.

Exactly why the Bush administration chose to place ETIM on a terrorist list is unclear. It's possible that it took China's claims seriously, but despite claiming to have 'independent evidence', the justification it offered directly quoted the Chinese white paper. There were many other likely reasons, such as wanting Chinese support for its military actions in Iraq and Afghanistan, or because it was trying to get China to restrict its weapons sales to countries the United States distrusted. No one seemed to remember President Bush's promise from October 2001 that 'the war on terrorism must never be an excuse to persecute minorities'.

The US endorsement was hugely damaging for any attempt to discuss the problems in Xinjiang without linking them with violence and terrorism. While it did raise the profile of Uyghurs, it did so in a mostly detrimental way. As James Millward commented in 2004, for 'many Western media outlets it is arguably only the idea of a nexus of Islam, terrorism, and China that justifies running a story about Xinjiang at all' – a statement that still holds true.

Many of China's neighbouring countries followed the lead of the United States. In January 2002 Nepal extradited three Uyghurs to Xinjiang, despite them already being granted refugee status by the UNHCR; one of them was subsequently executed. China's partners in the Shanghai Cooperation Organisation also showed their support. In December 2002 a small explosion in Bishkek's Dordoi bazaar (where there were many Chinese traders) that had initially been attributed to a container of fireworks became the work of 'Uyghur terrorists'. The explanation for an explosion at a foreign-exchange office in Osh, in south Kyrgyzstan, went through a similar transformation. Initially thought to be the work of the Islamic Movement of Uzbekistan, it was subsequently blamed on Uyghurs. In 2004 China and Russia jointly called for help in their fights against separatists in Xinjiang and Chechnya.

The placing of ETIM on a US terrorist list also put Xinjiang on the radar of the many 'experts' on global security that proliferated after 9/11, such as SITE Intelligence Group (a monitoring service that offers material on 'the Jihadist threat'), the *Long War Journal* news website (whose aims are the same as SITE's) and IntelCenter (another subscriber service offering counterterrorism intelligence). Many of these organisations treated the Chinese government's assertions as hard facts, and in doing so helped to establish the narrative of a Uyghur terrorist threat. The repetition of such claims muddied the waters so that Uyghurs became, as one analyst put it, 'guilty until proven innocent'. Unfortunately such organisations often do not carry out investigative or fact-checking work. In a 2006 interview with the *New Yorker* magazine, SITE's founding director Rita Katz 'conceded that her group doesn't check the scientific accuracy of each [terrorist] manual or the legitimacy of every threat'. Long before the Tiananmen explosion in October 2013 and the Kunming attacks in 2014, searching on the internet for credible information about terrorism in Xinjiang quickly led down a rabbit hole of spurious and alarmist claims about there being a network of jihadis poised to unleash violence throughout the region.

Yet if there were obvious reasons why SITE and similar groups might not be overly concerned about repeating claims they couldn't verify (these are, after all, commercial ventures: fear is good for business), it seems fair to ask whether there was a similar, if contrasting, bias in the scepticism of those who doubted (and continue to doubt) China's claims about terrorism. Just because the Chinese government had a long history of being an unreliable source, did that mean it couldn't be trusted about anything? Could every aspect of its argument about being a victim of terrorism be dismissed?

There were certainly *some* instances of planned violence, principally the assassinations of local officials and some Uyghur religious figures accused of collusion. And while few experts had heard of ETIM before 2001, an organisation by that name does appear to have existed in Afghanistan in the late 1990s and early 2000s. There was also the matter of the Uyghurs in Guantánamo accused of fighting with al-Qaeda. While such facts weren't enough to prove China's claims, they required explanation.

Of all the incidents the Chinese government presented in the white paper, the assassinations seemed most likely to merit the label of 'terrorism', except that the identities and motivations of those who ordered and carried out these acts remain unknown. There are many possible reasons for the killings. Local officials are generally unpopular throughout China, usually because of corruption and abuse of power, with the result that violence against them is far from uncommon. In 2008 a man confessed to killing six Shanghai police officers in revenge for allegedly being tortured while interrogated about a possibly stolen bicycle; in the same year a teenager stabbed a Communist Party official through the heart for seizing farmers' land and extorting money. Neither act was officially described as terrorism.

As for the Guantánamo Uyghurs, the announcement in 2003 that 15 of them were to be released because they were deemed low-risk was tantamount to saying that their detention had been a mistake. Four were given asylum by Albania, where they got jobs as pizza chefs. Their testimonies suggested that they had just been in the wrong place at the absolute worst time. Most of them had essentially been refugees. The reason they had gone to Afghanistan was not to join a terrorist cell, but because it was the easiest bordering country to enter without a visa. As one detainee told Sean Roberts, 'as soon as they know we are in Kyrgyzstan and Kazakhstan, they will send us back to the Chinese'. As for the 'terrorist camp' they were supposed to be part of, it amounted to little more than some ramshackle buildings near Jalalabad, in Afghanistan. Thus although ETIM did exist in 2001, and with the stated purpose of training Uyghurs for militant activity against the Chinese state, it had no operational capacity. When the United States began bombing Afghanistan, the Uyghurs fled to northern Pakistan, where they were quickly turned over to bounty hunters and sold to the US military. The condition of the camp, as well as the lack of weapons, suggests that if there had been contact between ETIM and anyone from the Taliban or al-Qaeda, it had not led to financial or logistical support – perhaps nothing more than permission to be in Afghanistan.

The evidence thus suggested that neither in the 1990s nor in the early 2000s had there been a significant Uyghur terrorist threat. At most, the facts were inconclusive. Though few Xinjiang scholars were willing to go so far as to say that there was *no* possible threat from Uyghur militant groups, many felt that the case that these groups existed, and had carried out attacks in Xinjiang, hadn't been sufficiently made. As for those who argue that such caution was (and is) unwarranted – arguing, perhaps, that it is surely better to be over-vigilant than lax when it comes to national security – views of this kind tend to neglect the consequences for those so accused. In China, as in many other countries, the authorities used the pretext of 'terrorism' to tighten their control of social, religious and cultural life, especially in Xinjiang.

CLOSING THE WEST

Just as the Open Up the West campaign was really an extension of existing economic policy, so was China's overall approach to 'security' in Xinjiang from 2001 onwards. In late 2001 the government made wide-ranging changes to many of the country's criminal and security laws. It became a criminal act simply to be a member of a designated 'terrorist organisation', even if no other crime was committed, and without any definition of what constituted such a group, meaning that this label could be easily applied. The number of crimes punishable by the death penalty was also increased. There were also amendments to the religious laws. The new rules specified that imams couldn't preach outside their own towns, and that mosques couldn't accept worshippers from other places. The new definition of 'illegal religious activities' involved such diverse (and secular) activities as 'slandering the authorities', 'stirring up trouble', 'spreading rumours' and 'distorting history'. In essence, the legislative changes had the effect of criminalising almost any form of dissent.

The new laws were quickly implemented. Another 'Strike Hard' campaign saw thousands arrested – one official figure was 18,000. Though such high numbers are partly the result of arrest quotas (not a uniquely Chinese problem), reports that many families have to (illegally) pay law-enforcement suggests another reason that law-enforcement officers have an incentive to detain large numbers of people. For those who were subsequently charged, a conviction was almost certain. Chinese courts have only to provide 'basic truth' and 'basic evidence' for a guilty verdict. In 2003 the conviction rate was a staggering 98 per cent.

As the supposed main cause of terrorism, 'religious extremism' became the main target of the new laws. This led to a general disruption of all aspects of Uyghurs' religious practices. While there was no outright ban on new mosques being built, it was clearly discouraged. The number of places for religious activities was said to be 'adequate', meaning that 'we should not have to build new places'. Further restrictions on renovating existing mosques were also issued.

The transmission of religious knowledge to young people – an integral part of Uyghur socialisation – was also subject to new restrictions. In 2005 Xinjiang University gave out a handbook with religious guidelines for students, warning them of expulsion if they were repeatedly caught engaging in religious activities. At many mosques notices were placed above the doors warning that it was against the law for anyone under the age of 18 to enter. There was also a campaign against informal religious teaching. This extended to storytelling and folk songs being transmitted by community elders, a traditional rural practice. Xinjiang party secretary Wang Lequan's comments on the risks of 'folk cultural activities' being vehicles for 'reactionary propaganda' could have been uttered during the Cultural Revolution.

Religious personnel in settlements larger than villages were also required to undergo 'political re-education', with the aim of 're-establishing correct ideological understanding and improving the political qualities of the religious leaders'. During these sessions imams had to listen to speeches from government officials and then answer questions about the religious regulations. They were also required to perform 'self-criticisms' (a long-standing feature of Chinese Communism) during which they admitted past errors. These re-education sessions sometimes went on for weeks – in Yining the father of a friend of mine was an imam at the time and the strain of the classes on him was evident. Officially, all imams were very enthusiastic – at the end of the re-education campaign clerics apparently reported that they 'had seen the light as if we had just walked out of a dense fog'.

SHRINE TOURISM

There were, however, some aspects of Islam that were deemed to be of value. A number of local authorities began promoting *mazar* as tourist sites. This was by no means a uniform initiative – Ordam, the main shrine festival in Xinjiang, which was based around the tomb of the tenth-century martyr Ali Arslan Khan, had been banned since 1997. But in other places Chinese-owned companies were allowed management rights to the sites, meaning they could charge admission. Some local governments did improve access to sites (most of which are in the desert). The Hotan authorities built a road and ensured a water supply for pilgrims (and more importantly, tourists) at the tomb of Imam Asim Khan, an eleventh-century martyr.

Opening up these sites to tourism inevitably had an impact on their spiritual function. It wasn't just the entry charge that disturbed the activities of pilgrims – in some places Chinese tourists were allowed to smoke and drink or behave in other intrusive ways. According to Rahile Dawut from Xinjiang University, at one shrine in Aksu Han tourists are encouraged to buy ribbons from the gift shop that say 'a long life' in Chinese characters and then to tie them among the pieces of cloth left by pilgrims.

Such cultural insensitivity is likely to breed resentment, especially when few of the proceeds go back to the community in which a shrine is located, as with the Tuyuq Khojam *mazar* in Pichan, a small village near Turpan.

The *mazar* is based around a series of caves in which saints are buried. Some believe that the place is so holy that to visit it is worth half a trip to Mecca. One explanation for its holiness is the story that once there were two travellers passing through the village who stopped to rest under a tree. Both fell asleep, and when they woke there was a tall man dressed in white standing over them. He had very black eyes and his nails were long and pointed, but what was strangest was that he cast no shadow. Even though the stranger's lips were still, the two men seemed to hear a voice. It told them he was a servant of God and that they should stand and follow him. When they hesitated, the sky darkened and the figure moved towards them. As the two men fled they seemed to hear the sounds of thousands of hooves behind them. They ran into a cave and prayed to God for deliverance. Immediately they heard a sweet singing and looked out of the cave. The air was full of birds, bearing twigs and grass in their beaks. They swooped down on the cave entrance and within seconds had covered the cave mouth with small nests. Still the sound of hooves approached, and so the men threw themselves to the floor. Suddenly, all went quiet. The travellers got up and looked outside. The sky was blue, the birds were singing and there was no sign of the dark figure. The birds' nests had fooled the evil spirit into thinking the cave was empty.

When I visited Pichan in 2000 I saw adobe houses, donkey carts and a small girl selling melons at a table. The village square was a space of cleared earth around two twisted trees.

When I asked a group of villagers where the shrine was they pointed to a whitewashed room with a green carpet. Money only changed hands when an old man put his hand on my shoulder, raised one finger, then produced a folded piece of paper from his pocket. He carefully unfolded it to reveal a large banknote, which he handed to me for inspection. It was dated 1898, and one side was orange, the other blue, both of which bore a double-headed eagle.

The shrine was reached by small stairs on the far wall of the mosque. These led up to a rough-walled tunnel, which soon widened to a small cave. There two women and a man sat around a fire, chanting at first together, then in alternation. The air was thick with smoke and the women were crying. One of the women broke off chanting and began to keen. The man kept chanting, but his voice was cracked.

In 2000 pilgrims (and even casual visitors like myself) were freely welcomed to the shrine and the village. But after 2003, when a private company bought the rights to the site, a ticket was needed to enter both. There were even proposals that the villagers wear identity badges so as not to be confused with tourists. As in many other *mazar* tourist sites, villagers receive little of the profits.

This kind of commodification of Uyghur culture, while obviously insensitive, is most likely motivated only by profit. But at some Uyghur *mazar* other agendas are being pursued. At the shrine of Afaq Hoja in Kashgar there is also a tomb for Iparhan (Xiang Fei in Chinese), an eighteenth-century Uyghur woman better known as 'the fragrant concubine'. According to popular myth, her beauty and perfume were so great that the Qianlong emperor (who was Manchu) had her brought all the way to Beijing. On the way she was said to have received daily rub-downs with butter and baths in camel's milk. In an early version of her story that circulated in novels and plays in the late Qing and Republican period, Iparhan was said to have resisted the Qing emperor's advances by keeping daggers in her sleeve, until she was poisoned. This story appealed to those who saw the Qing as an invading force – her defiance was seen an act of resistance.

The basic message remained the same in the 1930s, albeit with the additional resonance of the Japanese invasion. But the story told today at the shrine is very different – instead of a story of abduction, attempted rape and murder, the tale of Iparhan and the emperor is now presented as a great romance. The emperor is said to have wooed her by building a miniature Kashgari village outside her window in Beijing and showering her with the sweet melons and flowers of Xinjiang. The intended lesson is that the peoples of Xinjiang and those of the interior have always had good relations with each other. Iparhan's tale has been used to convey this message since the 1980s, when it was announced that 'Xiang Fei and her whole family made a definite contribution by opposing separatism and protecting nationality harmony [i.e. ethnic harmony] and national unity'. But its great popularity now in China is as much to do with commerce as ideology (though one obviously helps the other). In recent years, the Xiang Fei story has become a brand, with a chain of roast-chicken restaurants named after her, as well as a type of raisin and a line of perfumes. An animated series about her early life is currently in the works.

Unsurprisingly, many Uyghurs have a different take on Iparhan's story. In a nice piece of circular irony, some see it as yet another iteration of the 'virtuous woman resisting an invader' narrative, only now the symbolic target is the current Chinese government.

'SEPARATIST' ART

Uyghur culture also came under greater scrutiny in the early 2000s. The first indication of this was at the beginning of January 2002, when Tursunjan Amat, a Uyghur poet, was arrested for having read out a poem at a New Year's performance in Urumqi. He was accused of attacking 'social reality by innuendo' and advocating 'ideas of ethnic separatism'. Several weeks after the reading of the poem, the chairman of the regional government emphasised the need to 'strengthen the anti-separatism struggle in the ideological field'. He claimed there were 'a very small number of people making use of the literary and art stage to peddle their anti-people works that spread ideas of ethnic separation'.

The next phase of the campaign was an attempt to regulate Uyghur folk music. There were reports of lyrics having to be vetted before songs could be performed or recorded, and an inspection of concert set lists. This was accompanied by a purge of books with religious content published without state approval, and of novels and history books with an apparently separatist theme. Once again, there were book burnings.

By the middle of the decade even allegory, or the suspicion of it, was being heavily punished. In 2005, the writer Nurmemet Yasin was arrested for publishing a story allegedly 'inciting separatism'. It told of a blue pigeon that travelled far from home. When it returned, different-coloured pigeons captured him and locked him in a birdcage. Although the other pigeons fed him, the blue pigeon opted to commit suicide by eating a poisoned strawberry rather than remain imprisoned in his hometown. Because many pro-independence Uyghur groups use a blue flag, the Chinese authorities read the story as referring to Uyghur resentment of government policies. Yasin was tried in closed hearings and sentenced to ten years in prison for splittism, while the editor of the journal in which the story appeared was given a three-year sentence.

Neither the intensity of the rhetoric, nor the quest for 'security', showed any signs of slackening during the mid-2000s. In 2003 Wang Lequan called for the forces of East Turkestan separatists to be dealt 'devastating blows without showing any mercy'. The list of alleged terrorist groups was extended to include organisations in the Uyghur diaspora. China claimed that both the World Uyghur Youth Congress and the East Turkestan Information Centre were engaged in terrorist activities, and asked for international support in its fight against them. Though this claim had the merit of naming organisations whose existence could at least be validated, there was no evidence to support these accusations. Most likely, it was a response to their increasing prominence.

Daily life in Xinjiang became increasingly disrupted, especially by an escalation in the duration and intensity of 'Strike Hard' campaigns. In 2003 there was a special 100-day campaign, while in 2004 a 'High-pressure Strike Hard' had no end period specified. Such campaigns often involved a whole neighbourhood being cordoned off while armed police conducted house-to-house searches. The police checked residents' identity cards and searched for illegal publications. Given how nebulous the law had become by this point, it probably wasn't hard for them to fill their arrest quotas. In some cases, the searches were conducted with considerable brutality, just as they would be in Urumqi in 2009 after the riots.

NO LONGER 'VOLATILE'?

The Open Up the West and anti-terror campaigns in Xinjiang made great, albeit familiar promises of development and stability. Whether or not these campaigns can be deemed successful inevitably depends on the criteria that one chooses. Given the vagueness of the aims of the Open Up the West campaign, it wasn't hard for the government quickly to declare it a triumph. As early as November 2002, Xinhua was breathlessly reporting that

> three years have gone by, and the roads have become passable, the lights have become lit, the mountains have become green, the rivers have become clear and the travelling traders more abundant. One after another, wonderful stories about the homeland of the western region have been circulated and sung.

Propaganda aside, the campaign undisputedly had a beneficial effect on Xinjiang's economy. Between 2001 and 2010, its GDP grew by 300 per cent, which, though impressive, needs to be put in a wider context – the national average was 304 per cent. If the only criterion for success was the unambitious one of preventing the gap between western provinces and those in the east from getting any wider, then the campaign did succeed. What it did not do was ease the inequalities within Xinjiang, especially between Han and Uyghur. Though there were, as before, some prosperous regions with sizeable Uyghur populations, the majority of these were in eastern Xinjiang. In the south, where Uyghurs were concentrated, the economic situation remained significantly worse than in the north. By 2010 the average income in Kashgar was only half of what it was in the northern town of Changji (a suburb of Urumqi that is 75 per cent Han). In Hotan the average income was only a third of what it was in Changji. The per capita GDP of both Kashgar and Hotan prefectures was lower than that of Guizhou, the poorest province in China.

Economic inequalities have by no means been the sole (or even the primary) cause of confrontations between Uyghurs and the authorities in Xinjiang, but they have certainly created a general context of resentment. Officials in Xinjiang stressed the link between poverty and social instability throughout the 1990s, but without acknowledging the causes of the 'backward' conditions of minority areas. By this logic, and what's known about the causes of previous incidents, one might have expected the 2000s to have been a decade in which the region actually deserved some of the adjectives – 'restive', 'troubled', 'volatile' – that the Western media often burdened it with. If one also factors in the provocations caused by state interference in Uyghur cultural, social and religious life, you could almost be forgiven for thinking that Xinjiang was liable to witness some of the 'terrorism' the government was so concerned about.

At times, officials seemed to be guaranteeing it. In 2003 Wang Lequan went against the prevailing logic of the 1990s by attacking the notion that 'after Xinjiang's economy develops, people's living standards will improve so the issue of stability will be resolved naturally. This belief is wrong and dangerous. Economic development cannot eliminate separatists.' In some ways, this was a clever argument. By weakening the causal link between 'separatism' and economic conditions, the occurrence of any public disturbance could no longer be used as a basis on which to infer that there were problems with the governance of Xinjiang. It also shifted the issue onto apparently problematic aspects of minority society and culture.

Yet despite worsening conditions for Uyghurs in Xinjiang, the years from 2000 to 2007 had the lowest number of incidents of any period since 'opening up', perhaps even since 'liberation'. Even compared with other parts of China, Xinjiang had fewer violent incidents. Those that did get reported weren't of much substance. In October 2005 the Xinjiang authorities announced that they had arrested 19 foreign militants, but few other details emerged. In 2007 Chinese state media reported a raid on a training camp in the mountains near Kashgar, and that weapons and explosives had been seized. According to official sources, 18 'terror-ists' were killed and another 17 were captured. However, Rafael Poch, a Spanish journalist, after investigating the incident found no evidence that there had even been such a camp.

Whether or not there was any truth to these reports, there was certainly a general absence of explosions, assassinations or major protests during the majority of the 2000s. To the limited extent that any of these incidents had previously been 'terrorist' acts, the Chinese government appeared to be winning their war on 'terror'. However, one doesn't need to endorse the official narrative about 'separatism' to argue that the increasing securitisation of Xinjiang during the decade, of which the 'Strike Hard' campaigns were a core element, prevented most forms of public dissent. It's also possible that the crackdown on Uyghur organisations in the former Soviet republics had an effect, though probably not a large one, given their marginal role in prior incidents.

Another, more likely, explanation is that for many Uyghurs it was no longer possible to sustain the quixotic optimism that had led some to believe that another country or agency was going to intervene. The brutal response to the Yining protests also made it absolutely clear that the state would only respond to criticism or dissent with repression and violence. Faced with these prospects, many Uyghurs opted to leave Xinjiang, either for other cities in China, or for other countries. Education was probably the easiest way for people to shift their *hukous* to another city. In 2001, of the 12,000 students from Xinjiang who went to university in other provinces, only 20 per cent came back.

Given that many Uyghurs had poor Chinese and few connections in cities outside Xinjiang, most ended up getting badly paid jobs. If one travelled around China in the 2000s it was common to come across Uyghurs running small restaurants or working in university canteens, especially in north-western cities like Xian and Lanzhou. Beijing has also had a sizeable Uyghur community since the 1980s – officially around 3,000 at present, though certainly higher due to the many people who are unregistered.

Leaving the country was far more difficult. Uyghurs with state jobs had a better chance of getting permission to study or train abroad, but most were denied a passport. Many were forced to leave illegally, which meant that they faced arrest if they returned. The desire to leave, at least for a while, led to an explosion in private English classes for Uyghurs.

In the early 2000s, the only way for Uyghurs to learn English through state education was if they were *min kao han*. For students learning in minority languages, their second language had to be Chinese. Even in higher education, access to English was restricted. In many colleges English departments only accepted minority students on alternate years, apparently as a trade-off, since they needed lower test scores to gain admission.

In Yining I taught one of these classes to Kazakh and Uyghur students, and visited many more. What was immediately apparent was how motivated the students were, and how quickly they made progress. Many were self-taught and had far greater confidence than my Han students who had been learning English at school for almost ten years. For some Uyghurs, the experience of already having had to learn a second language (that is, Chinese) definitely helped them learn English. Private English schools are still just as popular today among Uyghurs in Xinjiang, and speaking English has become something for many Uyghurs to be proud of. Since 2004 Uyghurs have reached the finals of most national English-speaking competitions, many of which are televised, and thus constitute one of the rare depictions of Uyghurs in Chinese media that is both positive and empowering.

THE PEACOCK FLIES NORTH

When writing about poverty, whether relative or absolute, there's a tendency to neglect the ways in which people find methods of coping in adverse circumstances. This is especially likely when a marginalised group of people is predominantly from an ethnic minority. The idea of them as 'victims', with no capacity to effect change in their lives, then receives greater emphasis. In the 2000s the situation for Uyghurs, especially in the south, was probably worse than during any period since the end of the Cultural Revolution. Other than with those determined to paint Uyghurs as Islamic terrorists, the notion of Uyghurs as an oppressed and powerless ethnic minority thus still had great currency in the Western media (which now strives to have it both ways, especially since the Kunming attacks).

There was obviously ample material for such a characterisation of the situation of Uyghurs in Xinjiang. Uyghurs *were* subject to repressive state policies; they *were* subject to institutionalised discrimination. There was nothing wrong with journalists and human-rights campaigners highlighting these inequalities. The problem was that little mention was given to the way in which Uyghurs in Xinjiang might be responding to these issues – or, to put it another way, were *resisting* – without overtly challenging authority.

The popularity of English classes is one example of the ways that Uyghurs in the 2000s sought to provide themselves with ways to over-come the economic discrimination they faced. But perhaps the most common solution was the one that people were using all over China: they moved to the big city. Throughout the country, young men and women were leaving their villages and small towns and going to find work in factories, on construction sites, in restaurants and karaoke bars. Generally the work was unskilled, and not well remunerated – though it still paid more than a farmer earned. Migrant workers like these are known as China's 'floating population', and are to be found in any major urban centre. Because their *hukous* are registered elsewhere, they are usually disqualified from medical care, affordable housing or any welfare privileges. They are often the subject of prejudice and discrimination from local residents. As a result, many lead a precarious existence – a study in 2003 found that migrants were twice as likely as urban residents to suffer from absolute poverty.

In Xinjiang, the main migration by Uyghurs was from the south to Urumqi, which was also a destination for Han workers from other parts of China (as encouraged by the Open Up the West campaign). By 2009 there were around 630,000 registered migrant workers in Urumqi (the actual number was undoubtedly higher). However, whereas most Han came to Urumqi principally for work, more than a third of Uyghurs interviewed in a study in 2005 said they had come for other reasons, such as the greater social, political and religious freedom they experienced compared to living in Kashgar and Hotan (something that parallels the way that some Uyghur artists in the 1990s, like the singer Askar, took advantage of the more permissive climate of cities outside Xinjiang).

The greater religious tolerance of the authorities in Urumqi was still evident in Er Dao Qiao, one of the main Uyghur neighbourhoods in the south of the city, as late as 2012. According to Rachel Harris, there were signs in southern cities like Aksu warning women it was illegal for them to wear a veil in public, and men praying in the bazaar were being arrested, whereas fully veiled women, some dressed in black, were able to walk around Urumqi freely.

This illustrates once again the considerable differences in the way that policies of all kinds are applied at a local level in Xinjiang, with factors like the demographics of the area, its political history and its economic conditions all affecting the manner in which any given policy is implemented.

The influx of Uyghurs from south Xinjiang over the last decade has been so great that Er Dao Qiao has lost its previously fashionable status, and become both poorer and more conservative. In 2013 I was told by a number of residents that several Uyghur girls had been attacked for wearing clothing thought to be immodest. Though some Uyghurs in Urumqi live in affluent areas, where the modern apartment buildings are well endowed with expensive Central Asian restaurants and halal supermarkets, most Uyghur migrants in Urumqi live in Er Dao Qiao and other southern districts. Some of these areas are virtual slums, with houses that are small brick structures with corrugated iron roofs, many of which lack access to water or power. Migrant workers throughout China are often forced by lack of funds to live in poor housing – windowless basements, cramped dormitories, makeshift structures under bridges – but in Urumqi conditions for migrants were especially bad. In 2003, on average 15 per cent of urban migrants lived in absolute poverty in China's cities; in Urumqi it was 54 per cent.

Though conditions were bad for all migrants in Urumqi, they were worst for Uyghurs, who were more likely to end up doing low-paid work. In 2005 they earned 30 per cent less than Han in Urumqi, mainly because they were confined to particular economic niches. Given China's rapid urbanisation, construction is one of the main employers, yet one study found that almost no Uyghurs in Urumqi were able to get jobs in this sector. Employer discrimination against Uyghurs is often explicit: some job advertisements state that only Han Chinese can apply. This somewhat undermines the Chinese government's rationale for bilingual education. If it's not Uyghurs' poor Chinese that makes it hard for them to find a job, then there's no reason to favour Chinese as a language of instruction.

While this kind of employer discrimination is indefensible, it's perhaps relevant to note that Chinese employers also discriminate according to provincial origin – some refuse to hire people from Guizhou or Anhui on the basis that they are supposedly lazy and unreliable. The drawing of such distinctions should serve as a warning against viewing Han Chinese as a monolithic ethnic group, something there is a tendency to do when comparing the general situation of Uyghurs in Xinjiang with that of Han. In Urumqi both Han and Uyghur migrants suffered, albeit to different degrees.

One of the main differences between the two groups was that Han migrants were more likely to have contacts with potential employers in construction and manufacturing, which is often crucial for finding a job in any part of China. Uyghurs' lack of contacts with Han employers, as well as the mutual distrust between them and Han Chinese, meant that the workplace replicated the social separation between the different ethnic groups (something that had been less prevalent in the public sector). Uyghurs in Urumqi tended to work for, and with, other Uyghurs, mainly in demolition, or a culturally specific sector (like halal restaurants) from which Han workers were excluded. Until 2002 many Uyghurs sold goods in the bazaar in Er Dao Qiao, but it was then demolished to make way for a new Chinese-owned complex thought to be more tourist-friendly. The new International Grand Bazaar was a huge, light-brown, faux-Islamic building with a Kentucky Fried Chicken, a Carrefour supermarket and rents that were too high for most stallholders.

Those Uyghurs who couldn't find a cheaper stall elsewhere peddled goods on the street, shone shoes or turned to petty crime (all survival strategies of migrants throughout China). In defence of the new bazaar, one might add that it did help to raise property values in the surrounding Uyghur districts (at least until the riots in 2009).

The Uyghurs in Urumqi who were best off were those with the capital to start their own business, which was usually borrowed from relatives. Many traded in goods imported from Turkey and Central Asia. In Urumqi and also Yining it was common to find small shops selling henna, biscuits, flavoured black tea and sweets from Uzbekistan or Kazakhstan. This preference for buying Central Asian goods rather than ones from elsewhere in China reflects not only fears that Chinese products might not be halal, but also the stronger sense of identification with the cultures of these countries. Nowhere was this more evident than in the music heard in shops, nightclubs and restaurants, which, if not Uyghur, was usually Turkish or Russian, or from Uzbekistan or the other Central Asian states.

Though such businesses did good trade in the early 2000s, there were limits to how far they could grow, given they were competing with other Uyghur firms in a fairly limited market. Access to greater capital was hampered by the lack of Islamic banking facilities in Xinjiang, and a lack of *guanxi* with Han investors. Very few companies had the ability to compete with larger, Han-owned firms.

In Urumqi, as in many other places in Xinjiang, there were thus many sources of friction between Han and Uyghurs. Some of this was caused by local issues, like competition between Uyghur and Han migrants for jobs and business, but this was arguably only the latest iteration of the long-standing resentment of Han immigration. The increased cultural and religious repression after 9/11 was also merely a new version of an old injustice. Whether or not one regards Chinese rule of Xinjiang as a colonial enterprise, there's certainly one lesson from the history of colonisation that the Xinjiang authorities in the 2000s would have done well to heed: people who see themselves as oppressed invariably find a way to attack those they blame. By 2006 some were already warning that Uyghurs were being driven to desperation. The scholar Jennifer Taynen commented:

> If anything, tension below the surface is even greater because of the lack of emotional outlets, and although the Chinese seem oblivious to it, the minority populations' lack of hope for the future poses a very serious threat to regional security.

Even within China – where Xinjiang has long been one of those sensitive issues that Chinese intellectuals generally avoid – there was some admission that the situation in the region was fast deteriorating. Wang Lixiong, who had written books about Tibet and helped set up Friends of Nature, one of China's first environmental NGOs, published a book in 2007 in Taiwan whose title translates as 'My far west, your East Turkestan'. Despite the use of 'East Turkestan' in the title, in the book Wang was against any form of independence for Xinjiang, but made other suggestions that were almost as radical. Wang argued that the restrictions on religion in Xinjiang amounted to a 'self-fulfilling prophecy': without more religious freedom, and some curbs on Han settlement, he predicted that a 'Palestinisation' of the 'Xinjiang problem' would occur.

It didn't take long for these predictions to be proved correct. In Kashgar in July 2008, just before the Beijing Olympics, two men drove a truck into a group of police officers jogging near their barracks, then threw explosives at the police station. Official sources claimed that 16 policemen had been killed, and that ETIM was responsible. Just over a week later, explosives were thrown at a police station and government offices in Kuqa city in southern Xinjiang. One security guard died and ten assailants were killed in the unrest, with police chasing down and firing at some of the attackers. On that occasion, the Chinese government said they did *not* believe that ETIM were responsible (but did not accuse anyone else). In neither case did any group accept responsibility, and the motives behind the attacks remain unclear.

What both incidents had in common was that the violence did not target civilians, something true of many previous incidents, even by official accounts. In Xinjiang government officials and security personnel have generally been the focus of popular anger, which is also the case with most protests in other parts of China. This would change the following year, when the worst outbreak of violence in Xinjiang since the Cultural Revolution took place in Urumqi. It wasn't a terrorist attack. But a line was certainly crossed.

7

URUMQI AND AFTER: LEARNING THE WRONG LESSONS

You could say the killing didn't begin in Xinjiang. You could say it started over 3,000 kilometres away, in the eastern city of Shaoguan, in Guangdong province, at the end of June 2009. Like many towns and cities in Guangdong, Shaoguan has factories where almost everything gets made: ball bearings, tractor gears, oil pumps, construction machinery, handbags, light bulbs, screws and spanners. The factory where the killing started made toys. It was owned by Early Light International, the world's biggest toy manufacturer, which is based in Hong Kong and makes products for multinationals like Hasbro and Mattel. Its Shaoguan factory employs 20,000 people; on its website there are photos of the workers' dormitories, rows of white- and red-tiled buildings stacked so close they seem like dominoes set up to fall.

In most factory towns in Guangdong, the labour force is primarily made up of migrant workers, especially young women from small towns or the countryside. But in Shaoguan most of the workers are from the local area, which makes for a stable labour pool, something many companies prefer. The 200 Uyghurs working in the toy factory were thus doubly an exception – the overwhelming majority of the workforce were Han. The Uyghur workers had arrived at the factory in May from Kashgar. Even by the standards of Chinese migrant workers – who often travel for several days on buses and trains to reach their workplace – they had come a very long way.

The Uyghur workers in the Early Light factory were part of a government scheme to send Uyghurs from economically deprived areas

183

with few employment opportunities to work in regions that had better prospects. Officials said that 96,000 people had been sent from south Xinjiang in the first half of 2009. Though there are claims by the WUC that this scheme represented forced labour and that the workers were threatened and coerced to go – in particular young women – the evidence for this is thin, at least in the majority of cases. While it's likely that some local officials, themselves under pressure to achieve migration targets, did use stricter methods than persuasion, the lack of major resistance to the scheme suggests that most workers were glad of the opportunity. It certainly wasn't a population transfer – their *hukous* remained in Xinjiang. As for the fact that many of the workers were young women, this doesn't suggest any intention on the part of the state to send the (supposedly) most vulnerable workers. Women outnumber men in most of China's southern factories, and generally have some control over their labour situation, as Leslie Chang's illuminating book, *Factory Girls* (2008), shows.

However, while the labour-relocation scheme was perhaps the most significant attempt by the Xinjiang authorities to tackle poverty in the south of the region for decades, it may have resulted from multiple agendas. Some officials spoke of the hope that it would allow minorities to get 'access to modernisation' and 'make them more open minded' – the usual rhetoric of integrating 'backward' minorities into (Han) Chinese society. There have also been suggestions that adding Uyghurs to a mostly Han labour force was intended to divide the workers on ethnic lines, so as to hamper the increasing activism of workers' organisations. While this isn't implausible, it's hard to see 200 Uyghurs making much difference to the solidarity of a workforce of 20,000.

But even with so small a group, there were still divisions. As in universities (and many neighbourhoods) in Xinjiang, the Uyghurs lived in separate dormitories. Most spoke poor Chinese, making it hard for them to communicate with their Han co-workers. Though the Xinjiang regional government claimed to be spending 400 million yuan on free technology and language training courses for the migrants, their linguistic skills were probably not a priority. And, as in Xinjiang, the separation of the Han and Uyghur communities fostered mutual misunderstanding and ignorance.

So when a disgruntled former worker wrote a post on an internet message board claiming that six Uyghur workers had raped two Han girls, there was already fertile ground for rumours. The inspiration for this accusation, which was completely unfounded (no such rapes were reported), may have been a previous incident in which a female Han worker got lost and ended up in the Uyghur men's dormitories. When they started talking to her, and she couldn't understand, she apparently screamed.

Whether it started with her scream, or with the man writing on the message board, the result was four hours of violence in the Early Light toy factory on the evening of 26 June 2009. Next day the authorities characterised it as a vicious brawl, but the amateur video shot that evening doesn't show any fighting. It begins instead with a blur of movement as one man runs through the brightly lit space between dormitories. Though the man is pursued, the camera keeps moving at walking pace along with hundreds of other people. Most of them are in short-sleeved shirts; one is wearing a yellow T-shirt on which it says 'Never Say Die' in English. For the next half a minute the crowd seems calm; though there are some scattered shouts, the clanking on the concrete of the metal poles and sticks held by many of the crowd is clearly audible.

People and the camera stroll forward, until there is a cheer, which spreads. Many of the men raise their arms in the air, some of them still holding their weapons. A man in a green basketball top jumps up and down as if a game has just been won. But the moment of triumph is over quickly. People lower their arms and start moving in another direction, allowing the camera to see the body of a Uyghur man on the ground. His face and hands are covered in blood and he is not moving. 'Another one,' someone says in Chinese, perhaps as a suggestion.

The camera retraces its steps till it reaches a parked ambulance. Through its windows, another man can be seen lying motionless on a stretcher, an arm over his face. Then there are the heavy thumps of something being beaten. The crowd parts to show five or six bodies lying in a row on the ground. Several men step forward to kick and hit them with poles. None of the bodies move when struck.

The official account of the Shaoguan violence said that two people had been killed, both Uyghurs, and over 100 people injured. However, even the brief video suggested the casualty count was higher, and when it was posted online many Uyghurs in Xinjiang, on the other side of the country, were furious. The riot police had taken several hours to arrive; even afterwards the comments of local-government officials suggested they didn't take it seriously. One official described the killings as 'a very ordinary incident'; another said that the problem between Han and Uyghurs 'is like an issue between husband and wife'.

The announcement on 28 June that one of the rumour-mongers had been arrested didn't assuage public anger. There was no mention of anyone being held responsible for the killings, and a lack of comment on the incident by the Xinjiang authorities. Their hope may have been that public anger would die down, but if so they weren't paying enough attention to Uyghur-language websites, where discussion of the incident led to the airing of broader grievances. At that point, the internet, though heavily regulated, was still probably the safest place for Uyghurs in Xinjiang to express dissent. The general mood of mourning and anger, which couldn't be publicly articulated, was eloquently conveyed by the darkening of the backgrounds of popular Uyghur-language websites like Diyarim.com and Uighurbiz.net (which was run by Ilham Tohti, who would be jailed for life in 2014).

Public outrage culminated in a call to demonstrate in Urumqi on the afternoon of 5 July. This was widely circulated by text message, especially among students, and on Uyghur message boards (many of whose webmasters would later be given prison sentences of between three and ten years for 'endangering state security'). The protesters were due to meet at the People's Square at 5 p.m., but were already gathering from 3 p.m. As a predominantly Han city, Urumqi doesn't have many

Uyghur areas, but most of those are in the south of the city. The closest thing to an ethnic dividing line is an area called Nan Men (in Chinese, 'south gate', named when the city was walled, as most of China's cities used to be). Nan Men is a few blocks south of the People's Square, so the protesters had picked a central, predominantly Han space, a place the authorities couldn't ignore.

By 5 p.m. around a thousand Uyghurs had gathered in the People's Square, many of them holding Chinese flags to signal their peaceful intent (and probably also to try to deflect accusations of 'separatism'). Given that the demonstration had been announced beforehand, the police were prepared. Their attempt to disperse the crowd seems to have been aggressive, though not violent. Eyewitness accounts describe them shouting at the protesters, taking photos and video of them, and making arrests. As this was going on, more joined the crowd, which soon left the square and headed south. Video taken from more than ten storeys up shows a crowd marching down the middle of the street, flowing around stopped cars. Their shouts and whistles echo.

News of what had happened in the square travelled fast. As the crowd moved south they were joined by groups from different neighbourhoods. Around 6.30 p.m. the crowd clashed with the police at a roadblock set up to prevent them going north (and thus into Han neighbourhoods). As in the square, the police made arrests, but considerably more force was used, most likely because PLA soldiers were also now involved. Tear gas and warning shots were fired, and, according to many accounts, there were beatings and shootings as well. It's unclear at what point some of the crowd started throwing stones at the soldiers and police, but this was when the protest became a riot.

The soldiers were able to push the crowd further south, towards Er Dao Qiao, after which there seems to have been little police presence. From there the rioters went into a number of mixed neighbourhoods, and it was here that the killings began. There are numerous reports of violence against Han civilians, ranging from opportunistic attacks to roadblocks being set up to stop traffic; any Han drivers discovered were dragged from their vehicles and beaten. The general chaos was increased by cars, buses and buildings being set on fire. The violence and confusion continued throughout the night. The whereabouts and actions of the police and army during this period remain unclear, though many residents reported hearing gunfire during the night. There would later be an official statement that the police had shot and killed 12 rioters, confirming their responsibility for at least some of the casualties.

THE AFTERMATH

Next morning the streets were marked with broken glass and blood. Burnt cars and shops still smouldered. The city was under virtual martial law. Armoured vehicles patrolled the streets while squads of armed police combed Uyghur neighbourhoods for anyone suspected of taking part in the riots. It was later estimated that around 20,000 additional security forces (including members of the XPCC) were brought into Urumqi. There was also a communications blackout that would last almost a year. Text messaging, international phone calls and internet access were blocked to stop the spread of 'rumours'.

The exact number of casualties had yet to be confirmed, but it was already estimated to be around 150 (the official figure given later was 197). News reports on state television showed footage of protesters beating and kicking people on the ground. Video shot at the hospital the previous night showed patients with blood streaming down their heads. Two lay on the fruit barrow that friends had used to transport them. A four-year-old boy lay on a trolley, dazed by his head injury and his pregnant mother's disappearance. He had been clinging to her hand when a bullet hit her.

The Xinjiang authorities' version of events mentioned neither the role of the Shaoguan incident, nor any other Uyghur grievance. A government statement described the protests as an 'organised violent crime' that had been 'instigated and directed from abroad, and carried out by outlaws in the country'. Xinhua, the state news agency, wasted no time in blaming Rebiya Kadeer. Wang Lequan said that the incident revealed 'the violent and terrorist nature of the separatist World Uyghur Congress'. According to him, it had been 'a profound lesson in blood'.

Unsurprisingly, Kadeer denied any role in organising the protests. The WUC claimed that the 'authorities' failure to take any meaningful action to punish the [Han] Chinese mob for the brutal murder of Uyghurs is the real cause of this protest'. The WUC also questioned the casualty figures, and would later claim they didn't include 400 Uyghurs killed by the police and army. The Chinese government later claimed to have recordings of international phone calls made by Kadeer with instructions for the rioters, in which she told her brother to tell the rioters to 'be brave' and 'make it bigger'. As usual, it failed to produce any such 'evidence'. Kadeer did acknowledge having made the call, but said it was only to get her brother to 'stay at home that day'. The demonisation of Kadeer in the Chinese media would go on for weeks, and while it gave the Chinese public someone to blame, it also had the unintended effect of raising her profile among Uyghurs in Xinjiang, most of whom had had little knowledge of her previously, especially outside Urumqi.

Her international profile was also raised by the Chinese government's attempt to block the screening of Jeff Daniels' documentary about Kadeer at the Melbourne Film Festival later in July. In an interview with me, Daniels said that both the festival and the Australian Broadcasting Corporation (ABC), the film's principal funder, came under intense pressure. A scheduled visit by Hu Jintao, then president, was postponed for six months, and the festival's website was hacked; Daniels said that, five years later, his own personal website still receives cyberattacks. While the Australian government withstood the pressure – despite the fact that China is Australia's second-largest trading partner – some other countries were intimidated. Daniels recalls that one broadcaster in South Korea told him: 'China's our biggest trading partner. We're not going to threaten that relationship by screening your film.'

But the fallout from the riots was most immediately felt by Uyghurs in Urumqi. As in Baren in 1990 and Yining in 1997, there was a huge wave of arrests in Urumqi over the following weeks. Almost 1,500 people were arrested on 6 July alone. Both Human Rights Watch and Amnesty International subsequently published reports on the brutality with which police and soldiers conducted house-to-house searches and arrests. These are corroborated by a video that later appeared on YouTube, which seems to have been shot for state TV. The footage shows Uyghur men being dragged from their homes, in some cases partially dressed, who are then handcuffed and made to lie face down. Many of the arrested have their shirts pulled over their heads so they cannot see. At one point the soldiers are shown entering a house, but the cameraman isn't allowed to follow. 'It's nothing,' says one of the officers, just before a suspect is beaten. Some arrests were justified by the young men allegedly having bruises or other injuries, or having been away from home during the previous evening, while in other cases the detentions were arbitrary. There were subsequently reports of families having to pay high sums for the release of relatives, or even for them to get medical treatment, which if true suggests that mass arrests are sometimes prompted by more than official zeal.

Though the mass arrests and blaming of hostile external forces were typical of the state's response, there was one departure. Foreign journalists were not only permitted, but encouraged to report from Urumqi. The hope was probably that the pictures of the wounded, and the damage to the city, would evoke sympathy (and thus support for the authorities' version of the events). While one should applaud this rare openness, in hindsight it was a terrible idea, at least from the government's perspective, and has not been repeated since for any other incident in Xinjiang. The problem wasn't just that most journalists did what they were supposed to do – describe the scene, interview residents and question the official account. This alone would have led to questions about the casualty figures, the use of force and the real causes of the riots. But their presence in the city on 7 July meant that they were able to witness two incidents the government would rather they hadn't.

The first was probably provoked by the presence of the journalists themselves. During an official tour of the riot zone, women in the market began to wail and chant as the reporters arrived. 'The policemen took away my husband last night. I don't know why and I don't know where he is,' said one woman. The crowd quickly grew to around 200, most of whom were shouting and waving their fists. Many held photos or ID cards of those that had been arrested. There were attempts by paramilitaries to push the crowd back, and some officers lashed out with batons and shields, though their superiors restrained them: they knew better than to attack an unarmed crowd in front of the global media. Nevertheless, the scene was still angry and tense, and might well have spiralled into violence, had it not been for an old woman propped up on a crutch. Tania Branigan, the *Guardian*'s China correspondent, described how

> [a]s older residents stepped forward and attempted to calm the crowd, she advanced steadily towards the line of armoured vehicles. She halted inches in front of one. The driver started its engine. For a long moment they faced each other. Then the carrier slowly began to roll backwards and the line of officers inched away, back down the road. She walked forward. They stepped back. She continued – while the officer pleaded with her to turn away.

This brought a temporary calm that allowed tensions to ebb. But later the same day the streets were once again full of anger. Han residents moved in groups through the city, armed with clubs, sticks, machetes, meat cleavers, iron pipes and shovels. Most were trying to reach the Uyghur districts in the south. When questioned, some said that it was because they were worried about further attacks, but many others said they just wanted revenge. 'They attacked us. Now it's our turn to attack them,' one man in the crowd said. Another, clutching a metal bar, told the AFP news agency: 'The Uyghurs came to our area to smash things, now we are going to their area to beat them.'

Though the police managed to block most of the armed groups from entering Uyghur neighbourhoods, some did get through. Uyghur shops were smashed and burnt, stalls were turned over, and there were a number of beatings and murders. While reports of the violence were still coming in, the WUC posted a hysterical list of atrocities on its website – 'a Uyghur woman who was carrying a baby in her arms was mutilated along with her infant baby [...] two Uyghur female students were beheaded [...] their heads were placed on a stake on the middle of the street' – none of which were later confirmed (the post was subsequently removed).

While for the most part the military did protect Uyghur districts, there were several incidents that suggested the authorities were just as concerned with winning the favour of the Han majority. Little attempt was made to disarm the hundreds of armed civilians. The inadequacy of these efforts was epitomised by Urumqi Communist Party secretary Li Zhi's turning up in a police car and appealing with the groups to go home, then leading them in a chant of 'Down with Rebiya'.

More seriously, some soldiers may have colluded with the armed groups. An amateur video shot that day shows about a hundred Han civilians waiting on the street, some of whom are subsequently given long metal poles by a soldier from the back of a lorry – which resemble the poles that were later used by the mobs that attacked Uyghur districts. There's no way to know whether this was an isolated incident or not, but it raises questions about the impartiality of some sections of the police and military, as do the comments of one police officer to the journalists on the media tour. He asked them: 'Why are you reporting on the Uyghurs? The Uyghurs chopped the heads off 100 Han Chinese.'

What both the killings and the attacks on 7 July illustrated was the sharp deterioration in Han–Uyghur relations. Though prejudice and mutual dislike between the two had long been common, inter-ethnic violence was generally something that arose only from personal conflicts.

But what the Uyghurs who dragged Han out of cars and beat them and the Han who wanted to hurt Uyghurs with cleavers and shovels had in common was that they wanted to hurt strangers purely on the basis of their ethnicity. After July 2009 few people in either community would put much stock in the repeated calls for 'ethnic unity' that were made in the media, proclaimed from the red banners hung in the streets or blared from loudspeakers on the police cars and military vehicles that drove through the city. Among both communities stories circulated about the savagery of the other. Thomas Cliff was told a story by a Han businessman about 'a little Uyghur girl whose role was to pick up a brick and smash the skulls of Han people lying beaten on the ground – to make sure that their brains were splattered'. Though this story, like that on the WUC website, was surely a fabrication, both illustrate how much relations between the two communities had worsened.

There were further detentions of Uyghurs in Urumqi throughout July and August, though many of these were targeted arrests, rather than the neighbourhood raids of 6 July. Much of the blame for the violence was placed on the Uyghur floating population in the southern slum areas, especially Heijiashan district. According to Wang Lequan: 'The hard-core elements who participated [...] are mostly concentrated in the social dregs of the key sensitive areas [...] For many years the domestic separatist forces have clustered there.'

While it's debatable whether the Uyghurs who targeted the Han did so because of 'separatism', this was perhaps one of those rare instances when the official explanation of events did acknowledge, however inadvertently, some of the causes of Uyghur dissatisfaction. When I visited Urumqi in April 2010 many Uyghurs told me that street traders had been responsible for much of the violence. Many lived in the areas Wang referred to, and constituted the poorest, most marginalised section of Urumqi society – those who had the greatest reason to feel socially and economically excluded.

After almost a decade of growing economic hardship, as well as cultural and religious repression, some explosion of Uyghur anger was inevitable. Yet while the protest was certainly an expression of wider anger and not just a reaction to the Shaoguan killings, without the severe response from the authorities it probably wouldn't have escalated. This is not to justify the killings – merely to suggest an explanation for how the peaceful protests descended into ethnic violence.

Perhaps the only attempt to appease Uyghur anger after the riots was the announcement that 15 people had been arrested for their part in the Shaoguan riots: 13 for the violence, and two for spreading rumours (and of these two, one was subsequently given life imprisonment, while the other was given the death penalty). But despite this gesture, and the continuing presence of security forces, the situation in Urumqi was anything but safe.

'KILL WANG LEQUAN'

Conditions in Urumqi that August could not have been more conducive to rumour. The continuing tensions, coupled with the lack of internet access and the general mistrust of state information, made people especially susceptible to misinformation.

So when it was reported in mid-August that people on the streets of Urumqi were being attacked with hypodermic syringes, there was a swift outcry. The fact that it was unclear who was responsible only made things worse. Over the following weeks, the stabbings continued – none of which was fatal. Han residents began to claim that they were being targeted. The government confirmed that most of the victims were Han (as would be expected from the demographics of Urumqi), but stressed that Uyghurs and other ethnic groups had also been attacked. By 3 September hospitals had reported 531 cases. Perhaps the most remarkable part of the episode was that 80 per cent of the 'stabbings' didn't actually happen. Only a fifth of the 'victims' examined by doctors had actual puncture wounds. The rest had mosquito bites, or no marks at all – some only claimed to be wounded because the state was offering compensation to victims. Fear, social hysteria, and a degree of opportunism had created yet another source of tension between Han and Uyghur in Urumqi.

These concerns were further inflamed by posters that went up around the city on 2 September that described the stabbings as a 'serious terrorist crime', and as an attempt 'to destroy the city's peace and unity'. People were even sent SMS texts by the local government that claimed the attacks were a continuation of the 5 July riots. The aim of these messages, as with all China's post-9/11 rhetoric about being a victim of terrorism, was to encourage sufficient public fear to justify the increasing restrictions on Uyghur culture and religion in the name of 'security'. While this was arguably effective throughout the 2000s, there was always the risk that the sense of insecurity it promoted, primarily among the Han Chinese, would create further public disorder.

This finally happened on 3 September 2009, when around 10,000 Han gathered at the North Gate in Urumqi to protest against the government's failure to protect them. Wang Lequan was singled out for blame, which was somewhat ironic given his long track record of severity (among many Uyghurs his nickname was 'Wang Shicai', in reference to Sheng Shicai, the draconian ruler of the 1930s). The crowd chanted 'The Han are angry!' and 'Kill Wang Lequan!' When Wang tried to placate them, some threw plastic bottles at him. Eventually, tear gas had to be used to disperse the crowd; in the chaos five people were killed and 14 were injured.

It was the biggest Han challenge to the Xinjiang authorities for decades (the last was the 1979 protests by those who wanted to return to Shanghai). The Xinjiang government responded quickly, and in a manner that contrasted both in speed and kind with its handling of many Uyghur protests. There were no mass arrests in Han neighbourhoods, nor were 'hostile foreign forces' blamed for inciting trouble. Instead, several days later it was announced that four Uyghurs had been prosecuted for endangering public safety, three of whom were drug addicts. Officials stated that it had been a calculated scheme to 'undermine ethnic unity', and that anyone found guilty of stabbings with syringes containing poisonous or harmful substances could face the death penalty. While Wang Lequan was not dismissed at that time, two of his chief officials were: Li Zhi, Urumqi's party secretary, and Liu Yaohua, the Urumqi police chief. A Xinhua news report went out of its way to emphasise that all was now under control in Urumqi by describing an idyllic scene in a park where 'more than 60 people, mainly senior citizens, were dancing to the tune of Paso Doble, while a father played badminton with his teenage son'. Such reassurances did not prevent many Han who had lived in the south of the city from moving to northern districts with a greater Han majority.

The announcement in October of the first convictions of those involved in the 5 July riots was probably also intended to placate Urumqi's Han citizens. Six death penalties and one verdict of life imprisonment were handed out; all those sentenced were Uyghur. No such verdicts were announced for those who had carried out revenge attacks on Uyghur neighbourhoods.

The profound difference in the handling of Han and Uyghur violence in Urumqi undermined what little 'ethnic unity' remained. Even if this concept had more than rhetorical value to the Xinjiang authorities, their actions after the September riots, and over the following year, illustrated that their main priority was to convince Han Chinese that Xinjiang was a safe and economically beneficial place for them. One crucial difference between the governance of Xinjiang (and the rest of China) in the Maoist era and governance after 'opening up' is that in the earlier period Han Chinese could basically be forced to go to Xinjiang. But since the 1980s most of the migration had been voluntary, albeit state-encouraged. After the Urumqi riots the authorities had to confront the fact that while the Han might be 'the greatest force for stability in Xinjiang' (as Ma Dazheng had previously claimed), this arrangement was perhaps more contingent, and thus more fragile, than they had realised. Most Han Chinese who have come to Xinjiang since 'opening up' don't regard themselves as being *from* the region – even after a decade or more, they perceive their hometown (*laojia* in Chinese) to be elsewhere. Their continuing presence in the region was thus due to purely functional reasons.

The Urumqi riots didn't just call into question the safety of Han civilians in Xinjiang: they also shook confidence in the region's economy. The growing perception of Xinjiang as a dangerous place had a calamitous effect on tourism – 98 per cent of tourist groups had cancelled their trips by mid-July alone, which also meant serious losses for small businesses. The lack of full internet access (until early 2010) further hampered trade. The booming construction industry also slumped, as did property prices.

In some respects the security issue was easiest to address. In the months after the Han riots in September thousands of security cameras were installed in the streets and on public transport. Checkpoints and security scanners were set up at many railway and bus stations in Xinjiang, and there was a huge increase in the numbers of soldiers and police on the streets. When I visited Urumqi in April 2010 I counted 45 soldiers and policemen on Er Dao Qiao in a ten-minute period, as well as three police vans and two army trucks.

The most intimidating of these were the soldiers of the PLA, who wore lightweight black body armour, carried compact automatic weapons and marched up and down the streets, clearing a path through the crowd. Though most soldiers were Han, a recent recruitment drive had added many Uyghurs to the police force. By contrast, there were few police or troops in the northern, predominantly Han areas of Urumqi.

In addition to the regular forces, there were also large numbers of men wearing green camouflage outfits emblazoned with red armbands. These had been recruited via advertisements promising a salary of 1,000 yuan a month in return for an ill-defined role in keeping order: most had received little or no training, and in general seemed aimless. While wandering round the city's derelict zoo, I found three next to what had been the peacock enclosure. One was lying on a stone bench, a newspaper over his face, while his companions stood and smoked. Both were middle-aged and heavy-set, and lacked a military demeanour.

When I asked them if they liked their jobs, one said, 'Yes, because it's very important.' 'That's right,' said his friend, and stood up straighter. 'We will stop any trouble.' They looked as if even the slightest threat would send them lumbering in the opposite direction.

Though these figures appeared ineffectual, they nonetheless added to the pervasive security presence in Urumqi. At night, police cars and army vans patrolled the streets, especially outside Xinjiang University (where many of the protesters on 5 July came from).

The increased securitisation was not confined to Urumqi: in Yining, 700 kilometres to the west, there were also soldiers and police patrolling the streets, as well as numerous checkpoints throughout the city, at which both drivers and pedestrians were stopped and questioned. Anyone entering the bus station was checked for weapons; the college at which I used to teach had riot shields and batons stacked at its gates.

Overall, 5,000 police were recruited in the region, with the ranks of the People's Armed Police being strengthened especially in Yining and Kashgar, no doubt due to their history of previous incidents.

Given the central role of the internet in organising the 5 July protests, it was unsurprising that the Xinjiang authorities sought to regulate it further. When internet access was restored in May 2010, it was with new restrictions. One official justified these by saying that 'the internet has become a major platform for the "three evil forces" – extremists, separatists and terrorists – to spread rumors and plot sabotage activities. So reinforcing the management of Xinjiang's internet is extremely important for national security.'

One of the new rules was the requirement that people show their ID cards before being allowed to access computers in internet cafes. It also became a crime to post comments online about separatism or independence. Network operators and internet service providers were made responsible for monitoring and reporting any such online activity. The result was a drastic reduction in the diversity of Uyghur-language websites, and a rise in self-censorship among many commentators and bloggers. However, just as with previous restrictions on internet use in

China, some were able to get round these restrictions by using proxy servers and virtual private networks, or unregistered black-market disposable phone cards on their mobiles. However, this didn't prevent a torrent of arrests in 2013 in a number of cities in Xinjiang for viewing 'illegal' websites, downloading 'illegal recordings' and sharing information, the sentences for which varied from two to 13 years in prison.

THE XINJIANG WORK FORUM

The removal of Wang Lequan from his post in April 2010 was meant to signal a shift in policy in Xinjiang, and was prudently timed: in China anniversaries are often politically sensitive. His successor, Zhang Chunxian, began by restoring full internet access in the region (probably one of the few policies in recent years to be welcomed by *all* the peoples of Xinjiang). But the biggest sign that the authorities were trying to address concerns about Xinjiang's economic situation was the convening of a special 'work forum' in May, which was attended by 350 high-level officials and was the first of its kind for Xinjiang (others had been previously held for Tibet). Its main aim was to set out a plan of 'leapfrog development' for the next ten years that would produce, once again, prosperity for all.

While this lofty goal had also been the aim of the Open Up the West campaign – which had only boosted regional inequalities – the economic stimulus package did at least acknowledge that the south of Xinjiang was most in need of help. To this end, it was announced that a number of eastern and central cities would be twinned with 82 poorly developed regions in Xinjiang. The partnership was not only financial – the municipalities were supposed to allocate between 0.3 and 0.6 per cent of their annual budgets – but would also involve the transfer of personnel and expertise. The flagship project of the scheme was the establishment of economic-development zones in Kashgar and Horgos, the two major interfaces with Central Asian markets. According to the policy outline, the scheme would 'basically complete' their infrastructure.

There were also policies that sought to alleviate poverty directly, many of which would benefit Han and Uyghurs equally. State support for the unemployed was introduced and wages were increased, as were living allowances for rural boarding-school students, thus reducing the financial burden on parents. In an effort both to attract new investment and to ease the burdens on existing companies, major tax exemptions were granted. For two years, businesses would pay no income tax, and for the following three, only half.

But the biggest change in taxation was in the region's highly profitable energy sector. In 2010 Xinjiang accounted for 30 per cent of China's oil reserves, and 34 per cent of its natural gas. Yet of the huge revenue this created, little went to the Xinjiang government (only 1.5 per cent in 2008), mainly because it was taxed by volume, not price. The vast inequality between Xinjiang (the source of the energy) and the eastern provinces that relied on its energy for their manufacturing was perfectly encapsulated by the fact that people's gas bills were cheaper in Shanghai, at the end of the pipeline, than they were in Xinjiang, because Shanghai could afford to subsidise gas prices. The Xinjiang Work Forum addressed this by introducing a tax on the price of the oil or gas, which led to a huge increase in revenue. Some of this was probably earmarked for the poverty alleviation schemes in Xinjiang, and so on the face of it this was a good policy shift. However, as Ilham Tohti argued at the time: 'Xinjiang's problem isn't a lack of money […] it's how it is allocated.'

There was also speculation about the political trading it had taken to get the central government (which essentially owns the oil and gas companies that operate in Xinjiang) to agree to pay more tax to the Xinjiang authorities, which intensified when the central government allowed the price of gas to rise shortly afterwards. The result of all this was that people and companies in Xinjiang were to some degree bearing the costs of this latest great development plan.

Though the Xinjiang Work Forum was an improvement on the previous trickle-down, north-centred development plan, its main thrust was still aimed at helping sectors of the economy from which most Uyghurs were excluded or in which they were under-represented (which argu-ably made a perverse kind of sense, given that no Uyghurs had been involved in drafting the new plan). Some of the proposed partnerships with eastern and central cities amounted to little more than providing finance for the XPCC. In many cases, this was certainly needed. While the city of Shihezi, near Urumqi, was prosperous, due to its proximity to the capital and the nearby resources, many other *bingtuan* were in poor financial shape. In 2010 the average wage for XPCC workers was 1,000 yuan a month, which, though more than most farmers earned, was still very low.

But by choosing to prop up some of the least profitable parts of the XPCC, the central government was essentially prioritising their welfare over that of Uyghur farmers. It's arguable that this is the main reason that poverty has proved so persistent in south Xinjiang. Given the region's ecological constraints – a scarcity of water and cultivable land – and the requirements of the quota system, Uyghur farmers have never been able to compete with the large-scale, state-subsidised farms of the XPCC.

However, the Xinjiang Work Forum did offer the prospect that southern Xinjiang might begin to develop its industrial sector, which would thus generate non-agricultural jobs. The pairing of Kashgar's new development zone with Shenzhen, the former fishing community that became the centre of China's economic miracle, was intended to raise expectations (and attract investment). A banner with the slogan 'Learn from Shenzhen, Pay Tribute to Shenzhen' was hung in Kashgar's People's Square, next to the huge statue of Mao Zedong. The core of the scheme was to be a large industrial park, touted as a future centre of textile and electronics production. While no one thought Kashgar was going to be another Shenzhen – the success of the latter depended on its coastal location and access to supply chains – the hype nonetheless succeeded in making Kashgar seem a good investment bet. In 2010 there was an increase in property prices of between 30 and 40 per cent, with most of the buyers coming from inner China. When a salesman for a high-end apartment complex was interviewed by the *New York Times*, he said: 'We can't build apartments fast enough for the demand [...] Come back here in five years, and you won't recognise the place.'

THE DEATH OF OLD KASHGAR

When I first visited Kashgar in 2000 it was already two places. Walking between tall white-tiled buildings, past shops selling engine parts, steamed dumplings and fireworks, was like being in the small town in Hunan province, 5,000 kilometres to the east, where I'd spent the previous year. It wasn't what I'd expected (or wanted) from an almost 3,000-year-old city that had been a major hub of trade and culture on the Silk Road, a place Marco Polo had praised ('there are a good number of towns and villages, but the greatest and finest is Cascar itself'), albeit while damning its inhabitants ('The natives are a wretched, niggardly set of people; they eat and drink in miserable fashion').

But in 2000 all I needed to do was turn off the main street. Then the buildings quickly lowered and the streets grew narrow. The adobe houses had heavy old doors through which, if ajar, you could see courtyards with rose gardens and tethered sheep, or into rooms where men hammered metal and wood. The lanes twisted, forked and wound, some quiet and shaded, others thronged with bicycles, horse-drawn carts, women wearing bright headscarves, men in square, stiffened skullcaps stepping from a mosque. In the market I saw knife-sellers, saddle-makers, sheets spread with dried snakes and seahorses, swathes of dried fruit and nuts, walls of golden dowry caskets, gaily painted cribs. I smelt the smoke of grilling lamb, saw boys whipping wooden tops, heard the ring of anvils, the bleat of sheep, the rising call to prayer.

When I was tired, or the sun too hot, I sat beneath a tarpaulin by the Id Kah mosque and slurped sour yoghurt with golden syrup through splinters of ice. Or I rested in a teahouse on a first-floor balcony, its walls turquoise with golden panels, its row of beds dark green. Birds in wicker cages chirped. An old man gifted me a red plastic heart. Later, he played a wooden flute, and then, from deep inside his canvas bag, produced the bright-red plastic of a View-Master. He offered it to me and when I looked I saw Mecca in colour: it was a hadj in 12 easy clicks.

In the streets of the Old City it was easy to succumb to orientialist notions about Kashgar being unchanging. Yet there had already been major changes since 'liberation'. As in many other Chinese cities, the 25-foot-thick city wall had mostly been torn down, and a main street was built through its centre. But in 1985 a visiting scholar to Kashgar could write that its 'only Chinese feature' was 'the towering, incongruous statue of Mao in the newer part of town'. Even throughout the 1990s and the 2000s, when every major city in China was convulsed by paroxysms of demolition and construction, Kashgar remained mostly unscathed. In 2006 the city was still able to stand in for 1970s Afghanistan in the film of *The Kite Runner*. The core of the Old City was large enough that many experts viewed Kashgar as one of the greatest examples of mud-brick settlement anywhere in the world.

The end came quickly. In early 2009 it was announced that 220,000 people from five neighbourhoods in the Old City were going to be relocated. According to the Chinese government, the old brick houses were too great a danger in the event of an earthquake. Xu Jianrong, the vice mayor of the city, sought to justify the proposed demolition of two-thirds of the Old City by asking: 'What country's government would not protect its citizens from the dangers of natural disaster?' Yet although there had been major tremors in the region during the previous two years, there was no shortage of alternative explanations for the demolition. Many saw it as a deliberate attack on Uyghur culture and identity, prompted by the violence in the city in 2008, when a truck had been driven into a group of police recruits. There were also rumours that the demolitions were an attempt to disable a network of tunnels that ran beneath the Old City.

By law, municipal authorities in China have to offer compensation to households they evict. The city also offered cash bonuses to residents who moved out early. Most homes were razed as soon as they became empty. Meanwhile, state media sought to present the demolitions as a great achievement. A nightly 15-minute infomercial combined fear-evoking statistics on seismic activity with scenes of Uyghurs dancing in front of their new concrete apartments: 'Never has such a great event, such a major event happened to Kashgar,' said the announcer. The local authorities even went so far as to put up a billboard falsely claiming that UNESCO approved of the demolitions.

While some residents of the Old City did prefer to live in a modern apartment building, for many the move was a profound disruption to their daily lives that in some cases jeopardised their livelihoods. Though it was frequently claimed by the authorities that local residents had been thoroughly consulted about the plans, no such process seems to have occurred. Crucially, there was no public discussion about alternatives to demolition. A number of organisations with experience on such issues, such as the International Scientific Committee on Earthen Architectural Heritage, had already argued that the improvements necessary to make many Old City dwellings earthquake-safe didn't require rebuilding.

Given the Communist Party's frequent suppression of many aspects of Uyghur culture, and its often-expressed assimilationist rhetoric, it's easy to view the destruction of Kashgar's Old City as yet another attempt to dilute Uyghur identity. What should caution us against accepting this as the only, or even the main reason for the demolitions is the explanation offered by Jane Jacobs, a journalist who wrote about urban issues, for the death of old neighbourhoods in American cities: old Kashgar was doomed because no one was making a fortune from it. Two stubbornly entrenched features of the Chinese system made the demolition almost inevitable: landownership and city finance. In China, all land is owned by the state; residents only have ownership rights for their homes, not the land they're built on. Even in the countryside, farmers only lease their land from village collectives. For most cities in China the main source of revenue since the late 1980s has been selling land leases to real-estate companies, who can then build on it, even if the land is currently occupied, so long as they offer compensation to the inhabitants. Residents usually end up having to move to new homes in different areas, and while for some this can mean an improvement in their material circumstances, they have no say in the matter.

Perhaps the most glaring recent example of this is the destruction of Beijing's old *hutong* neighbourhoods in the preparations for the 2008 Olympics. The fact that these buildings, so rich in Chinese heritage, and at the symbolic heart of modern China, could be destroyed, suggests that profit was at least as strong a motive for the destruction of old Kashgar. Being Han Chinese provides no more protection against market forces for China's citizens than does being Uyghur.

By the end of 2010 more than 10,000 houses in the Old City had been destroyed. When I visited the city in 2013 it was barely recognisable. Bright ten- and 15-storey buildings lined the eight-lane roads. There were shops selling gourmet cakes, Apple phones and computers, expensive bottles of wine. It all seemed to confirm what Chinese news reports were saying: that the 'once prosperous Silk Road hub' was 'experiencing something of a renaissance' and had 'a bright future ahead'.

The only thing that didn't fit this picture was the Uyghur man riding a horse through the traffic. On the back of a truck moving alongside him two men were beating a large drum while a third played a two-stringed lute; in front a man with a video camera leant precariously from the back of a battered white Mercedes. And there were still some landmarks that had been unaffected, like the Id Kah mosque. But in 2000 the mosque had been the hub from which noisy, chaotic streets of traders radiated. Now the shops near the Id Kah are housed in new buildings whose architectural style could be described as Islamic Lego: blocky, light-brown structures graced with ornamental arches. Above their doors are wooden signs saying 'Minority Folk Art' or 'Traditional Ethnic Crafts' in English and Chinese. But while it all looked far too kitsch, the notion of an 'authentic' tourist shop is an oxymoron. The shops sell the same knives, hats and musical instruments they sold a decade ago.

Further up the street I saw the first sign of the Kashgar I remembered. Bakers were prising flat circles of nan bread from the walls of clay ovens, stacking them in piles, spreading them in rows. It's hard to overestimate the centrality of nan bread to Uyghur life: it has a sacred status. Nan mustn't be thrown away, or put on the floor; in Uyghur there's a saying: 'I'd rather step on a nan.' Seeing the bread, and the people lining up to buy it, made me think that, whatever the destruction, something would endure.

The rest of the street allowed me to sustain this optimism. There were stalls selling fruit from other cities in the region – yellow melons from Hami, green grapes from Turpan – parts of sheep hanging from hooks, cobblers soling shoes. Noodles were being banged onto wood; smoke from kebabs moved slowly through the day's last light. Admittedly, the street lacked bustle, the kind you'd expect at the dinner hour. But at least there were ordinary Uyghur people buying ordinary things.

It was not until climbing Yar Beshi, a hill in the east of the city, that I understood the scale of the destruction. The path leading up was thick with dust, dust that had been houses, homes: despite being one of the two main sections designated for protection, large areas of Yar Beshi have been completely razed. From the top I could see a panorama of clay- and white-coloured six-storey buildings, more of which will probably fill the huge area – around ten city blocks – that have been cleared at the foot of the hill. It was strange to see such a vast open space in the heart of a city; it was as if there'd been some kind of disaster.

Yar Beshi has been spared for tourism. I had only gone a few streets in when I saw a sign that said 'Route 1'. A few moments later I came across a large party of tourists from Shanghai. They were wearing yellow hats and listening to a guide; perhaps they had been inspired to visit after seeing a recent Chinese state TV programme proclaim the joys of old Kashgar. In the segment the presenter announces:

Here we are in old Kashgar. It has a history of more than 2,000 years. Walking in the old town is a real experience of touring the Uyghur folk culture. With more than 20 streets, it is the only well-preserved labyrinth town in an Islamic style in China.

206

I waited for the tour to pass; after they left the streets were deserted. There was a strange hush that made me doubt whether people were still living behind the walls and doors.

Wandering through the narrow streets I came across more absence. I found staircases that went nowhere. There were fragments of walls that still had their shelves.

I saw houses in every stage of demolition: swathes of broken brick and metal; roofless shells filled with rubbish and faeces; houses that looked as if they'd been smashed by a giant fist.

I was taking photos of one house when I heard glass break. I turned and saw a Uyghur boy bend, pick up a rock, then launch it into the wreckage of a nearby house. After this, he picked up another rock, then another, each time throwing the rock fast and hard into the crater of tiles and bricks, breaking what was already broken.

The most intact house I found had been abandoned for several years. I crawled through a broken window and found a room bare except for an old Islamic calendar for 2008–9. In the next room there was enough light from the holes in the roof to see wooden shelves, carved panels, the workmanship of the ceiling.

When I exited I met a man coming out of the house next door. I asked him where the people had gone. 'I don't know,' he said. 'Maybe to one of the new places outside the centre. Many people went there.'

In this respect, the fate of old Kashgar's population was like that of Beijing's *hutongs*. In both places, the compensation the residents were given was only enough to live in new apartments located outside their former area; the property prices in their old neighbourhoods had increased too much for them to remain. The official descriptions of the drastic changes wrought on both old cities was also similar. Instead of 'demolition' or 'destruction', the street posters and newspaper articles spoke of 'renovation' and 'rejuvenation'. In 2010, the manager of the planning department for Kashgar was quoted as saying that the restoration of 10,799 'dilapidated houses' of the Old City would be completed by the end of that year.

But three years later, though most of the demolition was over, the 'restoration' was far from complete. The most finished houses were the ones on the streets behind the Id Kah, which resemble a kitsch fantasy of a southern-European street. The houses and the road bricks were complementary shades of terracotta; the balconies and doors were made from wood that had a plastic sheen. Even on these mostly residential streets, there were the same heavily varnished signs placed above the shops as could be found hanging over the souvenir shops.

But to say that these streets resemble a model village would be unfair to model villages – usually they are built with some degree of care. The houses on the fantasy street looked to have been built using the construction style common all over China. Quickly laid brick is smoothed over with concrete and then a skin of white (or terracotta) tiles applied. The aim isn't to make a durable building, just to make a building fast. The quality of replacement accommodation outside the Old City is also questionable. In the Pomegranate Compound, a new development five kilometres outside the Old City, one reporter for the *Australian* found 'an unprepossessing collection of buildings only a few years old and already showing signs of wear and tear that look like decades of decay'. These also were only built of simple bricks, and lacked quake-protection features like strengthening steel girders.

Some of the 'restored' buildings in the Old City weren't as bad. A number of these had had their adobe replaced with brick and wood, and bore some resemblance to traditional Uyghur architecture. But many of these buildings were unfinished and uninhabited. There was the same hush that prevailed in the tourist zone. It wasn't walls and doors that were missing: it was communal life that had gone.

A WIDER TRANSFORMATION

Kashgar's iconic status meant that its destruction received considerable media attention, but the same processes were at work throughout Xinjiang. The regional authorities told reporters that, by 2015,

1.5 million houses would be 'transformed'. As in Kashgar, the possible causes of this aggressive approach to urban planning were probably as much economic as ideological. But whether deliberate or not, the result in many cities in Xinjiang was a fragmentation of Uyghur communities, which in cities like Yining tended to be organised according to particular neighbourhoods (in Uyghur, *mehelle*). These communities were far from static – in Yining's *mehelle* in the early 2000s there were two- or three-storey houses with metal gates, usually a sign of recent wealth – but in the past most changes to people's homes had been of their own choosing. When I visited some of Yining's *mehelle* in 2010 there were many evident changes, the most obvious being that the muddy streets had been paved, and that there was more street lighting.

Though these changes were popular among the Uyghur residents I spoke to, the fact that many houses had been destroyed for being 'unsafe' was a source of contention. While it's common for people to feel an emotional attachment to their homes, in many cultures the home is also a rich repository of beliefs, customs and spiritual experiences. As mentioned in Chapter 4, the preparation of food is one such practice in some Uyghur communities. For some of the residents of Yining's *mehelle*, especially the older generations, the home is the site of many rituals that bring meaning to the domestic sphere. Jay Dautcher writes about how, after a stove was rebuilt or mended, it was common for family members to gather around it and laugh when it was lit for the first time, in the belief that it helped the smoke progress. Similarly, it has often been the custom to bury things under the threshold of Uyghur houses in the belief that they will provide good fortune. In the house where Dautcher lived in Yining there were toenail clippings buried under the threshold, which on Judgement Day were supposed to grow into 'a thick barrier of thorns and keep the infidels, the *xitay* [i.e. ethnic Han Chinese] out of the house'. In one variation of this story Satan will appear riding a donkey whose hairs are the strings of musical instruments. This infernal music will draw people from their homes to join him; only the hedge will stop the people from running to damnation.

Destroying the homes in which such practices occur jeopardises both the memory and the transmission of this intangible culture across generations. The overall aim of the changes to these neighbourhoods was arguably not even for the benefit of the residents. In Yining a large brick gate had been erected at the entrance to one of the *mehelle*. Next to it was a large notice in Chinese, Uyghur and English that announced this was a 'Folk Tourism Spot':

> There's no mansions and high buildings, but tiny bridge over a spar-
> kling steam, and on the far bank, a pretty little village. She is just like
> an allopatric princess with purdah, and sleeping deeply, peceful [*sic*],
> concine [*sic*] and mystery, to let yourself be seduced into love her, and
> be charmed.

As with Kashgar's Old City, people's homes had been turned into a kind of ethnic theme park, only, in Yining, there was also an eroticised element to the way in which Uyghur culture was framed. One of my Uyghur friends described the gate as 'a fucking cage'.

In other cities there was also an explicitly political rationale for the demolitions. In Hotan, where 65 per cent of the population lived in the old city, the working committee of the city government concluded that up to 17,000 houses needed to be 'transformed'. The committee justi-fied this by saying that the old city had 'always been a centre for bad elements, with many religious sites'. The slums of Heijiashan in Urumqi were also slated for demolition, and were described in state media as 'a hotbed of poverty and crime'. A local official said: 'Due to the poor management of the area, the migrants were easily incited by rioters.'

While the need to improve conditions in Heijiashan wasn't in ques-tion, as in Kashgar and elsewhere there were concerns that compen-sation would be inadequate and that replacement housing would be poor. These doubts were especially pertinent after the city authorities announced that owners of 'unlicensed' houses would only be allocated replacement homes that were 70 per cent of the original dwelling's floor area. Most Uyghurs were living in Heijiashan because they couldn't afford anywhere else, due to their low incomes. In an interview with Radio Free Asia, Dilxat Raxit of the WUC suggested: 'The real aims are firstly to take away a place where Uyghurs can go, and secondly to prevent large numbers of Uyghurs from congregating in a single place.' Support for this notion came from the announcement that the population of Urumqi was projected to double by 2020, most of whom would come from other parts of China.

Though there was no official admission that the main reason that Uyghurs were concentrated in Heijiashan was employment discrimination, Xie Min, deputy director of the slum-transformation office, did allude to the complexities of the housing issue. In an interview with the *Global Times*, he said: 'The relocation is harder in Urumqi than in other cities because this is a multi-ethnic city with a huge floating population.' Perhaps the most constructive suggestion came from Pan Zhiping, a professor at the Xinjiang Academy of Social Sciences, who proposed that after the demolition work was complete, the government should bring in new industries that would allow the different ethnic groups to work and live together.

Another aspect to the demolitions in Urumqi, Kashgar and elsewhere was how they affected urban space. The winding, labyrinthine streets of Uyghur neighbourhoods were being replaced by broad, well-lit avenues arranged on a grid system. Many cities have sought to impose this kind of organisation on their citizens – perhaps most famously Paris, radically transformed in the eighteenth century by Baron Haussmann – but it has been especially popular with colonial and authoritarian regimes. As James C. Scott, a professor of political science at Yale, argues in his book *Seeing Like a State*:

> A far-flung, polyglot empire may find it symbolically useful to have its camps and towns laid out according to formula as a stamp of its order and authority. Other things being equal, the city laid out according to a simple, repetitive logic will be easiest to administer and to police.

The changes to urban space in Tibet over the last few decades are suggestive of what is likely to occur in many cities in Xinjiang. In Lhasa the old districts have been reduced and surrounded by new construction for Han settlers. The use of a grid-like social-management system, with regularly spaced police stations, has allowed for a high degree of surveillance in many neighbourhoods.

In Xinjiang, Korla is an example of a city that has already undergone a similar transformation. Korla is a centre of oil and gas production, and has undergone a major demographic and economic shift over the last few decades. In addition to its new roads and high buildings, it has erected new public statues and monuments that present a version of its past that ignores the long history of Uyghur settlement in the area. This trend is likely to increase, as there have been proposals to expand the city's jurisdiction to incorporate the surrounding *bingtuan* areas. Given the predominantly Han Chinese composition of these areas, this will further marginalise the Uyghur community in Korla, a pattern likely to be repeated elsewhere.

Yet although the demolitions in Korla, Kashgar and elsewhere were unpopular with many residents, there's no record of any major protests against them. One possible reason is that residents didn't see it as something that was specifically targeting them, as Uyghurs, and in one sense they were right. The razing of old neighbourhoods has taken place throughout China. The primary purpose of most of the demolitions was to make property developers and city officials rich; eroding Uyghur culture was just a fringe benefit.

LOOKING FORWARD

The violence in Urumqi in 2009 (as well as in Tibet the previous year) was seen by many in China and elsewhere as a sign that their policies for minority areas needed rethinking. While a greater permissiveness towards minority culture and religion, as had occurred in the 1980s, didn't seem likely, some of the economic sources of Uyghur grievances might have been addressed. What the government chose to do instead was strengthen the economic and social position of Han Chinese in Xinjiang. While the Xinjiang Work Forum overlapped substantially with the goals of the Open Up the West campaign the previous decade, it arguably went further. By promoting investment and settlement from other Chinese provinces into south Xinjiang, it sought to integrate more closely the entirety of the region into China. As with the Open up the West campaign, the proposals of the Xinjiang Work Forum seemed more likely to benefit Han Chinese in the region than Uyghurs.

These weren't the only signs that policy wasn't going to change substantially in Xinjiang. The Work Forum also called for greater progress in 'bilingual' education. A lack of qualified Mandarin-speaking Chinese teachers in south Xinjiang meant that in 2010 only 42 per cent of students were being taught in Chinese. It was proposed that by 2015 all classes should be fully 'bilingual' and that by 2020 all students should be fluent in Mandarin. The fact that the Han Chinese had become the de facto majority group in the region, whatever official population statistics said (in 2010, Han were still supposedly 40 per cent of Xinjiang's population, and Uyghurs 46 per cent), was underlined by one official's remark that 'not everyone can be provided with an interpreter when they interact with ethnic Han people'.

The lesson for the Chinese government from the Urumqi riots was thus not that Uyghurs had grievances that should be addressed, but that Xinjiang should become more like the rest of China, and, to put it bluntly, that Uyghurs should continue to be encouraged to become more like Han Chinese. This latter proposition was controversial even within Chinese intellectual circles, with scholars like Hao Shiyuan and Wang Xi'en arguing that the state didn't need to take an active role in forging a *national* identity among ethnic minorities. Their view was that with continued social and economic development, ethnic identity would just fade away and be replaced by a stronger identification with the Chinese nation. While these views arguably didn't place much value on ethnic identity and its constituents (culture, language, community and so on), compared to the ideas of thinkers like Ma Rong and Hu Angang, who advocated that minorities should no longer be formally recognised, and that the system of regional autonomy for ethnic minority areas be abolished, it seemed a model of tolerance. For both Ma and Hu, the solution to 'the problem of Xinjiang' was to hasten the fusion of minorities and Han Chinese, with the aim of creating a mono-cultural state.

As I discuss in Chapter 8, the policies implemented in Xinjiang since 2010, especially in the religious and cultural spheres, strongly suggest that the Chinese government is keenly pursuing this objective. Another lesson that they drew from the Urumqi riots, and would apply during this period, was that there needed to be a greater focus on 'security'. The reasoning behind all the police and army patrols was that once the province reached a certain level of policing and surveillance there would be virtually no chance of any major incident occurring, a theory that has been proved wrong, and at great cost, in the last several years in Xinjiang.

But for many Uyghur communities in Xinjiang the lessons to be drawn from the violence in Urumqi were less clear. Though there would be an increase in violent confrontations between Uyghurs and the state – bombings, explosions and stabbings – there were also quieter forms of resistance.

8

'A PERFECT BOMB'

Alim was tall, skinny and in his early twenties; his upper lip had a
cloud of moustache through which a cold sore shone. When I met
him on a spring afternoon in Urumqi in 2010 he was standing by the
old camel on Er Dao Qiao that tourists have their photos taken
with. I knew little about Alim except that he had taken part in the
Urumqi protests and wanted to talk about it ('Alim' was not his real
name). When I arrived we did not shake hands or exchange greetings.
Instead he turned away, muttered 'Let's go', and, after a moment, I
followed. There were many soldiers and police on the streets, and he
did not want to be seen talking to a foreigner. Several months later
the journalist Gheyret Niyaz was sentenced to 15 years in prison for
'endangering state security' by speaking to foreign journalists.

He led me into a backstreet where two Uyghur girls were selling
pink plastic belts. We passed a mosque covered in grubby white tiles, in
front of which a man was fixing a puncture. Alim turned down an alley
lined with old broken televisions. He stopped at a door and knocked.
There was no answer, so he knocked again. 'Please wait a minute,' he
said, then brought his tongue to his sore.

Inside we passed through a storeroom piled with rugs, then entered
a smaller carpeted room. We sat down on blue cushions spread around
a low table piled with nuts, dried fruit, sweets and hunks of nan bread.
A middle-aged woman, hair wrapped in a pink scarf, came in with a
teapot and bowls. 'My aunt,' said Alim as she poured the tea. After she
left he reached over to a small black briefcase. He opened it and brought
out a laptop, which he placed on the table.

'First you should see this,' he said, then played me a clip of the factory killings in Shaoguan. I saw the people running, heard the shouts. I saw the bloodied bodies.

After it ended we were quiet. Then he said, 'The police did not stop it. They do not arrest anyone. For them, it does not matter if some Uyghurs are killed.'

We spoke about the anger this caused in Urumqi, and the organisation of the 5 July protest. He then showed me another clip, in which at first the camerawork was shaky, so that all I could see were people walking quickly. Their faces were blurred, their speech unclear; then I saw someone I knew. Alim was waving his arms in the air and shouting. The expression on his face was joy. It suggested elation, a sense of release.

I could also hear chants and shouts. Alim said many of the protesters had been calling out 'Justice' or 'Wake up'.

'Because most Uyghurs do not understand what is happening. They think that if they do not do some political thing there will be no problem. It is because of this that we are not so strong. If you have a heart, there can only be three ways: you are arrested, dead or you go abroad.'

The video clip was from the early part of the protest, before the violence began. Alim was still there when the police began using force. He was also one of the protesters who threw stones in response.

'I will not do that again. But we were so angry.'

But despite the provocation of the security forces, Alim did not retaliate further: 'That night I stop two young men who were beating a Chinese very badly. They would kill him if I did not. Several days later, I did not know why I do this.'

The attacks by Han mobs on Uyghur neighbourhoods on 7 July changed his mind. He claimed the vigilantes had been shouting 'Exterminate Uyghur, make the Han stronger'.

When I asked him how the violence had changed life in Urumqi, he said the biggest difference was that 'many Chinese respect us now. They are scared of us. They have seen our strength.'

For Alim, the lessons of the riots were very different to those drawn by the authorities. He said, 'I have a question for you. Do you think the peaceful protest can work?'

'Yes,' I said, without hesitation. It seemed axiomatic.

'I thought so too,' he said. 'But now I do not think so. We try many times but they do not listen. Just arrest and kill our people. My brother is in prison now. For nothing. There is no trial, you are not the guilty man, but they keep you for two months, maybe half a year.' Alim shook his head. 'The only thing to do is fight. If I had a perfect bomb that could kill 100, or 1,000, I would use it. Or if we have 1,000 Uyghurs with AK-47s. We only need to kill 1,000 Chinese and the others will leave.'

'What if they don't?'

'I think most of them will. If not, we must kill 1,000 more,' he said calmly. 'Then they would go. The Chinese are not brave.'

'Maybe. But isn't there a difference between ordinary Chinese people and soldiers? What have they done to you?'

'If they are here in Xinjiang, they are guilty, unless they are the sick, women, old or the child.'

I pointed out that the rioters had killed a number of women.

'That was a mistake,' he said, then picked up a piece of paper. 'There are three ways for us,' he said, and drew arrows pointing in different directions. 'The first way is help from abroad. From America or Britain.' He looked at me pointedly – as if it was somehow my fault – then crossed out the arrow. 'This will not happen. No one will make the Chinese government do something. The second way is peaceful protest. We get closer to government. We hope they change our conditions.'

He drew a line through this.

'The third way is Taliban. In 2010 nothing will happen. But you should be here in 2011. If you are here then, you will see something.'

I never saw or spoke to Alim again. But in 2011, as the second anniversary of the Urumqi riots approached, I thought of him and wondered if I would indeed 'see something'. When the time came, nothing happened in Urumqi, but at the end of July 2011 there were two violent incidents in south Xinjiang. In Hotan on 18 July there was an attack on a police station, an incident the government described as 'an organised crime'. They claimed that 'several thugs' armed with explosives and grenades had broken into the police station and taken hostages, then displayed a flag 'with separatist messages'. Though this account could not be independently verified, the WUC didn't dispute that a crowd had stormed the police station, though they claimed it had been caused by mass arrests in the region.

The details of the violence in Kashgar on 30 and 31 July were also hazy. According to the authorities, on the first day there were two small explosions, after which several men hijacked a truck, killed its driver and drove to a street of food stalls, where they attacked people with knives. Though the motivation behind the attacks was unclear, the fact that they took place on a street with many Han-owned businesses was perhaps significant. On the following day, according to official sources, another explosion took place at a restaurant that was then stormed by attackers who killed the owner and a waiter. Several days later the government claimed that an attacker who had been captured had confessed that the group's leader had been trained in Pakistan to make bombs and guns by ETIM. The picture was further complicated by claims in September 2011 from an organisation calling itself the Turkestan Islamic Party (TIP) that it had been responsible for both incidents. In 2008, the TIP had released a video saying it had carried out bus bombings in Xinjiang and Yunnan.

While I never imagined that Alim had played any role in these incidents, they made me wonder how many Uyghurs had drawn the same conclusions as him from the violence in Urumqi. For Alim, the lessons from Urumqi were that even the most peaceful protest would be brutally suppressed, and that the Chinese authorities didn't value the safety and security of its Uyghur citizens. At this point it is of course vital to stress the considerable gulf between, firstly, expressing hatred for a government (or ethnic group) to a foreigner in private and the willingness to commit an act of violence, and, secondly, individual intent and having the organisational and financial capacity to carry out a planned attack. However, as Sean Roberts argued in an influential report on the possibility of terrorism in Xinjiang in 2012, 'given the animosity that many Uyghurs harbor for the Chinese state, it is difficult to imagine that there are not at least some who would seek to use violence'.

There were certainly more violent incidents in Xinjiang in the years after 2009 than there had been in the 2000s. At the end of December 2011 there were reports of a number of deaths in Pishan county, near the Pakistan border, following a confrontation with police. The government claimed that a small group of Uyghurs who were going to Pakistan to train in jihadist camps had taken several shepherds hostage. When confronted by the police, they apparently attacked the officers with knives, forcing the police to open fire. As with the incidents in July 2011, there was no way to verify this version of events. Some observers suggested that these Uyghurs might just have been trying to flee both the poverty of their remote cotton-growing region and the repressive religious policies of the local authorities – the WUC said they had been searching people's houses for prohibited religious materials.

There was more violence in Kargilik (known as Yecheng in Chinese) in south Xinjiang at the end of February 2012. Once again, there were very different versions of the incident. According to the Chinese government, a group of eight Uyghur men attacked pedestrians with axes and knives on Happiness Road. State media reported that 15 civilians died, as well as one police officer. All the attackers were killed by the police. Chinese officials characterised the event as a 'terrorist attack'. The WUC didn't deny that the attack was premeditated, but claimed it had only targeted security forces, and that it had been sparked by mass arrests in the region.

The next major confrontation took place in April 2013 in Bachu county (known as Maralbexi in Uyghur), in the Kashgar region. Officials said that 21 people died in what was 'certainly a terrorist attack'. They said a gang of 14 people hiding in a house had taken three community officials hostage after they found knives during a search. When the police arrived, they killed the hostages and 12 police officers, and set the house on fire. Six of the gang were killed and eight captured during subsequent clashes with law-enforcement agents. There were several other explanations for the violence, none of which could be confirmed. One resident told Radio Free Asia that the cause was a woman being made to lift her veil by a community-watch officer. Another explanation, offered by the WUC, suggested that there had instead been a protest against continual raids on Uyghur homes. The people opened fire on the protest, killing a young man, and then the crowd retaliated. The picture was further complicated by a police officer in a neighbouring county saying he had been told that the house searches in Bachu were for a suspect from the Turpan region, where security had been increased after a Han Chinese man stabbed a Uyghur boy to death several weeks before.

This incident in Turpan seems to have been behind the violence on 26 June 2013 in Lukqun, in the Turpan region, that left 35 people dead. According to official sources, in the early morning a group of Uyghur men armed with knives attacked a local police station, killing 24 people. Police then opened fire on the attackers, killing 11. According to state media, this was a terrorist attack that had been planned since January, when two men formed 'an illegal religious organisation' whose members listened to 'jihadist' propaganda distributed by ETIM. While the Chinese government provided no more evidence for this claim than had been offered in support for the many similar assertions in the past, what made the Lukqun incident unusual was that many of the conventional counter-explanations didn't apply. Lukqun is a mostly prosperous region that has had little Han settlement, and whose local officials seem to take a more relaxed approach to religion than their counterparts in many southern towns.

Though there are still many other possible explanations, to date the most plausible is the killing of a young Uyghur boy by a middle-aged Han man, who mistakenly thought the boy was trying to steal from his factory. Although the authorities in Lukqun initially pledged to punish the killer severely, local police later concluded that the man was suffering from mental illness and so was not responsible. Religious leaders were said to have warned that residents felt the authorities were underplaying the gravity of the crime. However, this still does not explain how this general dissatisfaction culminated in so many deaths – the crowd may have gathered to protest peacefully, and the authorities may then have reacted with violence. Establishing the facts of the incident was further hampered by the internet being cut off in the area, a tactic the authorities have used repeatedly since the 2009 Urumqi riots.

A NEW CYCLE OF VIOLENCE?

What should we infer from this sequence of violent confrontations between Uyghurs and the state? From the Chinese government's perspective, these incidents were all committed by terrorists motivated by religious extremism whose ultimate goal is to separate Xinjiang from China. Though they took place in different locations – in both north and south Xinjiang – they were almost all attributed to terrorist organisations like ETIM. Despite the official admission that south Xinjiang (where most of these incidents took place) is considerably impoverished compared to the north of the region, the official explanation for all dissent in Xinjiang thus remains the same as the line adopted after 9/11.

In the wake of the Kunming attacks in 2014, there has been an unfortunate tendency in some sections of the Western media to reclassify a lot of previously ambiguous incidents in Xinjiang as terrorist acts. But it's worth stressing that before Kunming there was considerable journalistic and academic scepticism about the Chinese government's terrorism narrative. While all the above-mentioned incidents were serious breaches of public order, in many of which violence seemed to have been committed by both Uyghurs and the security forces, there was no more evidence that these actions were instigated by Islamic terrorist forces than there had been in the 2000s. Though some of these incidents were claimed by an organisation identifying itself as the TIP, few experts regarded them as being able to do more than post videos online. According to Dru Gladney, the TIP are 'so shadowy and nebulous that almost anyone could step in and say they were this group and get support'. In the past this group had claimed – in videos assembled from materials easily available on the internet – to be behind incidents for which they were not responsible, including explosions on two buses in Kunming in 2008, claims that the Chinese government subsequently denied.

Too little is known about the causes of these incidents to rule out entirely the possibility that the TIP or some other organisation played a role in them. But the available evidence suggests that these were more likely to have been isolated events, born of particular, local complaints, rather than an expression of ideological grievances (such as a wish for independence) or inter-ethnic hostility. In many cases, the triggers of violence for those involved may have been the same as those that lead people to protest throughout China: the misuse of power by local officials; the overly strict application of religious or family-planning policies; the unlawful seizure of land. However, one difference is that most Uyghurs are more vulnerable to such injustices, owing to their marginalisation within the region's economy, itself the result of system-atic inequalities in employment and investment over several decades. This, coupled with the severe security policies applied to Uyghurs in the region, especially since the 1990s (such as house-to-house searches and mass arrests within their communities), has exacerbated resentment against the state, and often, by association, Han Chinese.

Another difference between violent acts in Xinjiang and those in the rest of China is the way in which they are described. When a man in a wheelchair tried to blow himself up at Beijing airport in July 2013, it was not described as terrorism, nor were the explosions outside Communist Party headquarters in Taiyuan, in Shanxi province, in November 2013. These different ways of framing events have profound consequences not only for those accused of being responsible (in terms of punishment) but also for the way that the police and army treat the communities they come from.

Ultimately, an opinion on whether or not China has been (or will be) a target for Islamist terrorism requires a judgement about what constitutes 'terrorism'. The incident in Tiananmen Square in late October 2013 was an especially contested event. On 28 October a jeep exploded in the square after crashing into the wall of the Forbidden City. Five people were killed, including the three passengers, and more than 40 were injured. The Beijing police said it was a terrorist attack, and that the driver and passengers were Uyghurs (it was later claimed that it had been a man, his wife and his mother). The police also claimed to have found knives and a 'jihadist flag' in the jeep. The government blamed the attack on ETIM.

Suggestions that it might have been an isolated incident born of a particular grievance (and thus not terrorism) were condemned by then Chinese Foreign Ministry spokesman Hong Lei as a 'slander on China's ethnic and religious policy' that amounted to 'connivance with terrorists'. Even the appearance of a video a month later on social media from a group identifying itself as the TIP, condoning (though not, as some claimed, admitting responsibility for) the attacks, failed to settle the issue. On Twitter Nicholas Bequelin of Human Rights Watch questioned the timing of the release of the video, suggesting that the temporal interval cast doubt on the veracity of their claim. But five months later there was a far less ambiguous incident.

KUNMING AND AFTER

The killings in Kunming in March 2014 were one of the most shocking acts of violence in China's recent history. They also seemed a major departure from other incidents linked with Xinjiang, not least because they did not take place in the region. Given the planned nature of the attack, and the targeting of civilians, it was unsurprising that the Western media followed the lead of the Chinese media by describing the incident as a terrorist attack. Chinese media called the event 'China's 9/11', and placed it in a context of supposedly similar terrorist acts 'over the past two decades'. The Chinese *Global Times* said that it and the Tiananmen explosion were indicative of a 'despicable trend that separatists are targeting civilians out of Xinjiang'.

This notion was also echoed by many Western media outlets, which offered different versions of the idea that the Kunming attacks represented 'a dramatic escalation of China's simmering Uyghur problem'. The BBC article from which this quote is taken was careful to say that this would only be true *if* the attack did turn out to be the work of Xinjiang separatists (which again, there was no evidence for, barring that the attackers were all thought to be Uyghurs).

Unfortunately a number of other media outlets were less cautious in offering explanations. The online news website *Quartz* ran a story with the headline 'China's bloody train station attack shows how terrorism is spreading out of Xinjiang', with an accompanying infographic of 'Terrorist attacks and ethnic violence since 2005'. In the article itself, the fact that the attacks 'took place far from the [*sic*] Xinjiang' was said to be 'a sign that insurgents are branching out'. There was little consideration given to the facts of the incident that argued against it being part of a wider movement. While some planning had obviously been required, the use of nothing but knives suggested a low level of funding and organisation.

But after the Kunming attacks there was more than just speculation masquerading as coverage. In order to be able to tie the Kunming attack into a longer narrative of violence involving Uyghurs, there was a selective presentation of facts about 'terrorism' in Xinjiang. Both CNN and the BBC mentioned that ETIM had been put on one of the US terrorist lists, but not that it had been later quietly removed. In a similar fashion, CNN also spoke of 'Uyghur groups' that 'claimed responsibility for bus bombs in Shanghai and Yunnan prior to the Olympics in 2008', without mentioning that these claims were discredited (including by the Chinese government). *The Economist* claimed that 'scarcely a week passes in Xinjiang without anti-government violence'. If this is true for Xinjiang, then the same can probably be said for every other province in

China. The Kunming incident was thus taken as a licence to reclassify prior, unconnected incidents as part of a terrorist campaign. The issue of how to refer to these events is more than just semantics: bolstering the Chinese government's claims helps to legitimise its repressive security policies.

Within China, the Kunming attacks led to an outpouring of online anger directed against Uyghurs. While the central government was at pains to stress that the ethnicity of the attackers wasn't a significant issue, a number of local-government offices added fuel to the fire. One government bureau in Guangxi province, which borders Yunnan, posted a notice asking residents to report any Uyghurs they saw in the area. Similar notices were posted in a number of other provinces.

However, there were also online voices who urged moderation. A post from popular blogger Han Han condemning terrorism, while also 'wishing that we don't place our hatred on an entire ethnicity or an entire religion', was shared over 200,000 times. The incident also exposed the wide distrust of state media coverage. Feng Xiang, a journalist for the investigate newspaper *Southern Weekend*, posted a comment on his Weibo account that the authorities 'never tell you what really happens'. Other bloggers went further by calling into question government policy in Xinjiang: 'I think using force to keep stability is not the right way. We should find the root of their hatred and that would be the right way to solve the conflict,' wrote another user, whose Weibo account was deleted soon after and who received a warning from Beijing police's cyber-security unit that 'as public figures you need to be responsible for what you say'. Under Chinese law, internet users can be imprisoned if their posts go viral and prove to be 'rumours'.

The four surviving Kunming attackers would be tried and convicted in September 2014. Three men were sentenced to death; a woman was given life imprisonment. But the reasons for the killings remained a mystery, unless of course one chose to suspend the usual (and justified) disbelief in the Chinese government's reflexive deployment of its narrative of terrorism fuelled by 'religious extremism'. The Kunming attack was awful and unjustifiable, but that didn't mean there was no need for evidence.

At the time of writing, the main alternative explanation to the Chinese government's is that the Uyghurs were asylum seekers who had planned to escape to Laos via Yunnan. Many Uyghurs had apparently left Hotan in late 2013 after a police crackdown, and then travelled to Yunnan, hoping to reach South East Asian countries. In October 2013 around 30 Uyghurs were apparently arrested at the Laos border. The Kunming attackers were supposedly among those not caught at the time, and would have been in a perilous situation, as arrest warrants for them had been issued and they lacked local ID cards. Being unable either to escape to Laos or to remain in China, the attacks may thus have been a last, desperate act of revenge.

The source of this idea was an anonymous resident of Kunming, interviewed by Radio Free Asia. There's often some reservation among academics and journalists about this organisation's coverage, mainly because its impartiality is often questioned (it is funded by the US government), but in this instance the idea seems plausible. Uyghurs have been fleeing to South East Asian countries in increasing numbers since 2009. Even those who managed to leave China have found little security, as most of these countries have been willing to send Uyghurs back to China, despite concerns for their safety. In 2009, Cambodia forcibly repatriated 20 Uyghurs who had taken refuge there, two of whom were sentenced to life in prison, another to 17 years. In 2010, seven Uyghurs were deported from Laos, while in 2011 Malaysia sent 11 Uyghurs back to China, even though they had all claimed political asylum. At the time of writing, China is seeking the return of Uyghurs from the Thai seaside town of Songkhla, claiming they are all terrorists trying to reach Syria. Though few facts are known about these people, the presence of many women and children among them seems to argue against their being jihadists seeking to fight abroad (most don't take their families with them).

Of course, this notion of the Kunming attackers as frustrated asylum seekers remains only a theory – as is usually the case with major crimes in China, little or nothing is known about the perpetrators (something that is unlikely to change without profound judicial reform or a free press in China). The closest thing to corroboration of the idea that the eight had previously tried to leave the country was a statement from Yunnan's Communist Party secretary, who said the terrorists had originally planned to leave China to wage holy war.

If much about the Kunming attacks remained uncertain, the same could not be said about the official response. Xi Jinping's administration reacted in the same way former leaders had to the Urumqi riots in 2009, the Yining protests in 1997 and the Baren incident in 1990. Throughout the remainder of 2014 the authorities emphasised the need for tighter security, and stricter responses to 'illegal activity'. Xi Jinping said he wanted terrorists to be like 'rats scurrying across the street, chased by all the people'. This had visible effects in many cities, and not just in Xinjiang. There was an increased security presence at airports and train and bus stations throughout China. In Beijing security was tightened around Tiananmen Square, with the addition of concrete barriers to prevent vehicles from driving along the pavement, as had occurred in the incident in October 2013. Though these were sensible precautions, the utility of some other measures was less obvious. For instance, the Urumqi authorities banned water and yoghurt from public buses, while in Kashgar matches were banned.

As in the previous year, internet usage was again placed under greater surveillance. In April 2014 the Aksu local government offered to pay informants for reporting suspicious behaviour, such as any indication that a person planned to use the internet 'to produce, extract, reproduce, post, or publish audio, video, pictures, or text which includes content that incites national separatism, ethnic hatred or discrimination'. The local authorities also offered rewards for information about 'someone watching a reactionary DVD, or download[ing] reactionary videos on mobile phones or computers'. In May 2014, a state newspaper reported that 232 individuals had been arrested since March 2013 for 'dissemination of violent or terrorist videos'.

But despite a high military and police presence throughout Xinjiang, there were two major violent incidents in Urumqi, less than a month apart. On 30 April 2014 an explosion outside the south railway station killed three people and injured 79. No one claimed responsibility for the attacks, though the TIP was misreported as having done so in a video, when all it did was offer approval. While the motivations behind the bombings remain unknown, some said it was timed to coincide with the arrival of a train bearing Han migrant workers from Chengdu in Sichuan province. One worker from Chongqing summarised the very different experiences and perspective of Han migrant workers and Uyghurs in Urumqi's labour market when he later told Reuters: 'We come this far because the wages are good […] Also, the Uyghur population is small. There aren't enough of them to do the work.'

The increased security in Urumqi was unable to prevent another attack on 22 May. In the early morning two cars crashed into a busy market in a predominantly Han area. One eyewitness described seeing two SUVs driving side by side, progressing quite slowly – because they were driving over people. 'They were all old people – they were hit once and did not get back up,' he said. Explosives were then tossed into the crowd, and then the vehicles burst into flames. One shopkeeper recalled: 'I thought it was an earthquake.' Over 30 people were killed in the incident, but as before, the reasons behind it were unclear.

During the summer of 2014 the authorities maintained their emphasis on security. At a mass-sentencing rally in Yining on 28 May an audience of 7,000 watched 55 suspects being pronounced guilty of a variety of crimes, including terrorism. Though these rallies used to be common, they have rarely been used since the 'Strike Hard' campaigns after the 1997 Yining protests. The aim of the mass sentencing was probably to reassure the Han population of Xinjiang that the government was in control of security, especially after the Urumqi attacks, while serving as a threat to potential criminals.

Predictably, Uyghurs' religious beliefs and practices also came under greater scrutiny. During the holy month of Ramadan many local authorities put pressure on state employees and students not to observe the fast. Though this had been common practice in previous years – at least as far back as 2001 – in 2014 the authorities made a particularly strenuous effort. In Kashgar, cafeterias at some government offices kept records of who ate lunch, while some university students were required to eat lunch with their teachers and forced to drink from bottles of mineral water before sunset (when the fast ends). There were also reports of surprise inspections of dormitories in the early hours of the morning to make sure students weren't eating before the fasting period. A number of students had their laptops and smartphones inspected to check they contained no religious content.

Religious education was also targeted. The government announced that 190 children had been 'rescued' from illegal religious schools in Urumqi, and that dozens had been arrested. Exactly what constituted an illegal religious school was unclear – but, under Chinese law, which only allows religious activities in government-registered venues, something as innocuous as a storytelling session to children is prohibited. Though such activities have long been subject to harassment, what was new was the implication that the children had been forced to take part in these activities.

But of all the religious restrictions imposed on Muslims in Xinjiang in 2014, the most invasive was the focus on personal appearance. Posters went up in public places with pictures of prohibited styles of dress and facial hair, while signs hung from government buildings repeated the message. In Karamay men with beards and women wearing headscarves were temporarily banned from taking public buses. In Kashgar and other cities, officials at checkpoints detained women wearing any clothing they deemed too Islamic, especially veils or niqabs, as part of an initiative called 'Project Beauty'. Some offenders were made to watch a film about the joys of exposing their faces and encouraged to be 'practitioners of modern culture'. An article in the *Xinjiang Daily* newspaper warned women of the potential dangers of Islamic dress, among which was the claim that black robes frightened babies and caused depression. In

Turpan the local government announced it was considering imposing fines of up to 500 yuan for anyone wearing a veil or a cloak in public. While all this was done in the name of fighting 'religious extremism', it's likely that many Uyghurs saw it as another attack on their cultural and religious beliefs.

'UTTERLY VILE': THE TRIAL OF ILHAM TOHTI

The Chinese Communist Party tends to promote an air of infallibility around itself, but there have been instances when it has admitted to mistakes in its approach. But in the case of Xinjiang and other minority regions, there has been no substantial re-evaluation of policy since Hu Yaobang's proposals in the 1980s. Throughout the violence of 2013 and 2014, state media published editorials in which Xi Jinping and other top officials were quoted as saying that government policy in Xinjiang was correct. The old Maoist strategy of identifying 'model villages' was employed; the development of Daxi village, in Weili county, was cited as proof that 'with the Party's good policies and the unity of people of all ethnic groups, locals will surely live comfortable and happy lives'. The problems in Xinjiang were thus not caused by government policy, but by those who blocked it.

In September 2014 the government signalled its refusal to reconsider its policies in Xinjiang by sentencing Ilham Tohti, one of the most prominent Uyghur intellectuals in China, to life imprisonment for the crime of 'separatism'. His real 'crime', however, had been to question government policy in Xinjiang publicly. At the end of 2005 Tohti founded the Uighur Online website 'to provide Uyghurs and Han with a platform for discussion and exchange'. However, according to Xinhua, China's state news agency, Tohti used the website to exploit 'his status as a teacher to bewitch, lure and coerce ethnic minority students' into 'forming a separatist clique'. It justified the life sentence by arguing that his 'attitude was utterly vile, and therefore he should be heavily punished'.

Tohti had been arrested in January 2014, along with ten of his students, but even then it wasn't obvious how much danger he was in. Tohti had been under surveillance for more than a decade, including in the classroom, and had been arrested on a number of previous occasions, most recently in 2009, when he was quickly released. But when the authorities charged him with separatism in July 2014, it became apparent that they meant to silence him for good.

What made the charge especially perverse was that Tohti has never advocated that Xinjiang should be an independent country. His attitude to Uyghur identity has also been flexible. Tohti had previously argued that 'any thinking that doggedly stresses a particular group's cultural uniqueness and superiority, thus making it non-inclusive, is closed-minded and a thing of the past. It will inevitably kill the culture it means to enshrine and protect.' However, he had also criticised the government's efforts to impose

a false and calculated ethnic harmony. Use of administrative means to keep ethnic groups together is, in essence, a use of force that breeds division, whereas tolerance as a means to encourage diversity will lead to mutual harmony and unity.

But the main reason Tohti was charged was the shift in the political climate in China since Xi Jinping took power in early 2013. Since then there has been a tightening of government control of the internet, the media (including foreign journalists) and civil society. When Tohti failed to parrot the official narrative about the October 2013 Tiananmen crash being the result of Islamic terrorism, and instead suggested other factors may have caused the incident, he became a target. His comment to a Reuters journalist that 'the use of violent means happens because all other outlets for expression are gone' was a direct repudiation of the official line.

After this statement, Tohti was followed by unmarked cars. In November 2013 plain-clothes security agents rammed his car while his two young children were in the back seat. The agents got out and threatened to kill him and his family if he kept speaking to the foreign press. After his arrest he was held in leg shackles for a month, even when he went to sleep, according to his lawyer. The prosecuting attorney's office defended this with the bizarre allegation that Tohti had been deliberately coughing to disturb other prisoners, which had led to fights with them. He was also not served halal food, forcing him to go on hunger strike for ten days.

The verdicts in high-profile trials like Tohti's are always predetermined. The actual trials take only a few days (Tohti's took two), which speaks volumes about the current state of China's legal system. Though China today is very far from being the totalitarian state that many people still imagine it to be, its judiciary remains in thrall to political power. Tohti appealed the sentence, but the appeal was denied in November 2014. Barring a major political shift in China, he is unlikely to be released for a very long time.

PLAYING THE SAME SONG

The need for the kind of constructive, reasoned discussion about Chinese policies in Xinjiang that Tohti sought to promote has never been greater. But just as the Urumqi riots were met with yet another phase of increased securitisation and repressive religious and cultural policies aimed at Uyghurs, so the incidents in 2013 and 2014 triggered a similar response. While it's difficult to know the extent to which the violence was itself a reaction to the mass arrests, surveillance and religious restrictions, these measures certainly appear to be unpopular with most Uyghurs, and thus can only worsen relations between Uyghurs and the state.

However, at the time of writing it seems that the authorities have all but given up trying to win Uyghur hearts and minds. Though a campaign was launched to do just this, its actual purpose appears to be to create a community surveillance system. The stated purpose of the

'Visit, Benefit, Come Together' campaign that started in early 2014 was for Communist Party officials to visit rural communities and to try to address their grievances. However, the fact that the teams were told to compile detailed reports on each village household that included not just demographic data, like employment status, but also the degree of religious observance in each family, including whether the men have beards or the women wear veils, suggests quite different priorities.

Further evidence that the government places more importance on the welfare of its Han citizens in Xinjiang comes from the most recent proposals to improve the region's economy. Just as with the Xinjiang Work Forum in 2010, these seem most likely to benefit the Han population. Unsurprisingly, the XPCC is at the centre of Beijing's latest vision for Xinjiang's economy; the government continues to encourage migration from other provinces to swell the ranks of the *bingtuan*. In June 2014 there were a number of articles in state media touting the advantages of joining the XPCC, the oddest of which was based around a mass wedding ceremony for 50 young couples from the XPCC in Urumqi. The event was 'designed to showcase the prosperous lives that most of them have forged working for the organisation' (which, as mentioned earlier, is certainly not the case for all XPCC members). One groom apparently gushingly remarked: 'I love this place where we can bring our talent into play.' His wife added, even less believably: 'Xinjiang boasts beautiful scenery and the locals are frank and great-hearted. I feel happy to do what I like to do in such a lovable region.'

One of the main tasks for the XPCC will apparently be the construction of a number of new cities in Xinjiang, which officials claim will bring employment, prosperity and stability. These are likely to resemble the kinds of grid-based, easy-to-police cities that many of Xinjiang's urban centres are already being transformed into. While few details of the new cities' locations have been provided, one will apparently be near Hotan, suggesting that the intention is to shift the demographics of south Xinjiang away from having a Uyghur majority permanently, and thus further marginalise Uyghur language and culture. Wang Dahao, a

Xinjiang-based writer, was quoted as saying that the cities could help promote 'modern culture'.

Neither the provision of this apparently rosy future for Xinjiang nor the heightened security presence throughout the region was able to prevent further violence in the summer and autumn of 2014. The particulars of the first incident, in Yarkant (known as Shache in Chinese) in south Xinjiang on 28 July, were especially opaque, even by the standards of reporting in Xinjiang. The authorities in Xinjiang claimed a large group of militants armed with knives and axes had attacked police stations and government offices in the area, killing 37 civilians. Police responded by shooting 59 'terrorists' and arresting 215 others. The mastermind of the attacks was said to have close ties to ETIM.

The version of events offered by a supposed 'eyewitness' that was published on the WUC website could not have been more different. The account contended that the incident had involved the killings by security forces of 45 women and children who had gathered together to celebrate the end of Ramadan. The account was both vague and contradictory, claiming first that 'everyone who was there was killed on the spot', then in a subsequent paragraph that after this 'armed forces went in and killed off those who were still alive, some wounded were strangled and their head [*sic*] were cut off. Among them there were newly born toddlers, old ladies and breast-feeding mothers.'

This kind of hyperbole recalled the exaggerated account of the 7 July attacks in Urumqi published on the WUC website in July 2009, and arguably went even further by estimating that the number of victims was 'from three thousand to five thousand', and then adding: 'it is possible that the actual numbers are much higher'.

If even the lower estimate was correct, then the Yarkant incident would have been one of the worst instances of violence in the history of the People's Republic of China. Yet even allowing for what appears to be a growing tendency for police in Xinjiang to shoot at suspects without warning (powers also granted to special police units in Beijing, Shanghai and Guangzhou), these numbers seem unbelievably high, and, most importantly, have not been backed up by another source. A different, if overlapping account was offered by the Uyghur American Association, who claimed that a Uyghur family had been killed on 18 July, and that the violence on 28 July was directed at a protest against the deaths. A WUC spokesman later said the number of dead and injured had been about 100.

The Yarkant incident was quickly followed by the murder on 30 July of Xinjiang's most senior imam, Jume Tahir, aged 74, who was not only the imam of Kashgar's Id Kah mosque, but also the president of the Xinjiang Islamic Association. Shortly after morning prayers he was fatally stabbed by three young Uyghur men. Two were shot and killed by the police while fleeing; the surviving attacker later said on TV that Tahir 'was the target of our jihad because he distorted the doctrine'. Like many such televised confessions in China, this had more than a whiff of coercion about it. Many instead blamed the assassination on Tahir's public support for the government's religious policies in Xinjiang. Whether or not the imam's murder was connected to the Yarkant incident (that is, whether or not it was revenge) remains unknown.

Details are also still vague about an incident in Luntai county, southwest of Urumqi, on 21 September. At first the government claimed that only two people had died in a series of explosions at a shop, a market and two police stations. Four days later it amended the death toll to 50 people, 40 of whom were the attackers (the government may have initially been trying to downplay the incident). It claimed that a Uyghur man named Mamat Tursun was responsible for the 'organised and serious' attack and that Tursun had been 'operating as an extremist since 2003'. Radio Free Asia quoted a local teacher's claims that the explosions were in retaliation for forced evictions in the area.

THE MAIN BATTLEFIELD?

At the end of November 2014 *China Daily*, a state-run English-language newspaper, carried a report on the anti-terror campaign since the

Urumqi market attacks. It described Xinjiang as the 'main anti-terrorism battlefield' and claimed that 115 terrorist cells had been eliminated in the previous six months alone through 'extremely tough measures and extraordinary methods'. This was intended to justify the intensive securitisation and religious restrictions that had been put in place; special mention was given to the utility of information gained from 'intensive inquests of detained suspects', which had apparently been responsible for stopping 40 per cent of terror cells.

The Chinese government's position was thus the same as it had been 13 years previously, when it announced in late 2001 that it was also a victim of Islamic terrorism. While this book has sought to point out the many flaws and inconsistencies in this argument, and instead highlighted the many other explanations for confrontations between Uyghurs and the Chinese state, incidents like the Kunming attack, and the Urumqi market bombing in May 2014, should raise questions about whether the Chinese government's claims must now be taken more seriously. It's undeniable that a small group of Uyghurs are choosing to use violence against the Chinese state, and are deliberately targeting civilians. For this reason, they qualify as terrorist acts (unlike many other previous incidents in Xinjiang). Can one thus conclude that Xinjiang is undergoing a surge in Islamic terrorism?

In some respects, the same counterarguments remain valid. At the time of writing, there's still no more evidence that ETIM, the TIP or any other 'terrorist' organisation has had any significant involvement in carrying out or enabling violent incidents in Xinjiang. No matter how often Chinese government officials (or terrorism 'experts') deploy these acronyms, the lack of credible evidence regarding their involvement means that we should continue to regard such statements as attempts to divert attention from the real causes of dissent. Though it's not inconceivable that the Kunming attacks and the Urumqi bombings represent the start of a different phase of more targeted and organised violence, at the time of writing this conclusion is premature. To the extent that recent violent incidents in Xinjiang follow any pattern, it's one where a local grievance triggers the anger of a community, whose members then quickly organise a protest (or riot) at a police station or government building, leading to clashes with security personnel.

As for the question of whether the violence, as either terrorism or a semi-spontaneous expression of public anger, is being driven by 'religious extremism', the answer is broadly the same as in the 2000s. While more conservative interpretations of Islam have gained in popularity in some Uyghur communities, religious ideology doesn't seem to be fuelling the violence. Some Uyghurs have undoubtedly been exposed to jihadist materials and ideas, mainly through the internet, but there's no evidence these have played any significant causal role. At most, one might argue that they have provided a source of inspiration for incidents like the Kunming attacks or the Urumqi bombings (though one could argue that they could just as easily have been inspired by the depiction of terrorism in Hollywood films or TV programmes like *24* or *Homeland*).

Ultimately, too little is known about the identities and motivations of those who carry out attacks like the Urumqi market bombing. Though the Chinese government often names those it holds responsible for such attacks, it usually only does so if the alleged masterminds are already dead. Almost nothing is known about the backgrounds and circumstances of those accused of involvement, mainly because of the severe restrictions on reporting in Xinjiang: access to local communities is hindered by obstruction and harassment by local officials and security personnel. A further obstacle is that for many Uyghurs talking to foreign reporters can have serious consequences. The lack of information about the identities and motivations of those involved means that there's often little option but to invoke what are perceived to be the wider set of Uyghur grievances: Han settlement, economic deprivation, religious and cultural repression, family-planning policies. Some or all of these grievances may have made someone throw explosives from a moving vehicle, or stab an elderly imam to death. But often we are just guessing.

If we don't know the causes (and in some cases, the details) of violent confrontations between Uyghurs and the state, then the basis on which we regard them as being connected incidents is also questionable. Should we regard all violent incidents in which Uyghurs are involved as being related to each other? While some incidents are certainly the result of Uyghurs being targeted by local officials and police on the basis of their ethnicity (such as the Yining protests in 1997), in other cases ethnicity may not have been a significant factor (which of course doesn't rule out the possibility that the problem stemmed from the *perception* that it was). If one accepts this argument, then it seems somewhat premature to draw conclusions about the state of Uyghur dissatisfaction in Xinjiang on the basis of a series of violent incidents about which we have vague, often contradictory accounts, and whose main or only common denominator may be that Uyghurs were involved. This is not to say that there's *no* connection between separate incidents in Xinjiang – one protest may inspire another – merely that in lumping incidents in Hotan or Kashgar with those in Urumqi or Yining we run the risk of ignoring some of the differences between (and within) these communities. At its worst, this tendency can lead to generalisations about 'what Uyghurs want'.

But if the violence of the last several years in Xinjiang hasn't been organised by terrorist groups, nor fuelled by 'religious extremism', how else can we explain the apparent rise in violent confrontations between Uyghurs and the state? An alternative explanation is that these incidents are the result of the increasing desperation of some Uyghurs in the face of a Chinese state that often seems indifferent to their concerns, yet subjects them to progressively more draconian systems of policing and control in the name of 'security'. Faced with this situation, would it be surprising if some Uyghurs, like Alim, have thus given up on peaceful forms of resistance?

If this is indeed the case, then the authorities' attempt to fight 'terrorism' has produced the very problem they have long claimed to be combating. It is also possible that the cumulative resentment against

state policy in Xinjiang over several decades – since the 1990s – has created an underlying anger and frustration in many Uyghur communities
that is more easily ignited. Though this would partially explain the way
that many recent large-scale violent incidents seem to have sprung from
very particular complaints, the problem with this argument is that it
relies on using one unknown quantity (the level of dissatisfaction in the
general Uyghur population) to explain the actions of another, equally
unknown quantity. The fact that there seems to be more violence, and,
in some cases, of a different kind, isn't necessarily because most Uyghurs
feel more resentment against the Chinese government. Essentially, one
can't assume that a bombing or assassination in any way represents
the views and concerns of most Uyghur citizens. The discourse in the
Western media tends to paint Han and Uyghurs as being at each other's
throats, and there's certainly considerable ill feeling and prejudice
between the communities in different cities. But usually this goes no
further than derogatory remarks and general avoidance of each other.
Despite frequent breathless reports about 'high tensions' in Xinjiang,
the atmosphere in most parts of the region is usually anything but (and
how does one measure 'tensions'?). If the lesson that some Uyghurs,
like Alim, drew from the Urumqi riots was that violence was the only
solution to the precarious situation of Uyghurs in Xinjiang, there were
many more who saw their future very differently.

A DIFFERENT TUNE

While the perceived link between Uyghurs and violence has probably
never been stronger in Chinese society (and the Western media), this
is thankfully not the only way they are represented. In China the long
association between Uyghurs and musical performance remains just as
strong. For many Chinese people, especially those from older generations, this perception probably derives from watching interminable
variety performances featuring people from ethnic minorities in colourful and exotic costumes singing state-approved folk songs. But for a

younger generation, pop videos on Youku (China's version of YouTube) have been more influential, as well as the appearance of performers like Perhat, a young Uyghur singer, on national TV talent shows. While music remains the primary focus in these encounters, these videos and appearances also provide mainstream Chinese audiences with a positive portrayal of Uyghurs and their culture. Perhat's conduct after winning his round of the competition in August 2014 was especially remarked upon by Chinese internet users. After beating his Han competitor, Perhat humbly refused to let his hand be raised in triumph. According to the author of the excellent blog *The Art of Life in Chinese Central Asia*:

> What is unique here is that Perhat is treating his Han counterpart in the same way that he would treat a close Uyghur friend. That level of respect across the ethnic divide is what makes Perhat seem so extraordinary; not only does he have the gift of an amazing voice but he also has the ability to transcend the usual social norms.

Perhat isn't the only Uyghur pop star reaching out to a wider Chinese audience. Ablajan, a 30-year-old singer who grew up in a small village, is often compared to Justin Bieber for his upbeat, catchy songs aimed at Uyghur children and young teenagers. His music is influenced by Uyghur folk, Sufi poetic forms and other Central Asian influences. His stage performances owe a lot to Korean pop and the dance moves of Michael Jackson. He first saw the latter on TV when he was 14, after which he started practising the moonwalk and writing songs. At 19, he went to Urumqi to study dance, and despite having no formal training or connections in the music industry was eventually able to get a record deal. The role of Ablajan's manager, Rui Wenbin, was obviously crucial: he formerly worked in Xinjiang's Ministry of Culture and so was well connected. Ablajan's first album sold more than 100,000 copies, which is a lot in the limited market of Uyghur-language pop.

Ablajan's success makes him an important role model for young Uyghurs, with the lesson being not that they can all become pop stars, but that they can lead a modern, successful life without giving up on their culture and language. In an interview with *Time* magazine he said: 'The message is that this is the 21st century […] We cannot make a living buying and selling sheep.' It's this kind of concern for social issues that distinguishes Ablajan from the ranks of anodyne Bieber-wannabes. While his music sounds like commercial pop, the lyrics often address social issues like pollution, the need for education and the loss of traditional patterns of living. It would be a stretch to say his songs are political – they certainly eschew the nationalistic sentiments of the folk songs popularised in the 1980s – but they do give voice to the concerns of many Uyghur communities.

Having said that, these aren't *uniquely* Uyghur concerns. The environment is one of the greatest worries of the Chinese public at present, as is the rapid pace of social change throughout the country (especially in terms of the shift to urban life). In 2013 Ablajan started recording songs in Chinese as well as Uyghur, obviously primarily for commercial reasons, but with this comes the possibility that a broader (Han) Chinese audience might get to hear a Uyghur singer articulating similar concerns to theirs. If more people outside Xinjiang can recognise that this common ground exists, some might also look more sympathetically (or at least with a more open mind) at other grievances expressed by Uyghurs in Xinjiang. As Rui Wenbin says: 'Ablajan's music can help bridge the divide between the Uighur and Han worlds […] He can be a messenger of peace.'

Like many other Uyghur musicians in different genres, Ablajan is using a modern musical form that nonetheless remains indebted to older Uyghur musical forms like the *muqam*. This combining of traditional and modern styles is likely to play an important role in the preservation of Uyghur culture and language, and, by extension, their identity. While Uyghur culture has been repeatedly targeted by the Chinese state, in many ways the 'threat' to Uyghur culture, if one perceives it as such, is just as great from globalising influences. In order to remain relevant, some growth and adaptation has to take place (as has had to occur historically).

This isn't to deny the importance of preserving Uyghur musical tradition. The famous tambur player, Mahmut Mehmet, has spoken of how, when he listens to the *muqam*, he remembers his grandfather, and his grandfather's grandfather, and which minority he's from, something that no other music can make him do. He's entirely right when he says: 'Music can represent a minority.' But there's more than one way to do this, as the documentary *The Silk Road of Pop* ably demonstrates. The film explores the vitality and diversity of the music being made by young Uyghur musicians in Xinjiang, focussing on the hip-hop, rap and heavy-metal scenes in Urumqi. Most of the groups involved in these aren't yet as popular as singers like Ablajan. As Sameer Farooq, one of the directors of the film told me:

> What was common among all of the musicians we spoke with was a shared struggle to make a livelihood through their music. It was very difficult to get the rest of China to know/understand what was going on in terms of new music production in Xinjiang. There was an enormous initiative on the part of many groups to organise showcases on their own, bringing together a number of bands to hold a concert.

The film shows that the music scene is at least one aspect of Urumqi society that isn't ethnically divided: Adil, a rock band, has Uyghur, Han and Manchu members; many of the bands sing in both Uyghur and Chinese; and, most importantly, a lot of the bands have a mixed fan base. Farooq says that shows 'draw thousands of young people from both the Uyghur and Han communities. The bands playing would also straddle many cultural groups. It was very encouraging to see that the audiences were mixed.'

Urumqi's rap scene began in the early 2000s; many rappers cite the influence of Eminem and his contemporaries. By the end of the decade there was a thriving scene, with groups like Hei Bomb, Soul Clap, Xikar and EIG, who rapped in Uyghur, Chinese, Kazakh and even English. In an interview in 2008, EIG said: 'My name is EIG, I am 20 years old, everybody calls me a genius. No one can defeat me in English rap.' After the 2009 riots the scene went quiet, due to a ban on public gatherings, and the inability to spread new music online.

Of the groups performing currently, the most prominent is Six City (a reference to the six cities of south Xinjiang). Most of its members come from the southern, poorer neighbourhoods of Urumqi, and have had to drive hospital shuttle buses and work in traditional Uyghur dance troupes to support themselves. The group raps half in Chinese, half in Uyghur, partly for commercial reasons, but also, according to one of Six City's members, because 'the Chinese government censors less when you mix in Chinese lyrics'. This is perhaps the flip side of bilingual education policies – though they do potentially endanger fluency in Uyghur, a command of spoken Chinese can also be empowering for far more than just getting a job. It can also be a tool with which Uyghurs represent their concerns in a manner that allows them to engage with wider Chinese society.

Like early hip hop in the United States, there's a focus on social injustice in Six City's lyrics, albeit within boundaries. Rather than writing about ethnic discrimination, they focus on topics like drug and gambling problems in poor areas, and on the need for self-respect and pride in their culture. Despite the limits of what they can express, their lyrics can still be challenging. During an informal performance in *The Silk Road of Pop*, in early 2010, less than a year after the riots, one member of Six City raps:

> The rhythm of life is speeding up.
> The rich have money, and they're going out.
> While the poor are still waiting.
> Some are crying, enduring.
> Often there are many fires.
> To get it real, lies are exposed.
> Don't get excited. Just wait till dusk.
> All the riots, all the cursing, for what?
> For my home. I'm staying here.

While the song makes no reference to ethnicity or nationalism, for many Uyghurs its references to economic inequality and suffering and the call for transparency, combined with the strong declaration of attachment to place, surely resonate.

Despite their different musical styles, Ablajan, Six City and other Uyghur groups have many things in common. One is that almost all of them, both in their music and in interviews, express an attachment to traditional Uyghur musical culture. Their music isn't intended to replace it, more to reinterpret it by filtering it through other musical styles. In many cases this is meant as more than a purely artistic project. For many of the groups, music is not only a way to comment on issues within Xinjiang, but also a way to engage with an international audience. As Eliar from Six City eloquently puts it:

> Every country, every ethnic group around the world is creating new ideas to help others understand their nation or ethnic group. They use all kinds of means. And us? Why do we want to do hip hop? Because we want the world to understand Uyghurs but we want to use a new method. If you go abroad to play *dutar* or *tambur*, maybe a small number of aficionados will know it is Uyghur music. But the average person won't know. They won't understand because they don't listen to classic or folk music. Most young people want to listen to pop music. So the point is to put our culture into popular culture. Then when people around the world hear our song they will say, 'Oh this is good, who is this? Six City. And what are they?' Uyghur. That's the most important thing.

Having a thriving Uyghur-language music scene is obviously helpful for preserving the language in the face of the virtually monolingual education system. Some musicians have also made an explicit effort to promote Uyghur. In 2013 Ablajan wrote a song to help language-learning, while the famous *dutar* player Abdurehim Heyit has recorded a version of the nineteenth-century poem 'Mother Tongue'. What makes the song particularly apt is that the poem was composed as a protest against the influence of Persian and Arabic in Uyghur education:

I will respect the person who knows his mother tongue
I will trade gold for the mother tongue spoken from their lips
Whether this mother tongue is in America or Africa
I will spend thousands of coins to go there (to hear the mother tongue)
Oh, mother tongue you are a mark left to us by our great ancestors

An especially impressive song for language-learning sung by a seven-year-old has also become popular. Berna, a child star from a wealthy family in Urumqi, and another teen star, Gulmire Tugun, include a lot of linguistic and cultural information in an apparently simple children's song. The lyrics manage to demonstrate spelling patterns, grammatical rules, how words can be formed by combining letters and, perhaps most of all, the importance of loving one's language:

Ba, Ba, bring it for me
Bring the alphabet for me
If you take it from the people give it back to the people
Give it back to the people who love it
Give the language to the people who love it
Purchase it again for me, buy an alphabet for me
With knowledge (of Uyghur) prosper for me
Rise and soar for me

At present, music and other cultural avenues are probably the safest way for Uyghurs to promote their language. Recent, more direct attempts have been curtailed by the authorities. In 2011 the linguist and poet Abduweli Ayup opened a Uyghur-language kindergarten in Kashgar, the success of which led him to try to do the same in Urumqi. Though there are numerous regulations for establishing private schools in China, Ayup presumably managed to follow these, as he was allowed to appear on state-run TV. According to one of his former students, he wasn't against Uyghurs learning Chinese: 'it's just that he thought they should also know their own language.'

But for reasons that remain unclear, the Kashgar kindergarten was closed down in March 2013, apparently for lacking the correct permit. Ayup and his two business associates were arrested in August 2013 for 'illegal fund-raising'. The brother of one of the arrested men told the *New York Times* that they had been trying to raise money for a kindergarten in Tianshan, a poor, predominantly Uyghur district in Urumqi (where most of Six City come from). Exactly what was so 'illegal' about their fund-raising was not specified – but they seem to have been engaged in such nefarious activities as selling honey and T-shirts.

The treatment of Ayup and his partners is illustrative of how limited the space for resistance of even the most peaceful kind has become for Uyghurs in Xinjiang. The increased restrictions on religion, the destruction of Uyghur neighbourhoods and the continuing economic marginalisation of most Uyghurs means that the material and cultural welfare of Uyghurs is increasingly under threat. There's little chance that government policy in Xinjiang is likely to become more tolerant in the near future in any of the areas that cause resentment.

Yet though a small number of Uyghurs may have concluded that there is no other way to resist except violence, musicians like Berna, Ablajan, Six City and Perhat all serve as examples of another way. They are representative of many young, city-dwelling, Chinese-speaking Uyghurs who are forging a different kind of Uyghur identity, one that may be able to negotiate the pressures, constraints and contradictions of life in contemporary China (not all of which relate to being an ethnic minority). While embracing global culture, and looking outwards, some also retain a sense of their history and culture, and are struggling to ensure these remain both vital and relevant.

AFTERWORD: 'AS CLOSE AS POMEGRANATE SEEDS'

When I wrote the preceding chapter, in October 2014, I made a conscious choice to end the book on a relatively upbeat note. After chronicling decades of repression I wanted to emphasise, perhaps belatedly, that Uyghurs weren't just an ethnic minority oppressed by an authoritarian state. I wanted to stress their agency and resilience, and not just for abstract, dutiful reasons: the majority of Uyghurs I've known over the last twenty years, both within and outside Xinjiang, have demonstrated a remarkable ability to adapt to shifting cultural, linguistic, religious and economic constraints, often by acquiring new skills and languages and moving within Xinjiang or to cities far from their homeland, either in China or in other countries. While I definitely wasn't optimistic about the future for Uyghurs in China, I believed that, even within a tightening web of restrictions, they still had viable options. At the start of 2015, most Uyghurs could at least still go to the market, attend prayers on Fridays or safely contact relatives and friends in other countries, what you could see as a semblance of normal life (inasmuch as walking down streets patrolled by armed police can be considered 'normal'). But it's also true that in order to see any grounds for hope in this situation, I had to squint very hard.

More than four years later, when perhaps 10 per cent of the Uyghur population are in detention, even that qualified optimism seems naïve. In addition to the many pitfalls of writing about Xinjiang – overgeneralising, framing everything in ethnic terms, ignoring regional differences, forgetting the wider Chinese context – there were perhaps also subtler, more personal ones for anyone who's spent time in the region and made local friends. Even with knowledge of the progressively worsening situation for Uyghurs in Xinjiang, and an awareness that new, harsher regulations on dress, belief and movement could be imposed by fiat, there was still a tendency (or temptation) to hope that official zeal might falter, or that policy might change.

But the construction of the internment camps signals a qualitative shift in the Chinese government's approach to the 'problem' of Xinjiang. The camps and other measures aim to provide a comprehensive system of control for all aspects of life in the region, one that recalls remarks made by Li Haiying, the military commander of south Xinjiang, who in an article in an influential Communist Party magazine wrote, 'We must cherish ethnic unity like we take care of our eyes ... nestle together with people of all ethnic groups as close as pomegranate seeds.'

This cosy, fruit-based metaphor (first used by Xi Jinping in 2014) is also an image of containment, of seeds trapped in place. Though the most dramatic changes would follow the appointment of Chen Quanguo as the new top official for the region in August 2016, his predecessor Zhang Chunxian laid the ground by imposing tighter curbs on freedom of movement in Xinjiang. In 2014, Zhang introduced a new type of internal passport for people in Xinjiang (which was in addition to the *hukou* permit every Chinese citizen is supposed to possess). This *bianminka* ('convenient for the people card') had the names and contact details of officials in the person's hometown and had to be shown at the numerous security checkpoints already in existence at hotels and in bus and train stations. The new card was in theory required by all Xinjiang residents, but few Han Chinese had to produce it. Many Uyghur migrant workers were forced to return to their hometowns to try to acquire their card – a long, expensive journey for many – and even then faced bureaucratic and financial obstacles that meant the card was very difficult to obtain. As a result many Uyghurs were unable to return to the cities where they had been working.

Further restrictions were imposed in November 2016 when Xinjiang residents were required to hand in their passports for 'safe-keeping', preventing people from leaving the country (though for many years it has been hard for Uyghurs to gain exit visas). Officials in Bayingolin Prefecture, in south-eastern Xinjiang, were so determined to control people's movements that all cars had to be fitted with GPS trackers.

Meanwhile, the authorities continued to represent Xinjiang as being rife with potential terrorists. In June 2015, just over a year after proclaiming the start of the 'People's War on Terror', the authorities announced that their efforts had been, unsurprisingly, a huge success (triumphant self-assessment is standard operating procedure for the CCP). They claimed to have broken up '181 terrorist groups', a number that seemed both arbitrary and inflated: China's definition of terrorism is so elastic that, in the past, crop burnings and robberies have been placed under that heading. As usual, there was no supporting evidence.

An incident in July 2014 in Elishku, a village near Yarkant, was the largest and most verifiable violent confrontation during that period. The official response to it is indicative of how many Uyghur communities in Xinjiang are caught in a vicious cycle of repression and violence that the state, at both the local and regional levels, seems unwilling to break. Local officials quickly boosted police presence and erected loudspeakers throughout the village that broadcast propaganda. Informers were promised huge financial rewards for information, and there was a description of the 'Seven Behaviours of a Religious Extremist' (which included refusing to drink with friends, quitting smoking and refusing to open a shop or restaurant during Ramadan).

Though all this was done in the name of promoting 'stability' and 'ethnic unity', the general restrictions on freedom of movement in Xinjiang also meant the villagers – many of whom grew cotton – faced economic hardship because they were unable to travel to seek better prices for their crops than the low ones offered by the state. Part of the justification later offered by the authorities for the 'vocational training centres' was their role in alleviating poverty (in their view, one of the roots of extremism). Yet the relative impoverishment of many rural Uyghur communities has been to some degree the result of such policies. And it is very hard for families to make ends meet when one or more of their members is unable to work because they are incarcerated.

The use of public loudspeakers to convey political messages has a long lineage in the People's Republic of China, as do slogans, public posters and murals, all of which have remained tools of persuasion, indoctrination and threat. But in Xinjiang the authorities have also reintroduced a method of indoctrination rarely used since the Maoist era. During the Cultural Revolution (1966–76) around sixteen million young people from the cities were 'sent down' to villages to 'undergo re-education' from the rural masses. In one editorial Mao was quoted as saying that 'the intellectual youth must go to the country, and will be educated from living in rural poverty'. Yet in Xinjiang, where non-Han culture, language and traditions are regularly portrayed in official discourse as 'backward' or low 'quality' (*suzhi*), in recent years this dynamic has been reversed by the visits of urban cadres whose aim has been to instruct the (Uyghur) masses. Under Chen, a similar campaign was launched in Tibet in October 2011, when twenty-one thousand political officers were sent to monasteries and villages.

In 2014, around two hundred thousand Party members (most of them Han Chinese) were sent to stay in Uyghur homes in villages in which, like Elishku, a violent incident had occurred or that had been identified as a potential source of 'religious extremism', all as part of a campaign to 'Visit the People, Benefit the People, and Bring Together the Hearts of the People'. The tone of the campaign could not have been more paternalistic – these essentially uninvited guests presented themselves as 'relatives' of the people they were imposing on. Having officially sanctioned strangers in their homes (who thus could not be asked to leave) was no doubt intimidating, yet there was also the patronising experience of having the errors of their cultural and religious traditions pointed out to them. Omarjan Alim's song 'I Brought Home a Guest' has now become literally true.

These home visits were also a sign that the state wasn't satisfied with merely public compliance among Uyghurs (e.g. not wearing veils or headscarves in schools or other government buildings). Though Uyghurs were without doubt being targeted, it's worth remembering that this is part of a larger renewed intrusiveness of the state under Xi Jinping. Despite his initial talk of 'putting power into a cage', there has been a purge of civil society, harassment and arrests of Christians, journalists, bloggers, professors, editors, human-rights lawyers and environmental activists. In China, repression is often simultaneously general and specific.

Since the 1990s Uyghurs have been subjected to periodic mass arrests and propaganda onslaughts (mainly the 'Strike Hard' campaigns), but in many cases these have come to an end with changes in policy and personnel (though arguably since 9/11 the war on 'terror' in Xinjiang, as elsewhere, has remained constant). But in 2016 a second cohort of 110,000 'relatives' was sent to Uyghur villages, followed by a larger third wave of one million in 2017. The aims of this latter group would be even more insidious: in addition to trying to indoctrinate and intimidate people in their homes, they would also play an integral part of the wider process of surveillance by which people were selected for the camps.

'LIKE SPRAYING CHEMICALS ON THE CROPS'

The vast – and still expanding – network of internment camps are not without precedent. During the Qing Dynasty the region was a place of mass detention (albeit for people from outside Xinjiang), while since the 1950s the concept of 'reform through labour' has been a core concept of the Chinese penal system. The new camps may technically not be prisons, since the detainees haven't been charged with any crime – a distinction that would be lost on the people kept in them – but they nonetheless resemble them in function and appearance, while also borrowing from the parallel system of 'transformation through education' centres set up in the 2000s to deal with Falun Gong practitioners and drug addicts.

Before Chen took office, there were some re-education programs in Xinjiang, though of much shorter duration (a few weeks) and on a smaller scale. Yet the fact that they were in three different areas (near Yining, in the north-west, and in Kashgar and Hotan in the south) suggests that these were pilot schemes for an idea that was already being generally considered. In Tibet in 2012, Chen had authorised the detention and 're-education' of several thousand Tibetans who had returned from attending religious teachings by the Dalai Lama in India (even though they had been granted permission to do so). One can only speculate as to when the camps were authorised on a grander scale, yet the speed with which mass detentions began after Chen took office in August 2016 – approximately nine months later – makes it reasonable to assume that the policy had its inception much earlier.

The initial detention facilities seem to have mainly been repurposed government buildings – schools, hospitals and factories – which indicates the perceived urgency of the campaign, and perhaps also a degree of caution. Yet the increased security presence all but guaranteed that there was unlikely to be much resistance, while the greater restrictions on (and sometimes harassment of) foreign journalists in Xinjiang prevented news of the camps escaping for some time. Establishing the existence and precise location of the camps required the triangulation of three kinds of information: (1) testimony from the very few people released from the camps thus far; (2) analysis of construction tenders and recruitment notices – mostly undertaken by Adrian Zenz, a lecturer at the European School of Culture and Theology; and (3) satellite images of the camps which have been provided by Shawn Zhang, a law student at the University of British Columbia. These images made it clear that the camps had been built from scratch or dramatically expanded since 2016: an analysis of twenty-eight camps by the Australian Strategic Policy Institute found that they had expanded by 465 per cent.

What has made the camps possible is the tighter control over all aspects of life in Xinjiang. Following the Urumqi riots in 2009, many cities in Xinjiang installed additional surveillance technology, set up multiple checkpoints and recruited more security personnel. By 2016, the contrast between cities like Urumqi and those in inner China was thus already marked, but after Chen Quanguo assumed control of the region in August that year, he quickly began to transform Xinjiang into a virtual police state. In Tibet, Chen had essentially used the tactics of an occupying army. Hundreds of surveillance posts were installed throughout Tibet, both in cities and in remote rural areas, each of which was responsible for a designated sector and the residents within, what Chinese officials call 'grid-style social management' (first trialled in Beijing in 2004). These sentry posts are known as 'convenience police stations' and are equipped with anti-riot equipment and advanced surveillance technology such as face and voice recognition software. State media have tried to make them sound like friendly places by touting their Wi-Fi, hot tea and free newspapers, but few are likely to mistake the function of these buildings and their armed personnel.

This increased police presence means that residents making a short journey may be stopped multiple times to have their ID checked or mobile phone inspected for banned software like Twitter or Skype. People's text messages are also checked for 'religious' or other suspicious language (many people appear to have been sent to the internment camps on this basis). Though both Uyghur and Han residents are stopped at checkpoints – especially in places, like Urumqi, that have a Han majority – anecdotal reports suggest that Uyghurs are far more likely to be stopped. In some cities people also now have to use their ID cards to enter some shops and may be barred from entering if they have been flagged as 'unsafe'. Anyone wanting to enter Urumqi's main mosques has to pass through metal detectors and have their face scanned. Elsewhere, many mosques have been destroyed or converted to other uses. One mosque in Kashgar is now a café for tourists.

As in Tibet, this radical effort to control public space has required a huge increase in security personnel. From 2016–17 Xinjiang posted vacancies for ninety thousand security-related positions, more than eleven times the number advertised after the Urumqi riots, according to Adrian Zenz and James Leibold, an Associate Professor in Politics and Asian Studies at La Trobe University. Most of these are low-level positions that require little training or experience – and yet are relatively well paid – which has made them especially appealing for people from rural communities with only basic education, particularly Uyghurs, who remain virtually excluded from many sectors of Xinjiang's economy. As a result, Uyghurs are now well represented in the security apparatus that is watching (and detaining) their own people, a fact that should caution anyone who thinks that the problems in Xinjiang are simply a question of interethnic conflict.

Even with all this human and digital surveillance, the authorities are apparently still so concerned about public safety that anyone buying a kitchen knife or meat cleaver must have their name and ID card number engraved on the blade; in many butchers and restaurants, kitchen knives are chained to the wall to prevent them being used as weapons. While this rule seems to apply to the whole region, there are also reports of additional local regulations. In Kashgar many shops and restaurants are required to have panic buttons for summoning the police, while in Hotan many businesses must have a part-time policeman on their premises. There have been restrictions on the sale of matches, cigarette lighters and other goods for some time, and even reports of people unable to buy sugar in large quantities in case they seek to manufacture explosives.

There have also been signs that the Chinese state is seeking to exert more direct pressure on Uyghurs outside the country. State security have contacted Uyghurs to try to gather information about their own activities, or Uyghurs they know, and told them that if they do not comply, their families might be detained. Uyghurs abroad have also been pressured to return to Xinjiang, often with the connivance of the country where they reside, the most blatant example of which was Egypt's deportation of a group of Uyghur students in June 2017. The overall goal seems to be to neutralise possible Uyghur dissent and spread suspicion (and thus division) within the Uyghur diaspora.

Almost every state would have increased security in the wake of an incident like the Kunming attacks; a few might even have tried to address the actual causes of the violence. But in my view the most distinctive, and thus most revealing, aspect of the Chinese government's response to the violence in 2013 and 2014 hasn't been the police stations and digital surveillance, or the curbs on freedom of movement. As recently as 2013 the authorities were still arguing that the problems in Xinjiang were due to a few 'bad apples'. After the violence in Lukqun, a Xinhua editorial blamed 'a few criminals' whose 'anti-human nature' made them 'the common enemy of all ethnic groups'. The aim here was to try and preserve the notion that, even after the Urumqi riots of 2009, there was still a 'harmonious society' in Xinjiang. But the specific targeting of Uyghur culture and identity that has accompanied Chen's 'convenience police stations' has made it clear that the authorities regard Uyghurs as a suspect population that needs to be watched, checked and, ultimately, changed.

One of the most egregious prohibitions has been the announcement, in April 2017, that parents in Xinjiang can no longer choose 'religious' names for their children (a rule that had been in place in Hotan since 2015). This included common first names like Fatima and Muhammad (as well as Saifudin, the name of the former chairman of the region, whose books are now banned). Residents who didn't comply were threatened with losing education, health care and other forms of child benefit. While it's customary (and not untrue) to refer to Uyghurs as a predominantly Muslim people, there are plenty of apparently 'religious' names favoured by secular Uyghur parents for whom the names have no stronger scriptural associations than names like 'David' and 'Christopher' have for people in English-speaking countries.

The state's view of how Uyghurs *should* be has been clearly communicated by a variety of initiatives that encourage Uyghurs not to speak their native language and adopt 'mainstream' behaviours. Even the Uyghur-language TV channels encourage Uyghurs to speak Mandarin. In Urumqi, shops and restaurants in predominantly Uyghur neighbourhoods that once would have played Uzbek or Turkish pop songs are now forced to broadcast Mandarin propaganda songs. In April 2017 a new regulation identified refusing to watch state television as a sign of religious extremism (other indicators included refusing to drink alcohol or smoke cigarettes).

In a similar vein, there have been reports of financial incentives for Uyghurs and Han Chinese to get married. Women wearing headscarves have been refused entry onto buses. Arabic writing has been removed from many shops, restaurants and street signs. A top official in Kashgar recently asserted that it's unpatriotic for Uyghur officials to speak Uyghur in public when they should be speaking the 'national language' (i.e. Mandarin).

There's virtually no feature of Uyghur ethnicity that the state approves of (barring them singing and dancing in bright costumes). If there was still any debate within Communist Party intellectual circles over what to do about the 'problem' of non-Han ethnicity, judging by recent policy in Xinjiang the debate seems to have been decisively resolved in favour of thinkers like Ma Rong and Hu Angang (and, more recently, Hu Lianhe), who favour aggressive assimilation.

The shift to viewing any expression of ethnic identity as a threat can be seen in how the home-visit program has changed since it was launched. While the households targeted by the programs in 2014 and 2016 apparently had some vague (albeit tenuous) connection to crime or 'religious extremism', the larger cohort of 'relatives' who descended on Uyghur villages in 2017 and 2018 had a broader mandate to watch and inform. The 'relatives' spent at least five days every two months in villagers' homes, during which many of them (in Kashgar Prefecture, at least) relied on a manual that told them how to make the villagers 'let down their guard'. They were advised to show 'warmth' and bring sweets for the children. They were also told to inform the household that all their communications had been monitored (which was probably true) and so they should not lie to any questions they were asked about religion.

From interviews conducted by Darren Byler, a lecturer in the Department of Anthropology at the University of Washington, it's apparent that these 'relatives' greatly disrupted their 'hosts'' lives during their stay. Residents had to attend a flag raising ceremony, watch state TV, practice Chinese calligraphy and sing patriotic songs; all conversations had to be in Mandarin. In both structure and content, this schedule resembles that of the people detained in the camps, emphasising that the home visits, like the camps, aim not just to watch and control people but also to shape them. These kinds of routines are thought by the state to be a way to transform 'low-quality' Uyghur habits into 'modern', better lives.

Byler describes some of the questions asked by the 'relatives' to assess their hosts' risk of 'extremism':

Did their hosts have any relatives living in 'sensitive regions'? Did anyone they knew live abroad? Did they have any knowledge of Arabic or Turkish? Had they attended a mosque outside of their village? If the adult little brothers and sisters' answers felt incomplete, or if they seemed to be hiding anything, the children should be questioned next.

Villagers were also tested by being offered cigarettes or alcohol, or seeing if they asked whether meat that the 'guests' had bought for them was halal. Their reactions, like their responses to the questions, were used to determine whether they should be sent for 're-education'. There is a wide range of 'offences', some of them signs of religiosity (praying, fasting, listening to a religious lecture), some apparently indicative of a 'terrorist' intent (owning multiple knives or a T-shirt with Arabic writing) and others that take a considerable effort of imagination to see how they might be viewed as suspicious (owning a compass or extra food, having WhatsApp, not smoking, forbidding crying at funerals).

The detention of so many people in the camps has, as can be imagined, had a shattering effect on communities throughout Xinjiang. And yet the estimate of one million in the camps doesn't include those incarcerated in designated prisons. In parallel with the mass detentions in the camps, there has been a huge increase in the number of people formally indicted (and, in most cases, convicted, since in China a 'guilty' verdict occurs 99 per cent of the time). In Chen's first year in charge, indictments leapt from 41,000 in 2016 to 216,000 in 2017, in itself an astonishing increase (422 per cent), but even more so when one considers that this accounts for 13 per cent of arrests *in China as a whole*.

Perhaps the most haunting evocation of the devastating effects of Chen's policies comes from an essay by Gene Bunin, a writer and translator who studies the Uyghur language. Over the course of eighteen months travelling around Xinjiang and inner China, Bunin spoke to over a thousand Uyghurs in a variety of informal settings – at the time of writing almost the only way to speak to Uyghurs in China without endangering them. The overwhelming mood of his interviewees was of sadness, despondency and fear. As one of his respondents said, 'Just look all around you. You've seen it yourself [here in Kashgar]. We're a people destroyed.'

The misery that Chen's policies have brought to Uyghurs and other non-Han peoples in Xinjiang has been exacerbated by the inability of people in the region to gain support from friends and family outside the country – a brief conversation can result in detention. Some Uyghurs' relatives in Xinjiang are so frightened that they have asked them not to call or write. Some have been unable to contact their families for over a year.

While to many external observers the targeting of so many Uyghurs, both in the home visits and in the camps, seems like the persecution of an entire ethnic group, the public comments of one official in Kashgar suggest that the authorities view this as a necessary method by which to purge society. He was reported as saying, 'You can't uproot all the weeds hidden among the crops in the field one by one – you need to spray chemicals to kill them all; re-educating these people is like spraying chemicals on the crops... that is why it is a general re-education, not limited to a few people.'

There is also evidence that local officials have been given detention quotas to fulfil, generally around 10 per cent of the population. This may be due to a desire to cast the net as wide as possible – given that all non-Han people are now suspects – though there may also be some rationale behind it. In late 2015 a judicial official is reported to have said that 70 per cent of people in a village 'merely change with the wider surroundings' and are thus 'easily transformed'. In his view the other 30 per cent were polluted by 'religious extremism', but of them only 5 per cent were true extremists. While it's unclear what basis (if any) the official had for making that assessment, it is not only of a similar order of magnitude to most of the reported quotas but also matches the limited statistical information there is about the numbers of people detained. In early 2018 a leaked document from a public security bureau quoted a total figure of 892,000 – not far from 10 per cent of Xinjiang's adult non-Han population. So although the much-repeated phrase of China detaining 'a million Muslims' remains only an estimate, it's not an unreasonable one. The Chinese government has been trying to spray the entire field.

ATTACKING THE PAST AND PRESENT

As soon as the Chinese government admitted the existence of the camps – if not their actual purpose – it began a domestic and international media campaign to present them as benevolent, necessary institutions that people attended voluntarily. Particular emphasis was placed on the educational aspect of the camps; these were, after all, supposed to be 'vocational training centres'. The TV reports showed art classes, Chinese lessons and, in one camp, a salon for training hairdressers. The tone of editorials in the state-run *Global Times* was typically bullish, arguing that it was China, not the West, that was a true defender of human rights because of its success in protecting its citizens from terrorism.

The authorities were so confident in their ability to present a convincing Potemkin village that in January 2019 they allowed international news organisations, including Reuters, into a few of the camps. The reporters were welcomed by a classroom of people wearing colourful costumes who then sang, in English, 'If you're happy and you know it, clap your hands', what was arguably a display of gross overconfidence, or a deliberate thumbing of the nose.

The responses of the inmates allowed to speak to the reporters had a sameness that spoke of fear and coaching. One inmate said, 'Before coming here, my brain was simple, my ideas impoverished. Now my brain has been enlightened with knowledge.' Shohrat Zakir, the Xinjiang governor, also stressed the corrective nature of the training, arguing that it helped people 'to reflect on their mistakes' and made them 'able to better tell right from wrong and resist the infiltration of extremist thought'.

Although the version of the camps that the government offered for scrutiny was misleading, its distortions still implicitly conveyed their core idea, namely that Uyghur culture, language and religious beliefs are of little worth and need to be corrected. This aim was baldly stated in November 2018 by Cui Tiankai, China's ambassador to the United States, who said that the aim of the camps was to turn Uyghurs and other Muslim minorities 'into normal persons [who] can go back to normal life'.

Yet while the Chinese state has targeted the whole Uyghur population with surveillance and the threat of detention, there has also been a selectivity to the detentions that betrays their real intent. More than a hundred Uyghur academics, artists and intellectuals have been detained since 2015, most of whom hadn't even voiced the mild dissent offered by Ilham Tohti. Many were establishment figures, occupants of university positions and recipients of state funding, which meant that in some cases their official biographies had to be quickly revised. In late 2017, Halmurat Ghopur, a former president of Xinjiang Medical University Hospital, went from being a well-respected medical researcher to a 'separatist' who had concealed his intention to create a Muslim caliphate in Xinjiang 'for the past 33 years'. The authorities claimed that he had 'planned to create an independent country according to his own wishes and become its leader'. He received a two-year suspended death sentence.

Ghopur and many other editors, officials and academics were charged with being 'two-faced', which meant paying lip service to policy but secretly opposing it. Concerns about the apparently divided loyalty of non-Han political cadres had already been expressed in December 2015, when Xu Hairong, secretary of Xinjiang's Commission for Discipline Inspection, complained that 'some waver on clear-cut issues of opposing ethnic division and safeguarding ethnic and national unity, and even support participating in violent terrorist attacks'.

Yet many of the artists and intellectuals detained had been far from equivocal in their public support for the CCP and, prior to their detention, had spoken out against 'religious extremism'. But even a cursory acquaintance with many of these people's work makes plain that their real crime has been seeking to preserve and maintain Uyghur language and culture for a new generation. Abdukerim Rahman, a 77-year-old specialist in Uyghur literature, who had been a member of the CCP for 40 years, disappeared in March 2018. Rahman had played an important role in the movement for teaching the Uyghur language to children, as had the singer Ablajan, who has also been detained. All of Ablajan's songs had been approved by the government censors, and some stress the importance of patriotism and secular knowledge, yet he too became suspect simply for promoting Uyghur culture.

Reading back through the first edition of this book, I've been struck by how many other Uyghur artists and intellectuals whose work I discussed, people who have spent their whole careers trying to protect and promote their rich, diverse culture, have been the victims of Chen's attempts to undermine Uyghur identity. The dutar virtuoso Abdurehim Heyit, whose song 'Mother Tongue' powerfully conveys his sense of attachment to his native language, was also detained in 2018. At the time of writing his status is unclear.

The detention of the academic Rahile Dawut is an equally blatant attack on a blameless individual. Dawut's work on folklore in Xinjiang, especially the traditions and contemporary practices surrounding *mazar*, has immeasurably aided wider understanding of Uyghurs' deep roots in the region. Despite her research being officially (and internationally) celebrated, and even though she too has been a member of the CCP for over 30 years, Dawut was detained in December 2017. At the time of writing she has yet to be charged, which means that she may be in a camp, rather than a prison, though her whereabouts are unknown.

By silencing Dawut, and others like her, the CCP is ultimately trying to erase its biggest 'problem', which isn't terrorism, or even separatism, but the fact of the region's distinct history, the present-day manifestation of which is the cultures and languages of the non-Han people in the region. This is why one religious-affairs official advised that the camps should 'break their lineage, break their roots, break their connections and break their origins'.

The extent to which the CCP wants to erode any sense of heritage among Uyghurs was conveyed by an article written by Yasheng Sidike, the mayor of Urumqi, who in August 2018 opined that Xinjiang wasn't the home of Uyghurs alone but of all ethnicities. He claimed that 'the Uyghur people are members of the Chinese family, not descendants of the Turks, let alone anything to do with Turkish people'. (At this point, it wouldn't be surprising if the region was renamed without 'Uyghur' as part of its title.)

NEXT?

Over the last ten years, Xinjiang has gone from being a place that few in the West had heard of to a Chinese region associated with Islamic terrorism and now, as a result of the international coverage of the camps, is widely seen as a troubled region in which terrible human rights violations occur. Global awareness about the situation of Uyghurs and other non-Han people in Xinjiang has never been greater. While this is no doubt a good thing, it hasn't translated into much conspicuous action from other countries. Most Western powers have done little more than express different flavours of 'concern' ('grave', 'strong', 'intense'). Although the United States has mooted sanctions, it has been more interested in fighting a trade war with China than in formulating a clear policy towards the camps. While Turkey has historically been one of China's Muslims' strongest defenders, harbouring Uyghur refugees and condemning the violence in Urumqi in 2009 as 'a kind of genocide', Turkey's Chinese trade deals and loans have made it more compliant. In August 2017, Mevlut Cavusoglu, the Turkish foreign minister, announced that the government would 'not allow in Turkey any activities targeting or opposing China'.

Even countries with a predominantly Muslim population have had little to say about the camps. Iran, Saudi Arabia, Egypt and Jordan officially condemned the treatment of Rohingya in Myanmar, yet they have been unwilling to challenge China's narrative about the camps. In these countries, as in Turkey, economic imperatives are thought to necessitate preserving good relations with China, which has been investing heavily in most of them as part of the Belt and Road Initiative that seeks to transform Eurasian infrastructure in China's favour. The Organisation of Islamic Cooperation, to which many of these countries belong, did eventually offer its 'concern' in December 2018, but its website has conspicuously less information about Xinjiang than about the situation of Palestinians, Afghanis and Rohingya.

Yet after almost two years since the camps opened there are beginning to be signs that Xinjiang policy is shifting slightly, though not necessarily for the better. In January 2019, Shohrat Zakir suggested, 'As time goes by, the people in the education training mechanism will be fewer and fewer.' As yet, there's no reason to think this is true, and the vagueness of Zakir's statement doesn't inspire confidence. (And the only acceptable number of people in the 'education training mechanism' is zero.) There has, however, been a cluster of releases of ethnic Kazakhs, some of them Kazakh citizens, from camps in northwest Xinjiang, at the request of Kazakhstan. In January 2019 the Chinese authorities also gave permission for two thousand Kazakhs to renounce their Chinese citizenship so that they could leave the country. Arguably, this isn't a big concession for China – it hasn't exactly demonstrated that it values their presence – but it's obviously beneficial to the people concerned and demonstrates that China's economic clout doesn't make it impervious to proposals by states who are willing to go beyond expressing 'concern' about human rights.

What complicates this story – and is possibly a harbinger of what is to come – is that some released Kazakh inmates have been sent to work in clothing and textile factories where they were expected to work 12-hour shifts in return for virtually no wages, as well as still undergo some 'political education'. Most of the factory's employees are said to be former camp detainees. Anyone who refuses to sign the employment contract gets sent back to the camps.

At present it's unclear how widespread this practice is, but satellite imagery, business registration documents as well as a small number of reports from former detainees confirm that factories are built in or near many camps. Officials in Kashgar in 2018 announced that they aimed to send one hundred thousand former inmates to factories (which for them would no doubt prove the success of the 'vocational training', as well as help defray the huge cost of the camps). It's unlikely that many officials will have qualms about adding exploitation to the arbitrary detention, intimidation and indoctrination suffered by the detainees.

Of equal concern are indications that some aspects of Chen's policies in Xinjiang are being considered for use in other parts of China. In December 2018 it was announced that the Xinjiang model of 'counter-terrorism' was being considered by Ningxia, the north-western region where roughly two million of China's ten million Hui Muslims live. While for the past several decades Ningxia's Hui have mostly been spared the repressive policies applied to Uyghurs and other non-Han ethnic groups in Xinjiang, over the last few years mosques have started being targeted for demolition or alteration if they look too 'Islamic' or 'Arabic'. The Grand Mosque in Weizhou was scheduled for demolition in August 2018, which was averted only after several of its domes were removed. As in Xinjiang, Arabic writing has been removed from shopfronts, street signs and halal food packaging. In January 2019, China announced that over the next four years China planned to Sinicise Islam. According to Gao Zhanfu, vice dean of the China Islamic Institute, the plan was not to change 'the beliefs, habits or ideology of Islam but to make them compatible with socialist society'.

China may reduce the numbers of people being detained, but it's unlikely to get rid of the camps in the near future. Their existence serves as a continuing threat to the non-Han population of Xinjiang (and perhaps elsewhere), a means of intimidation that, by its own awful logic, has to be kept in perpetual use if it's to remain a threat. By continually cycling a section of the population through Xinjiang's prisons and camps (and perhaps factories as well), while keeping the rest of the population under tight surveillance, the authorities will hope to either dilute or erode people's regional and ethnic identities, or at least make it impossible for these to be freely expressed in any meaningful way. Without wishing to draw any particular historical parallels – in my view, they tend to distract from and diminish the specifics of a particular case – it's inherently dangerous for any state, especially one as authoritarian as China under Xi Jinping, to possess such a vast apparatus of detention and surveillance. The existence of such a network of repression makes possible more extreme, violent and coercive actions against its citizens, especially in response to the acts of resistance they are likely to provoke.

SOURCES AND RECOMMENDED READING

PREFACE

My main source of testimony from former camp detainees is the Human Rights Watch report 'Eradicating Ideological Viruses' from September 2018. It is available at https://www.hrw.org/report/2018/09/09/eradicating-ideological-viruses/chinas-campaign-repression-against-xinjiangs# (accessed 29 January 2019).

For a list of offences that can result in detention, see Tanner Greer, *Foreign Policy* [website] '48 Ways to Get Sent to a Chinese Concentration Camp' (13 September 2018). It is available at https://foreignpolicy.com/2018/09/13/48-ways-to-get-sent-to-a-chinese-concentration-camp/ (accessed 29 January 2019).

A key early piece on the camps was by Megha Rajagopalan, *Buzzfeed News* [website], 'This is What a 21st Century Police State Really Looks Like' (17 October 2017). It is available at https://www.buzzfeednews.com/article/meghara/the-police-state-of-the-future-is-already-here (accessed 15 January 2019). Also see Emily Feng, *Financial Times* 'Security clampdown bites in China's Xinjiang region' (14 November 2017). It is available at https://www.ft.com/content/ee28e156-992e-11e7-a652-cde3f882dd7b (accessed 20 January 2019).

The U.N. Human Rights Panel's response can be found in a piece by Stephanie Nebehay for Reuters (10 August 2018) [website] 'U.N. says it has credible reports that China holds million Uighurs in secret camps'. It is available at https://uk.reuters.com/article/uk-china-rights-un/u-n-says-it-has-credible-reports-that-china-holds-

267

million-uighurs-in-secret-camps (accessed 3 November 2018).

The quotes from Shohrat Zakir are from *China Daily* [website] 17 October 2018 'Interview with Xinjiang government chief on counter-terrorism, vocational education and training'. It is available at http://www.chinadaily.com.cn/a/201810/17/WS5bc68c76a310eff303282c6f.html (accessed 4 January 2019).

INTRODUCTION

The eyewitness accounts of the Kunming attack are drawn from the following reports: 'Kunming station survivors speak of panic-stricken escape from attackers', *Guardian*, 3 March 2014; 'Survivors recount scenes of terror dubbed "China's 9/11" by state media', *Telegraph*, 2 March 2014; 'Chinese police "solve" Kunming massacre', *Telegraph*, 3 March 2014; 'Attackers with knives kill 29 at Chinese rail station', *New York Times*, 1 March 2014; 'China blames Xinjiang separatists for stabbing rampage at train station', *New York Times*, 2 March 2014; 'Witnesses tell of Kunming attack horror', *South China Morning Post*, 2 March 2014.

The *Daily Mirror* article that linked Uyghurs to the missing Malaysia Airlines flight appeared on 9 March 2014.

CHAPTER 1

The best history book on Xinjiang (which this chapter relies heavily on) is James Millward's *Eurasian Crossroads* (New York, 2007). Svat Soucek's *A History of Inner Asia* (Cambridge, 2000) is good for anyone wanting a broader Central Asian perspective. *Xinjiang: China's Muslim Borderland*, edited by S. Frederick Starr (Armonk, NY, 2004), is also a good starting point for a lot of general information on the region.

For more on *mazar* see the work of Rachel Harris and Rahile Dawut, such as 'Mazar festivals of the Uyghurs: music, Islam and the Chinese state', *British Journal of Ethnomusicology* xi/1 (2002), pp. 101–18. The best photos of *mazar* are in *The Living Shrines of Uyghur China* (New York, 2013) by Lisa Ross, whom I interviewed for the *Los Angeles Review of Books*. The article is available at http://lareviewofbooks.org/interview/eternal-sleep-the-uyghur-shrines-of-the-taklamakan-desert (accessed 28 January 2015).

Michael Clarke's paper 'The problematic progress of "integration" in the Chinese state's approach to Xinjiang, 1759–2005', *Asian Ethnicity* viii/3 (2007), pp. 261–89, was helpful for the Qing section. The section on the historical link between language and Uyghur identity is based on Eric T. Schluessel's paper 'History, identity, and mother-tongue education in Xinjiang', *Central Asian Survey* xxxviii/4 (2009), pp. 383–402. The quote from the Ministry of Information is taken from David Tobin, 'Competing communities: ethnic unity and ethnic boundaries on China's north-west frontier', *Inner Asia* xiii/1 (2011), pp. 7–25. The song about the Andijanis' departure is from Laura Newby's chapter '"Us and them" in 18th and 19th century Xinjiang', in Ildikó Bellér-Hann, M. Cristina Cesàro, Rachel Harris and Joanne Smith Finley (eds), *Situating the Uyghurs between China and Central Asia* (Aldershot, 2007), pp. 15–30.

For more on the development of Uyghur identity, see: Dru Gladney's work, in particular 'The ethnogenesis of the Uyghur', *Central Asian Survey* ix/1 (1990), pp. 1–28; David Brophy, 'Taranchis, Kashgaris, and the Uyghur question in Soviet Central Asia', *Inner Asia* vii/2 (2005), pp. 163–84; and Rian Thum, *The Sacred Routes of Uyghur History* (Cambridge, MA, 2014). For a thorough discussion of the uses and abuses of Xinjiang's history for nationalistic purposes see Chapter 1 of Gardner Bovingdon's *The Uyghurs: Strangers in Their Own Land* (New York, 2010). For more on the 'Queen of the West', see Alessandro Rippa, 'Re-writing mythology in Xinjiang', *China Journal* 71 (2014), pp. 43–64.

Ma Jian's quote about Xinjiang is from his travel book *Red Dust* (New York, 2001), translated by Flora Drew. For information about Xinjiang's role as a penal colony see *New Ghosts, Old Ghosts: Prisons and Labor Reform Camps in China* (Armonk, NY, 1999) by James Seymour and Michael Anderson.

The newspaper quote about Xinjiang being more advanced than China is from David Wang's paper, 'An oasis for peace: Zhang Zhizhong's policy in Xinjiang', *Central Asian Survey* xv/3–4 (1996), pp. 413–29.

CHAPTER 2

The bulk of the historical material in this chapter comes from Donald McMillen's *Chinese Communist Power and Policy in Xinjiang 1949–1977* (Boulder, CO, 1979) and James Millward's *Eurasian Crossroads* (New York, 2007).

The stories of early XPCC recruits are from the articles 'Migrants to China's west bask in prosperity', *New York Times*, 6 August 2009, and 'The story of the production and construction corps', which is available at https://beigewind.wordpress.com/2014/07/06/the-story-oft-he-production-and-construction-corps/ (accessed 28 January 2015).

The anecdote about the donkey punishment is in *Community Matters in Xinjiang 1880–1949* (Leiden, 2008) by Ildikó Bellér-Hann. The same author's paper '"Making the oil fragrant": dealings with the supernatural among the Uyghurs in Xinjiang', *Asian Ethnicity* ii/1 (2001), pp. 9–23, discusses domestic rituals.

A good overview of the XPCC's history is provided by James Seymour's paper 'Xinjiang's production and construction corps, and the sinification of Eastern Turkestan', *Inner Asia* ii/2 (2000), pp. 171–93. For material on population shifts since 1949 see: Yuan Qing-li, 'Population changes in the Xinjiang Uighur autonomous region (1949–1984)', *Central Asian Survey* ix/1 (1990), pp. 49–73; and Stanley Toops, 'The population landscape of Xinjiang/East Turkestan', *Inner Asia* ii/2 (2000), pp. 155–70.

The quote from the Ethnic Unity Education Board is taken from David Tobin, 'Competing communities: ethnic unity and ethnic boundaries on China's north-west frontier', *Inner Asia* xiii/1 (2011), pp. 7–25.

The Cultural Revolution song for schoolchildren is in Michael Friederich's chapter 'Uyghur literary representations of Xinjiang realities', in Ildikó Bellér-Hann, M. Cristina Cesàro, Rachel Harris and Joanne Smith Finley (eds), *Situating the Uyghurs between China and Central Asia* (Aldershot, 2007), pp. 89–108. The quote about the big stick of class struggle is from *Muslim Chinese: Ethnic Nationalism in the People's Republic* (Cambridge, MA, 1996) by Dru Gladney.

For more on the idea that members of ethnic minorities are of inferior quality (*suzhi*) see Michael Zukosky, 'Quality, development discourse, and minority subjectivity in contemporary Xinjiang', *Modern China* xxxviii/2 (2012), pp. 233–64.

CHAPTER 3

'The economy of Xinjiang' by Calla Wiemer in S. Frederick Starr (ed.), *Xinjiang: China's Muslim Borderland* (Armonk, NY, 2004), pp. 163–89, offers a wide-ranging analysis. For regional inequalities see: Cao Huhua, 'Urban–rural income disparity and urbanization: what is the role of spatial distribution of ethnic groups?', *Regional Studies* xliv/8 (2010), pp. 965–82; Yueyao Zhao, 'Pivot or periphery? Xinjiang's regional development', *Asian Ethnicity* ii/2 (2001), pp. 197–224; and Xiaogang Wu and Xi Song, 'Ethnicity, migration, and social stratification in China: evidence from Xinjiang Uyghur Autonomous Region' [Population Studies Center Report 13-810, November 2013].

My account of the Baren incident broadly follows that offered by Gardner Bovingdon in *The Uyghurs: Strangers in Their Own Land* (New York, 2010). William Peters' account can be found in 'Central Asia and the minority question', *Asian Affairs* xxii/2, pp. 152–7. Amnesty International's report 'China: gross violations of human rights in the Xinjiang Uyghur Autonomous Region' (1999) has material on the episode.

For rural policies and agricultural issues see: Ildikó Bellér-Hann, 'The peasant condition in Xinjiang', *Journal of Peasant Studies* xxv/4 (1997), pp. 87–112; Daniel Kelliher, *Peasant Power in China: The Era of Rural Reform 1979–1989* (New Haven, CT, 1992); and Xiaobo Lü, 'The politics of peasant burden in reform China', *Journal of Peasant Studies* xxv/1 (1997), pp. 113–38. For accounts of farming practices see Chris Hann, 'Peasants in an era of freedom: property and market economy in southern Xinjiang', *Inner Asia* i/2 (1991), pp. 195–219. Contemporary accounts of Urumqi are from Eden Naby, 'Uighur elites in Xinjiang', *Central Asian Survey* v/3–4 (1986), pp. 241–54, and Linda Benson's comment on that article, in *Central Asian Survey* vi/4 (1987), pp. 93–4 (which launched a minor spat).

On birth control and other preferential policies, see Barry Sautman, 'Preferential policies for ethnic minorities in China: the case of Xinjiang', *Nationalism and Ethnic Politics* iv/1–2 (1998), pp. 86–118. For the profits of family-planning fines see: 'China family planning officials levied £160m in fines in three years', *Guardian*, 19 September 2013; and 'How the Chinese government profits from the one-child policy', *Atlantic*, 4 September 2013.

The China Society for Human Rights report, 'Family planning among ethnic minorities: a review', is available at http://www.china-humanrights.org/CSHRS/Magazine/Text/t20090115_406184_1.htm (accessed 30 January 2015).

The assessment of the society's links to power is from the Chatham House Report 'China and the international human rights system' (2012) by Sonya Sceats with Shaun Breslin. It is available at http://www.chathamhouse.org/sites/files/chathamhouse/public/Research/International%20Law/r1012_sceatsbreslin.pdf (accessed 12 February 2015).

The account of the Minority Games is from Chris Hann's chapter 'Ethnic games in Xinjiang: anthropological approaches', in Shirin Akiner (ed.), *Cultural Change and Continuity in Central Asia* (London, 1991), pp. 218–36.

Justin Jon Rudelson's *Oasis Identities: Uyghur Nationalism along China's Silk Road* (New York, 1997) remains an important survey of Uyghur life, identity and culture in the 1980s and 1990s – the quotation from the poem 'Awaken!' is taken from here.

On religious policies and the Hui, see: Graham Fuller and Jonathan Lipman's chapter 'Islam in Xinjiang', in Starr (ed.), *Xinjiang*, pp. 320–52; Edmund Waite, 'The impact of the state on Islam among the Uyghurs: religious knowledge and authority in the Kashgar Oasis', *Central Asian Survey* xxv/3 (2006), pp. 251–65; Dru Gladney, 'Islam in China: accommodation or separatism?', *China Quarterly* clxxiv (2003), pp. 451–67; and Michael Dillon's overview 'Muslim communities in contemporary China: the resurgence of Islam after the Cultural Revolution', *Journal of Islamic Studies* v/1 (1994), pp. 70–101. For Hui protests, see: 'Ethnic clashes erupt in China, leaving 150 dead', *New York Times*, 31 October 2004; 'China unrest over mosque demolition in Ningxia', BBC News [website], 2 January 2012; and 'Muslims clash with Chinese police who destroyed mosque', *Telegraph*, 2 January 2012. For the *Sexual Customs* protests, see 'Chinese Muslims protest "Sex Habits" book', *Los Angeles Times*, 13 May 1989. For Hui rebellions, see David Atwill, 'Blinkered visions: Islamic identity, Hui ethnicity, and the Panthay Rebellion in southwest China, 1856–1873', *Journal of Asian Studies* lxii/4 (2003), pp. 1079–108.

For more on the Tarim mummies, see Elizabeth Wayland Barber, *The Mummies of Ürümchi* (New York, 2000).

The Nicholas Kristof quote is from 'A Muslim region is tugging at the ties that bind China', *New York Times*, 14 August 1993. The quote about what Uyghurs want is from '5 questions on Xinjiang separatists, Uighurs and the knife attacks at Chinese train station', *Washington Post*, 2 March 2014. The material on official views of religious extremism, including the quote from Nuer Bekri, is from 'Xinjiang leaders warn against religious extremism', *China Daily*, 8 April 2014.

CHAPTER 4

My sources for the Renshou protests are: Marc Blecher, 'Collectivism, contractualism and crisis in the Chinese countryside', in Robert Benewick and Paul Wingrove (eds), *China in the 1990s* (Basingstoke, 1999), pp. 105–19; Thomas P. Bernstein and Xiaobo Lü, *Taxation without Representation in Contemporary Rural China* (Cambridge, 2003); and 'China is sowing discontent with "taxes" on peasants', *New York Times*, 19 May 1993.

The links between demographics and GDP in Xinjiang are clearly shown in David Bachman, 'Making Xinjiang safe for the Han?', in Morris Rossabi (ed.), *Governing China's Multiethnic Frontiers* (Seattle, 2004), pp. 161–75. See also: June Dreyer, 'Ethnicity and economic development in Xinjiang', *Inner Asia* ii/2 (2000), pp. 137–54; and Nicholas Bequelin, 'Staged development in Xinjiang', *China Quarterly* clxxviii (2004), pp. 358–78. The quote from Cao Huhua about economic growth is in 'Urban–rural income disparity and urbanization: what is the role of spatial distribution of ethnic groups?', *Regional Studies* xliv/8 (2010), pp. 965–82. The 2009 white paper on development in Xinjiang is available at http://www.china.org.cn/archive/2009-09/21/content_18566736_2. htm (accessed 12 February 2015).

A useful overview of protest and violence is provided by James Millward's *Violent Separatism in Xinjiang: A Critical Assessment* (Washington, DC, 2004) and Brent Hierman in 'The pacification of Xinjiang', *Problems of Post-Communism* liv/3 (May/June 2007), pp. 48–62. Gardner Bovingdon, 'The not-so-silent majority: Uyghur resistance to Han rule in Xinjiang', *Modern China* xxviii/1 (2002), pp. 39–78, offers an invaluable perspective on everyday, non-violent forms of Uyghur resistance.

The best single volume on Uyghur identity and Han–Uyghur boundaries is Joanne Smith Finley, *The Art of Symbolic Resistance* (Leiden, 2013) – the quote from the Uyghur girl frightened of being seen with her Han boyfriend is from here. A good introduction to Smith Finley's work can be found in 'Four generations of Uyghurs: the shift towards ethno-political ideologies among Xinjiang's youth', *Inner Asia* ii/2 (2000), pp. 195–224, and 'Making culture matter: symbolic, spatial and social boundaries between Uyghurs and Han Chinese', *Asian Ethnicity* iii/2 (2002), pp. 153–74. Michael Dillon's argument that terrorism increased in the 1990s can be found in *Xinjiang: China's Muslim Far Northwest* (London, 2004).

M. Cristina Cesàro looks at the issue of food as an ethnic marker in 'Consuming identities: food and resistance among the Uyghur in contemporary Xinjiang', *Inner Asia* ii/2 (2000), pp. 225–38. For more on Han–Uyghur relations, see Ildikó Bellér-Hann, 'Temperamental neighbours: Uighur–Han relations in Xinjiang', in Gunther Schlee (ed.), *Imagined Differences: Hatred and the Construction of Identity* (Hamburg, 2002), pp. 57–81. See also Dru Gladney, 'Relational alterity: constructing Dungan (Hui), Uygur, and Kazakh identities across China, Central Asia, and Turkey', *History and Anthropology* ix/4 (1996), pp. 445–77.

For more on the *min kao han*, see Jennifer Taynen, 'Interpreters, arbiters or outsiders: the role of Min Kao Han in Xinjiang society', *Journal of Muslim Minority Affairs* xxvi/1, pp. 45–62. Smith Finley's *Art of Symbolic Resistance* also discusses their role.

My understanding of Uyghur music relies heavily on Rachel Harris' papers 'Reggae on the Silk Road: the globalisation of Uyghur pop', *China Quarterly* clxxxiii (2005), pp. 627–43, and 'Cassettes, bazaars and saving the nation: the Uyghur music industry in Xinjiang', in Tim Craig and Richard King (eds), *Global Goes Local: Popular Culture in Asia* (Vancouver, 2002), pp. 265–83.

Nathan Light's book *Intimate Heritage: Creating Uyghur Muqam Song in Xinjiang* (Berlin, 2008) was helpful for understanding more about *muqam*. I also found useful Nimrod Baranovitch, 'Inverted exile: Uyghur writers and artists in Beijing and the political implications of their work', *Modern China* xxxiii/4 (2007), pp. 462–504.

For more on HIV and drug problems, see: Jay Dautcher, 'Public health and social pathologies in Xinjiang', in S. Frederick Starr (ed.), *Xinjiang: China's Muslim Borderland* (Armonk, NY, 2004), pp. 276–95; and Anna Hayes and Abduresit Qarluq, 'Securitising HIV/AIDS in the Xinjiang Uyghur Autonomous Region', *Australian Journal of International Affairs* lxv/2 (2011), pp. 203–19. For a report on drug treatment, see the Human Rights Watch press release 'China: drug rehabilitation centers deny treatment, allow forced labour' (2010).

The quote downplaying the significance of the Yining protests is from Jay Dautcher's chapter 'Reading out of print: popular culture and protest on China's western frontier', in Timothy B. Weston and Lionel M. Jensen (eds), *China Beyond the Headlines* (Lanham, MD, 2000), pp. 273–95, while the report on the calm following the protests is from Michael Dillon, *Xinjiang: China's Muslim Far Northwest* (London, 2004). News reports on the protests are available at http://edition.cnn.com/WORLD/9702/11/china.unrest/ and http://www.apnewsarchive.com/1997/Report-Muslim-riot-in-northwest-China-kills-more-than-10-injures-dozens/id-a5bad9de5aaec4cac3a6c559e54efbe7 (accessed 12 February 2015).

More about Yining in the 1990s and early 2000s can be found in Jay Dautcher, *Down a Narrow Road: Identity and Masculinity in a Uyghur Community in Xinjiang China* (Cambridge, MA, 2009) and in my memoir of life in Yining, *The Tree That Bleeds: A Uighur Town on the Edge* (Edinburgh, 2011). For more on the *mashrap*, see Sean Roberts, 'Negotiating locality, Islam, and national culture in a changing borderland: the revival of the mashrap ritual among young Uyghur men in the Ili valley', *Central Asian Survey* xvii/4 (1998), pp. 673–700. Roberts' documentary, *Waiting for Uyghuristan*, is available at https://www.youtube.com/watch?v=mqX_3aUWujg (accessed 6 February 2015).

The EU response to the Yining protests is in *Bulletin of the European Union 1997*, 4. Amudun Niyaz is quoted in the Human Rights Watch report for 1998, available at http://www.hrw.org/legacy/campaigns/ china-98/sj_xnj2.htm (accessed 6 February 2015).

CHAPTER 5

For negative Chinese coverage of Kadeer, see: 'Evidence shows Rebiya Kadeer behind Xinjiang riot: govt', *China Daily*, 9 July 2009; and 'Rebiya Kadeer lies again', Xinhua, 11 August 2009. Yu-Wen Chen's *The Uyghur Lobby: Global Networks, Coalitions and Strategies of the World Uyghur Congress* (Abingdon, 2014) features earlier, more positive responses in the Chinese press (and other useful material on the WUC).

Most of my quotes from Rebiya Kadeer come from her book *Dragon Fighter: One Woman's Epic Struggle for Peace with China* (Carlsbad, CA, 2009). The claims about drugs are from a 2010 interview with the *On Islam* website. It is available here: http://www.onislam.net/english/ politics/asia/429578-meeting-the-uighur-leader-rebiya-kadeer.html (accessed 11 February 2015).

For Western coverage of Kadeer, see: 'The mother of the Uighur movement', *Washington Post*, 9 July 2009, and a very incisive interview with the *Diplomat* from 2013, available at http://thediplomat. com/2013/11/rebiya-kadeer/ (accessed 11 February 2015).

Jeff Daniels' film *The 10 Conditions of Love* (2009) is available on Amazon and iTunes. Quotes from Daniels are from an interview with me in October 2014. The source for the availability of hashish in Xinjiang is Nathan Light, 'Cultural pragmatics and the politics of resistance: reflexive discourses on culture and history', in Ildikó Bellér-Hann, M. Cristina Cesàro, Rachel Harris and Joanne Smith Finley (eds), *Situating the Uyghurs between China and Central Asia* (Aldershot, 2007), pp. 49–68. The quote explaining the *gulkhan* comes from here.

My analysis of the growth of Uyghur transnational organisations owes much to Gardner Bovingdon's treatment of the subject in Chapter 5 of *The Uyghurs: Strangers in Their Own Land* (New York, 2010). Also useful was Kristian Petersen, 'Usurping the nation: cyber-leadership in the Uighur nationalist movement', *Journal of Muslim Minority Affairs* xxvi/1 (2006), pp. 63–73. For more on the East Turkestan government in exile, see its website, which is available at http://eastturkistaninfo.com/english/ (accessed 12 February 2015).

The Channel 4 *Dispatches* documentary 'Death on the Silk Road', which Enver took part in, is available at https://www.youtube.com/watch?v=-PRb8Xcdxp8 (accessed 11 February 2015). I spoke to Richard Hering and Stuart Tanner in September 2014. For more on Chinese nuclear testing, see 'Did China's nuclear tests kill thousands and doom future generations?', *Scientific American*, July 2009. There is also a propaganda video at http://www.youtube.com/watch?v=F-B41TZw77Ms (accessed 11 February 2015).

CHAPTER 6

My understanding of the Open Up the West policy owes much to the following sources: Elizabeth Economy, *The River Runs Black: The Environmental Challenge to China's Future* (Ithaca, NY, 2004); Nicholas Bequelin, 'Staged development in Xinjiang', *China Quarterly* clxxviii (2004), pp. 358–78 (which contains Wang Lequan's claim that economic stability might not translate into social stability); Calla Wiemer, 'The economy of Xinjiang', in S. Frederick Starr (ed.), *Xinjiang: China's Muslim Borderland* (Armonk, NY, 2004), pp. 163–89; David S. G. Goodman, 'The campaign to "open up the west": national, provincial and local perspectives', *China Quarterly* clxxviii (2004), pp. 317–34 (which contains the breathless reports of the campaign's success); and Heike Holbig, 'The emergence of the campaign to open up the west', *China Quarterly* clxxviii (2004), pp. 335–57. For more on regional inequalities, see: Clifton W. Pannell and Philipp Schmidt, 'Structural change and regional disparities in Xinjiang, China', *Eurasian Geography and Economics* xlvii/3 (2006), pp. 329–52; and Henryk Szadziewski, 'Commanding the economy: the recurring patterns of Chinese central government development planning among Uyghurs in Xinjiang', *Inner Asia* xiii/1 (2011), pp. 97–116.

For arguments against Xinjiang being a colonial project, see Barry Sautman, 'Is Xinjiang an internal colony?', *Inner Asia* ii/2 (2000), pp. 239–71. For the ecological aspects of the Open Up the West campaign, see Elizabeth Economy, 'China's "Go West" campaign: ecological construction or ecological exploitation?', *China Environment Series* 5 (2002), pp. 1–11. The Hu Angang interview from 2000 is available at http://www. asian-affairs.com/China/huangang.html (accessed 12 February 2015).

The shifting role of the *bingtuan* is analysed in Thomas Cliff, 'Neo oasis: the Xinjiang bingtuan in the twenty-first century', *Asian Studies Review* xxxiii/1 (2009), pp. 83–106.

For the bilingual-education debate, the best place to start is Arienne M. Dwyer, *The Xinjiang Conflict: Uyghur Identity, Language Policy, and Political Discourse* (Washington, DC, 2005). See also: Linda Tsung and Ken Cruickshank, 'Mother tongue and bilingual minority education in China', *International Journal of Bilingual Education and Bilingualism* xii/5 (2009), pp. 549–63; and Ma Rong, 'The development of minority education and the practice of bilingual education in Xinjiang', *Frontiers of Education in China* iv/2 (2009), pp. 188–251. More on the Xinjiang Class can be found in Yangbin Chen, *Muslim Uyghur Students in a Chinese Boarding School* (Lanham, MD, 2008), and Timothy Grose, 'The Xinjiang Class: education, integration and the Uyghurs', *Journal of Muslim Minority Affairs* xxx/1 (2010), pp. 97–109. (The latter is the source of the quote on the ideology of the class.) For the history of Uyghur education, see Eric T. Schluessel, 'History, identity, and mother-tongue education in Xinjiang', *Central Asian Survey* xxxviii/4 (2009), pp. 383–402.

The quote from the Aksu teacher about Han and Uyghur children playing together is taken from Linda Tsung, 'Trilingual education and school practice in Xinjiang', in James Leibold and Yangbin Chen (eds), *Minority Education in China: Balancing Unity and Diversity in an Era of Critical Pluralism* (Hong Kong, 2014), pp. 161–86. Both the textbook material and the teacher's quote about the problems of useless material for Uyghur students are from Linda Tsung and Ken Cruickshank, 'Teaching Chinese as a second language in XUAR', in Linda Tsung and Ken Cruickshank (eds), *Teaching and Learning Chinese in Global Contexts* (London, 2010), pp. 97–116. Predictions on the *min kao han* are from Joanne Smith Finley, 'Ethnic anomaly or modern Uyghur survivor? A case study of the Minkaohan hybrid identity in Xinjiang', in Ildikó Bellér-Hann, M. Cristina Cesàro, Rachel Harris and Joanne Smith Finley (eds), *Situating the Uyghurs between China and Central Asia* (Aldershot, 2007), pp. 219–38.

The two best overviews of violence and 'terrorism' in Xinjiang are James Millward, *Violent Separatism in Xinjiang: A Critical Assessment* [Policy Studies 6] (Washington, DC, 2004) and Sean Roberts, 'Imaginary terrorism? The Global War on Terror and the narrative of the Uyghur terrorist threat' [PONARS Eurasia Working Paper] (2012). See also: Kendrick Kuo, 'Revisiting the Salafi-jihadist threat in Xinjiang', *Journal of Muslim Minority Affairs* xxxii/4 (2012), pp. 528–44; and Michael Clarke, 'China's war on terror in Xinjiang: human security and the causes of violent Uyghur separatism' [Griffith Asia Institute 'Regional Outlook' paper] (2007). For legal changes, see Michael Clarke, 'Widening the net: China's anti-terror laws and human rights in Xinjiang', *International Journal of Human Rights* xiv/4 (2010), pp. 542–58.

Wang Lequan's comments on Xinjiang pre-9/11 come from James Millward's *Eurasian Crossroads* (New York, 2007). The quote about Xinjiang being seen as a dangerous place is from Wen Bo, 'Xinjiang: a trip to the new territory', *China Environment Series* 5 (2002), pp. 66–8. For subsequent arrests and repression, see the report by Human Rights Watch entitled 'Devastating blows: religious repression of Uighurs in Xinjiang' (2005) (also the source of the quote from the government about expecting support for its anti-terror fight). The interview with Rita Katz from SITE is from 'Private jihad: how Rita Katz got into the spying business', *New Yorker*, 5 May 2006. It is available at http://www.newyorker.com/magazine/2006/05/29/private-jihad (accessed 12 February 2015). The comments on Tursunjan Amat are from an Amnesty International report from 2002, available at http://www.amnesty.org/en/library/asset/ASA17/010/2002/ar/feb1b2bb-d873-11dd-9df8-936c90684588/asa170102002en.html (accessed 12 February 2015).

For an overview of shrine tourism, see Rahile Dawut, 'Shrine pilgrimage and sustainable tourism among the Uyghurs: Central Asian ritual traditions in the context of China's development policies', in Bellér-Hann, Cesàro, Harris and Smith Finley (eds), *Situating the Uyghurs*, pp. 149–64. For a detailed analysis of the development of the 'fragrant concubine' myth and its uses, see James Millward, 'A Uyghur Muslim in Qianlong's court: the meaning of the fragrant concubine', *Journal of Asian Studies* liii/2 (1994), pp. 427–58.

For Urumqi's changes in the 2000s, see Adila Erkin, 'Locally modern, globally Uyghur: geography, identity and consumer culture in contemporary Xinjiang', *Central Asian Survey* xxviii/4 (2010), pp. 417–28.

The section on migration in Xinjiang is drawn from the following sources: Reza Hasmath, 'Migration, labour and the rise of ethnoreligious consciousness among Uyghurs in urban Xinjiang', *Journal of Sociology* (2012), pp. 1–15; Xiaowei Zhang, 'Uyghur–Han earnings differentials in Ürümchi', *China Journal* 65 (2011), pp. 141–55; Tyler Harlan and Michael Webber, 'New corporate Uyghur entrepreneurs in Urumqi, China', *Central Asian Survey* xxxi/2 (2012), pp. 175–91; Ross Anthony, 'Exceptionally equal: emergency states and the production of enemies in Xinjiang', *Inner Asia* xiii/1 (2011), pp. 51–72; and Ben Hopper and Michael Webber, 'Migration, modernisation and ethnic estrangement: Uyghur migration to Urumqi, Xinjiang', *Inner Asia* xi/2 (2009), pp. 173–203. For claims of forced migration, see the Uyghur Human Rights Project report 'Deception, pressure and threats: the transfer of young Uyghur women to eastern China' (2008).

For more on Wang Lixiong, see Sebastian Veg, 'Chinese intellectuals and the problem of Xinjiang', *China Perspectives* 3 (2008), pp. 143–50. The prediction of further violence was made in Jennifer Taynen, 'Interpreters, arbiters or outsiders: the role of Min Kao Han in Xinjiang society', *Journal of Muslim Minority Affairs* xxvi/1 (2006), pp. 45–62.

CHAPTER 7

Two of the best books on factory workers in China are Peter Hessler's *Country Driving* (New York, 2011) and Leslie Chang's *Factory Girls* (New York, 2008).

Xinhua's reporting of Wang Lequan's response to the riots is available at http://news.xinhuanet.com/english/2009-07/07/content_11663786. htm (accessed 12 February 2015). The WUC's denial of involvement is from 'Ethnic unrest in China leads to mass arrests', CNN [web-site], 7 July 2009. Available at http://edition. cnn.com/2009/WORLD/asiapcf/07/06/china.uyghur.protest/index. html?eref=onion (accessed 12 February 2015). The claim that order was quickly restored is available at http://news.xinhuanet.com/english/2009-09/07/content_12010305.htm (accessed 12 February 2015).

For the Melbourne Festival controversy, see 'Beijing pressures film festival to dump documentary', *The Age*, 15 July 2009. Available at http:// www.theage.com.au/news/entertainment/film/beijing-pressures-film-festival-to-dump-documentary/2009/07/14/1247337123701. html (accessed 12 February 2015). See also 'Jeff Daniels: one year later', *Filmink*, 28 September 2010. Available at http://www.filmink. com. au/features/jeff-daniels-one-year-later/ (accessed 12 February 2015).

Tania Branigan's report for the *Guardian*, 'Woman's lone protest calms tempers as Uighurs confront Chinese police' (7 July 2009), is available at http://www.theguardian.com/world/2009/jul/07/uighur-protest-urumqi-china (accessed 12 February 2015).

The video of the arrests in Urumqi is available at https://www. youtube.com/watch?v=tj0X2bEgYcI#t=6m25s (accessed 12 February 2015).

For accounts of the post-July 2009 arrests, see: Human Rights Watch's report 'We are afraid to even look for them' (2009) and Amnesty International's '"Justice, justice": the July 2009 protests in Xinjiang' (2010). For more on the post-2009 riots response, see: David Tobin, 'Competing communities: ethnic unity and ethnic boundaries on China's north-west frontier', *Inner Asia* xiii/1 (2011), pp. 7–25; and my own article 'After the Xinjiang protests', *n+1* [website] (2010). It is available at https://nplusonemag.com/online-only/online-only/ after-xinjiang/ (accessed 12 February 2015).

More on internet restrictions can be found in the Uyghur Human Rights Project report 'Trapped in a virtual cage' (2013) and Rachel Harris and Aziz Isa, '"Invitation to a mourning ceremony": perspectives on the Uyghur internet', *Inner Asia* xiii/1 (2011), pp. 27–49. The official's quote on the internet is from 'Security of internet, phone top priority in Xinjiang', *China Daily*, 20 May 2010. Available at http:// www. chinadaily.com.cn/china/2010-05/20/content_9870467.htm (accessed 12 February 2015).

Good analysis of the Xinjiang Work Forum proposals can be found in Henryk Szadziewski, 'Commanding the economy: the recurring patterns of Chinese central government development planning among Uyghurs in Xinjiang', *Inner Asia* xiii/1 (2011), pp. 97–116. See also: Liu Yong, 'An economic Band-Aid: Beijing's new approach to Xinjiang', *China Security* vi/ 2 (2010), pp. 13–23; and Shan Wei and Weng Cuifen, 'China's new policy in Xinjiang and its challenges', *East Asian Policy* ii/3 (2010), pp. 58–66. For more on the importance of placating Han immigrant concerns, see: Thomas Cliff, 'The partnership of stability in Xinjiang: state–society interaction following the July 2009 unrest', *China Journal* 68 (2012), pp. 79–105; and Isabelle Côté, 'Political mobilization of a regional minority: Han Chinese settlers in Xinjiang', *Ethnic and Racial Studies* xxxiv/11 (2011), pp. 1855–73.

The quotes about Kashgar by Marco Polo are from the 1903 translation by Henry Yule and Henri Cordier of *The Book of Ser Marco Polo*. An account of my 2013 trip to Kashgar first appeared as 'The death of old Kashgar', *Unmapped* 6 (2014). For more on the destruction of Beijing's *hutongs*, see Michael Meyer, *The Last Days of Old Beijing* (New York, 2008). The Uyghur Human Rights Project's report 'Living on the margins: the Chinese state's demolition of Uyghur communities' (2012) has a region-wide overview of the destruction of Uyghur neighbourhoods. The quote about Kashgar becoming unrecognisable in five years is from 'Aid fuels change of fortunes on Silk Road', *New York Times*, 14 November 2010. The quote from Xu Jianrong is from 'To protect an ancient city, China moves to raze it', *New York Times*, 27 May 2009. The report from the Pomegranate Compound is from 'Uighur tensions persist as Kashgar's Old City is demolished', *Australian*, 6 January 2010. For more on Uyghur *mehelle*, see Jay Dautcher, *Down a Narrow Road: Identity and Masculinity in a Uyghur Community in Xinjiang China* (Cambridge, MA, 2009). The Dilxat Raxit quote is from 'China razes Uyghur homes', Radio Free Asia [website], 13 July 2010. Available at http://www.rfa.org/english/news/uyghur/raze-07132010120547.html (accessed 12 February 2015). Xie Min is quoted in 'The vanishing slums of Urumqi', *Global Times* [website], 29 July 2010. Available at http://www.globaltimes.cn/content/557130.shtml (accessed 12 February 2015). See also James C. Scott, *Seeing Like a State: How Certain Schemes to Improve the Human Condition Have Failed* (New Haven, CT, 1999).

For an excellent look at the changes in Korla, see Thomas Cliff, 'Peripheral urbanism: making history on China's northwest frontier', *China Perspectives* 3 (2013), pp. 13–23. David Tobin's blog for the China Policy Institute, 'Xinjiang dreams: worrying about ethnicity' (6 November 2013), is very informative about the assimilation and ethnicity debate in Chinese policy circles. The point about the position taken by scholars like Hao Shiyuan and Wang Xi'en is taken from here. It is available at http://blogs.nottingham.

ac.uk/chinapolicyinstitute/2013/11/06/xinjiang-dreams-worry-ing-about-ethnicity/ (accessed 12 February 2015).

CHAPTER 8

A longer version of my conversation with Alim appeared in the article 'A Perfect Bomb', *n+1* [website] (2010). It is available at https://nplu-sonemag.com/online-only/online-only/a-perfect-bomb/ (accessed 12 February 2015).

For bombings that weren't terrorism, see: 'Wheelchair-bound Beijing airport bomber Ji Zhongxing jailed', *South China Morning Post*, 15 October 2013; and 'Police nab suspect in fatal Taiyuan bombing', *South China Morning Post*, 8 November 2013. The BBC article about the 'escalation' is John Sudworth, 'Shock and anger after Kunming brutality', BBC News [website], 3 March 2014. Available at http://www.bbc. co.uk/news/blogs-china-blog-26380542 (accessed 12 February 2015). See also Sean Roberts, 'Imaginary terrorism? The Global War on Terror and the narrative of the Uyghur terrorist threat' [PONARS Eurasia Working Paper] (2012). Dru Gladney was quoted in 'Audio recording attributes Tiananmen crash to Uyghur armed group', Al Jazeera America [website], 24 November 2014. Available at http://america.aljazeera.com/articles/2013/11/24/audio-attributesti-ananmencrashtouyghurarmedgroupbutdoesitexist.html (accessed 12 February 2015).

For a good piece on the Lukqun violence, see 'Xinjiang: reassessing the recent violence', *Diplomat*, 4 August 2013. Available at http://thediplomat.com/2013/08/xinjiang-reassessing-the-recent-violence/ (accessed 12 February 2015).

The alternative explanation for the Kunming attacks is well expressed in 'The Kunming train station attack: a hypothesis', *East by Southeast* [website] (9 March 2014). Available at http://www.eastby-southeast.com/kunming-train-station-attack-hypothesis/ (accessed 12 February 2015).

There's a lot of great material on *The Art of Life in Chinese Central Asia* blog, especially 'Perhat, a gracious Uyghur rock star on the voice of China', 'Playing with serious space in Ürümqi: Sufi poetry and the Uyghur Justin Beiber [*sic*]' and 'Gendered futures, "Mother Tongue" and Berna the Uyghur city girl'. The blog is available at https://beige-wind.wordpress.com/ (accessed 12 February 2015). The translations of Berna's song and 'Mother Tongue' were done by Beige Wind and originally appeared on that site.

For a good piece on Six City, see 'China's Uighur minority finds a voice through American-style hip-hop', *Atlantic*, 29 October 2013. My interview with Sameer Farooq is available on the *China File* website, at http://www.chinafile.com/reporting-opinion/media/silk-road-pop (accessed 12 February 2015).

AFTERWORD

For a valuable overview of policy in Xinjiang see Sean Roberts' 'The biopolitics of China's "war on terror" and the exclusion of the Uyghurs' in *Critical Asian Studies* 2018.

Li Haiying's pomegranate quote is from Reuters, [website], 'China's military on mission to bring 'modern civilization' to Xinjiang' 1 July 2015. It is available at https://www.reuters.com/article/us-chi-na-xinjiang/chinas-military-on-mission-to-bring-modern-civiliza-tion-to-xinjiang (accessed 15 January 2019).

A useful summary of Zhang Chunxian's policies can be found in an *Economist* piece, 'The race card', 3 September 2016. It is availa-ble at https://www.economist.com/china/2016/09/03/the-race-card (accessed 23 December 2018).

I wrote about the '181 terror groups' for the *London Review of Books* Blog 3 June 2015. It is available at https://www.lrb.co.uk/blog/2015/06/03/nick-holdstock/181-terrorist-groups/ (accessed 7 January 2019).

For Benjamin Haas' report on the loudspeakers in Elishku for

AFP see, 'Hear this now: propaganda drive in Xinjiang village' 28 April 2015. It is available at https://news.yahoo.com/hear-now-prop-aganda-drive-xinjiang-village-071248735.html (accessed January 20 2019).

An essential piece for understanding the home visit campaign is Darren Byler's 24 October 2018 *ChinaFile* [website] 'China's govern-ment has ordered a Million Citizens to Occupy Uighur Homes. Here's What They Think They're Doing'. It is available at http://www.chin-afile.com/reporting-opinion/postcard/million-citizens-occupy-ui-ghur-homes-xinjiang (accessed 11 December 2018).

Chen Quanguo's Tibet policies are summarised by the International Campaign for Tibet [website] 10 December 2018, 'The origin of the 'Xinjiang model' in Tibet under Chen Quanguo: Securitizing eth-nicity and accelerating assimilation'. It is available at https://www.savetibet.org/the-origin-of-the-xinjiang-model-in-tibet/ (accessed 2 January 2019).

For more on the construction of the camps, detention quotas, and re-education in general, see Adrian Zenz's paper in *Central Asian Survey* 2018, 'Thoroughly reforming them towards a healthy heart attitude: China's political re-education campaign in Xinjiang'.

To see Shawn Zhang's images of the camps, see https://medium.com/@shawnwzhang/detention-camp-construction-is-booming-in-xinjiang-a2525044c6b1 (accessed 8 January 2019).

The analysis of the camps for the Australian Strategic Policy Institute [website] was by Fergus Ryan, Danielle Cave and Nathan Ruser. 'Mapping Xinjiang's 're-education' camps' 1 November 2018. It is available at https://www.aspi.org.au/report/mapping-xinjiangs-re-education-camps (accessed 3 January 2019).

For Adrian Zenz and James Leibold's work on securitisation and recruitment under Chen see 'Xinjiang's Rapidly Evolving Security State' in *China Brief* [website] Vol. 17. No. 4, 14 March 2017. It is available at https://jamestown.org/program/xinjiangs-rapidly-evolv-ing-security-state/ (accessed 6 June 2018).

A good idea of how invasive surveillance is in Xinjiang can be gleaned from Timothy Grose and Darren Byler's article for *Dissent*, 'China's Surveillance Laboratory' 31 October 2018. It is available at https://www.dissentmagazine.org/online_articles/chinas-surveillance-laboratory (accessed 7 November 2018).

The post-Lukun remarks can be found at http://www.china-consulate.org.nz/eng/zt/zhuantixinwen/t1055062.htm (accessed 6 November 2018).

For more on the spike in arrests in Xinjiang, see Chinese Human Rights Defenders [website], 25 July 2018, 'Criminal Arrests in Xinjiang Account for 21 per cent of China's Total in 2017'. It is available at https://www.nchrd.org/2018/07/criminal-arrests-in-xinjiang-account-for-21-of-chinas-total-in-2017/ (accessed 21 January 2019).

Gene Bunin's powerful account of the effect of the camps on Uyghur communities appeared on *The Art of Life in Chinese Central Asia* [website] 31 July 2018. It is available at https://livingotherwise.com/2018/07/31/happiest-muslims-world-coping-happiness/ (accessed 10 January 2019).

The quote about spraying the field comes from Rachel Harris' post 'Securitisation and Mass Detentions in Xinjiang' on the Central Eurasian Studies Society Blog, 18 August 2018. It is available at http://thecessblog.com/2018/08/securitisation-and-mass-detentions-in-xinjiang-by-rachel-harris-soas-university-of-london/ (accessed 2 November 2018).

Rob Schmitz's piece for NPR quotes the former camp inmate - 'Families of the Disappeared: A search for Loved Ones Held in China's Xinjiang Region', 12 November 2018. It is available at https://www.npr.org/2018/11/12/665597190/families-of-the-disappeared-a-search-for-loved-ones-held-in-chinas-xinjiang-regi (accessed 3 December 2018).

On the media visits to the camps, see Ben Blanchard's Reuters piece, 'China says pace of Xinjiang 'education' will slow but defends camps', 6 January 2019. It is available at

https://www.reuters.com/article/us-china-xinjiang-insight/
china-says-pace-of-xinjiang-education-will-slow-but-defends-camps

For an overview of the campaign against intellectuals in Xinjiang, see the Uyghur Human Rights Project report 'The persecution of the intellectuals in the Uyghur Region: Disappeared Forever?', October 2018. It is available at https://docs.uhrp.org/pdf/UHRP_Disappeared_Forever_.pdf (accessed 1 February 2019).

Halmaurat Ghopur's arrest was reported by Radio Free Asia [website] 'Prominent Uyghur Intellectual Given Two-year Suspended Death Sentence for 'Separatism', 28 September 2018. It is available at https://www.rfa.org/english/news/uyghur/sentence-09282018145150.html (accessed 8 December 2018).

Xu Hairong's remarks on 'two-faced' officials were quoted by Reuters, 'China official says some Xinjiang Party members back 'terrorist acts', 24 November 2015. It is available at https://uk.reuters.com/article/uk-china-security-xinjiang (accessed 1 February 2019).

For more on Abdukerim Rahman's career, see Amy Anderson's warm and nuanced piece on the *The Art of Life in Chinese Central Asia* [website] 'How is Abdukerim Rahman Surviving Without His Books?', 2 October 2018. It is available at https://livingotherwise.com/2018/10/02/abdukerim-rahman-surviving-without-books/ (accessed 3 January 2019).

I wrote about Rahile Dawut for the *London Review of Books* Blog, 'Where is Rahile Dawut?', [website], 16 August 2018. It is available at https://www.lrb.co.uk/blog/2018/08/16/nick-holdstock/where-is-rahile-dawut (accessed 25 November 2018).

The comments of the Urumqi mayor about Uyghur history were reported by the *Global Times* [website] 'Uyghurs are not descendants of Turks: Urumqi mayor', 26 August 2018. It is available at http://www.globaltimes.cn/content/1117158.shtml (accessed 3 January 2019).

The crackdown in Ningxia is explored in depth by David R. Stroup on *China at the crossroads* [website] 'The Xinjiang model of ethnic politics and the daily practice of ethnicity', 19 December 2018. It is available at http://davidrstroup.wixsite.com/china-crossroads/single-post/2018/12/19/The-Xinjiang-model-of-ethnic-politics-and-the-daily-practice-of-ethnicity (accessed 5 January 2019).

China's plans to Sinicise Islam are covered in a story by Chris Baynes for the *Independent* 'China passes law to 'make Islam more compatible with Socialism' amid outcry over Muslim abuse', 7 January 2019. It is available at https://www.independent.co.uk/news/world/asia/china-uighur-muslim-crackdown-xinjiang-islam-united-nations-sinicize-a8715506.html (accessed 17 January 2019).

INDEX